John Guy

WOVEN CARGOES

Indian Textiles in the East

THAMES AND HUDSON

To the memory of John Irwin (1917–97)
Keeper of the Indian Department, Victoria and Albert Museum, 1960–77,
and a pioneer in the study of Indian trade textiles

ON PAGE 1 Hanging scroll depicting a scene with a south Indian woman and two Portuguese men. Fragment of an early seventeenth-century Indian mordant-dyed cotton cloth in a scroll mount, bordered with Indian cotton and Japanese stencilled cotton. Kobe City Museum. (See p. 171.)

ON PAGES 2–3 Detail of fig. 29.

ABOVE *Patolu,* ceremonial cloth with two pairs of caparisoned elephants. Gujarat, for the Indonesian market; nineteenth century. Silk, double ikat, 480 x 100 cm. Victoria and Albert Museum, London. (See p. 88.)

Maps appear on pp. 15, 27, and 70.

Measurements Where a complete cloth is illustrated, both dimensions are given in the caption; where only the weft or width is shown entire, that dimension is given. For the size of cloths of which only details are illustrated, see Illustrations: Credits and Notes, p. 188.

First published in hardcover in the United States of America in 1998 by
Thames and Hudson Inc., 500 Fifth Avenue, New York, New York 10110

Library of Congress Catalog Card Number 98-60188
ISBN 0-500-01863-4

Printed and bound in Singapore

TEXTILES, CULTURE AND SPICES

◆◆◆◆◆◆◆◆◆◆◆◆◆◆◆◆◆◆◆◆◆◆◆◆

The Indian subcontinent has been renowned throughout history as a centre for cotton weaving. India was also a great entrepot for early international trade, the axial point through which the East–West commerce in aromatics, spices and other luxuries passed. It is these two themes, textiles and trade, which form the subject of this book. Textiles were a principal commodity in the trade of the pre-industrial age and India's were in demand from China to the Mediterranean. Indian cottons were prized for their fineness of weave, brilliance of colour, rich variety of designs, and a dyeing technology which achieved a fastness of colour unrivalled in the world.

The most comprehensive collection of Indian textiles in existence is that of in the Victoria and Albert Museum, London. A much admired and studied aspect of these holdings is the European-market chintz collection, published by John Irwin and Kathrine Brett in their *Origins of Chintz* (1970). This work broke new ground in drawing heavily on English East India Company records to construct a comprehensive account of the production of and trade in high-quality chintzes to the West. Since then an impressive series of regional studies have been published revealing a wealth of information on the commercial operations of the European trading companies in the East.[1] A recurring feature is the pivotal role played by Indian cloth. *Woven Cargoes* seeks to present the story of chintz in the broader sense in which the word '*chint*' is used in those records, denoting not only fine but also coarse painted and printed dyed cottons. These were the cloths which, together with *patola*, the famous double-ikat silk cloth of Gujarat, which we will also consider, dominated the textile markets of Asia.

And whereas the orientation of most chintz studies to date has been to the West, here the focus will be on the East [1]. The European chintz market, which began as a by-product of the eastern spice trade, was initially characterized by high-quality, low-quantity trade. India's cotton exports to the East present a different story: they extended across the full gamut of quality, and were widely used as a favoured medium of exchange. The sheer volume and variety of the Indian textile trade to the East meant that it was a far more complex and significant phenomenon than its better-known western counterpart. Estimates of its scale are problematic, as only European records survive, and there is abundant evidence to suggest that the greater volume was carried by Asian merchants in Asian vessels. Nonetheless, a sense of the magnitude of the trade is suggested by the fact that in the mid-eighteenth century the Dutch East India Company – Verenigde Oostindische Compagnie, or VOC – warehouses in Batavia (now Jakarta) stocked between 500,000 and 1,000,000 items of cloth, the vast majority of which was of Indian origin.[2]

Textiles are an important medium in cultural studies because of their universality and mobility. They circulate within specific cultural milieus and also serve as a vehicle for the transmission of ideas between cultures. They play a central role in the ceremonial and ritual life of most Asian societies, as signifiers of rank and as bearers of other social messages, and as the recipients of influences from the process of trade and exchange. Textiles lie at the heart of the

1 A wedding in Lampung, south Sumatra, at which the substantial dowry paid to the bride's family is publicly displayed. A rich variety of cloths is to be seen, along with matting, baskets and other items suspended from bamboo poles. The opulence of the display indicates the high rank of the bride and groom, seen enthroned as 'king and queen for a day'. Photograph by A. W. Nieuwenhuis, 1913 (detail). Koninklijk Instituut voor Taal-, Land- en Volkenkunde, Leiden.

exchange mechanisms of many societies. These processes are not only economic: many social, political and spiritual contracts are sealed through the giving and receiving of cloths. Gift exchange is a widely practised means of ensuring the circulation of commodities in Southeast Asian societies.

The cloths which are the focus of this study add a new dimension to our understanding both of the history of Indian textiles and of their role in Southeast Asia and Japan. Yet they remain little-known in India: as commercial commodities produced to the requirements of a foreign consumer, they never entered Indian princely or noble collections and remain today almost entirely unrepresented in Indian textile collections; a few pieces acquired by the Calico Museum, Ahmedabad, are the only examples in the subcontinent, apart from isolated and late survivors in royal libraries (preserved in bookbindings), museums and schools of art where their true identity is not generally recognized. Outside India, the only substantial pre-twentieth-century collections are the legacy of colonial acquisition policies, as seen in the Victoria and Albert Museum and a number of Dutch institutions.[3] In recent decades, however, significant holdings of Indian textiles for the Asian markets have been built up in Europe, Japan, the United States of America and Australia, of which those of the Victoria and Albert Museum are among the richest.

The existence of these textiles has been known from the beginning of trading records, but what they actually looked like has largely remained a mystery. It is only with the recent discovery of cloths preserved in Southeast Asia and Japan that their identity and distinctive character has begun to emerge. Their provenances, most notably in Indonesia and Thailand, reveal that regional style preferences were operating in these markets. The biggest concentrations have emerged from Sumatra, Sulawesi (the Celebes), Buton, Maluku (the Moluccas) and Timor. Significantly, these regions correspond with the historical centres of the spice trade, underscoring the key role of Indian textiles in the procurement of spices.

The circumstances of the survival of trade cloths in Southeast Asia vary dramatically. In insular Southeast Asia they were typically preserved by upland communities as treasured heirloom objects, often stored in rattan baskets high in the rafters of ancestral houses and only brought out for use as part of the regalia of office. In Thailand members of the nobility received these prestigious cloths as signifiers of rank, and families retain high-quality Indian cloths even today, a legacy of a dress etiquette which required their use on ceremonial and state occasions. In Japan they are preserved as garment linings and as wrapping cloths for prized objects. Samples were also included in albums assembled in the Edo period by textile connoisseurs.

When provenanced examples are studied, a picture begins to emerge of the types of cloth used in the spice trade, classifiable according to their specific regional markets. Sometimes it is possible to link them with the textile names that appear in dry lists filling the records of the European trading companies and abound in European travellers' accounts, but the brevity of the descriptions and the use of terms no longer current have made it exceedingly difficult to establish a detailed concordance. After John Saris led the first English expedition to Maluku in 1613 he reported that twenty-one varieties of Cambay (i.e. Gujarati) and Coromandel cotton cloths could be profitably bartered for cloves. A typical entry in the VOC *Daghregister* (daybook) records only the cloth's name, measurement, and its cost, expressed either in florins or, more commonly, in weight of pepper or cloves. Occasionally a reference to the dominant

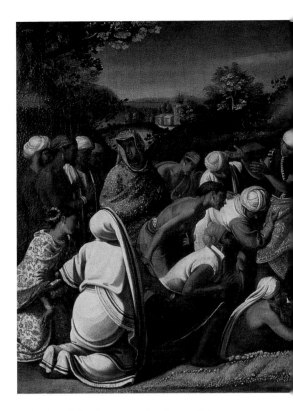

2, 3 *Francis Xavier resurrecting the chief of a caste in Ceylon in 1541* (ABOVE), and detail of *Francis Xavier preaching in Goa* (BELOW), by André Reinoso. Oil on canvas, 1619. Sacristy of São Roque, Lisbon.

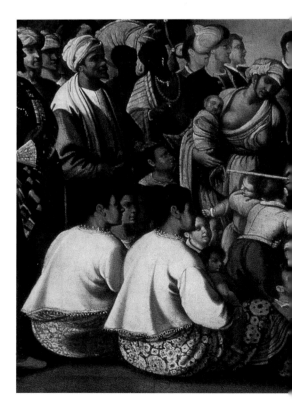

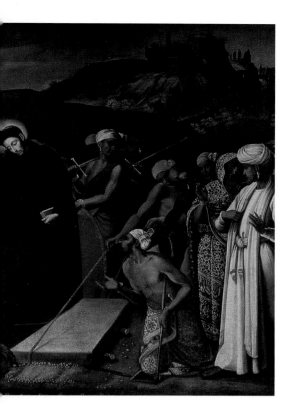

colour would be added, but the design was assumed to be understood from the name attached. As these names ceased to be used, so knowledge of the designs was lost. Glossaries of textile types have been constructed from the historic records, but the problem of specific identifications largely remains.[4]

There are surprisingly few reliable depictions of Indian textiles as dress among the innumerable engraved images prepared to illustrate the European travel literature of the seventeenth and eighteenth centuries. Most of the patterns depicted are generalized beyond recognition, and the costumes have come to resemble Roman togas rather than saris and *dhotis*. A rare exception is a series of twenty paintings commissioned by the Society of Jesus in Lisbon in 1619 to mark the beatification of Francis Xavier. The paintings, by the Portuguese artist André Reinoso, relate episodes from the life of the saint, including his missionary activities in India, Maluku and Japan. Several show Indian crowd scenes in which the local population are dressed in textiles the designs of which are consistent with known south Indian types [2, 3]. The specific nature of the designs, and the number of different varieties that are distinguished, strongly suggest that the artist was given actual examples to copy. Interestingly, Reinoso is also reasonably accurate in recording the manner in which the cloths were worn, a remarkable achievement for his time. All this points to a range of south Indian textiles being sent to Lisbon in the early seventeenth century. Their presence in Portugal is not in itself exceptional (see pp. 166), but the fact that these were sari and *lungi* cloths in the Indian manner, rather than to European taste, is. Records are early as 1508 record the presence of vestments and accessories made of Cambay and Calicut (coastal western India) cloth in church inventories in Lisbon, though they were probably not widespread at this time.[5] A century later the situation had changed dramatically: painted cottons (*pintados*) and embroidered silks in Western taste and adapted to European domestic needs were in wide circulation as wall hangings and bedcovers. Why Indian textiles intended for Indian domestic use were sent to Lisbon remains a mystery unless it was expressly to serve as models in these paintings. They include what appear to be cotton black-and-white check *lungis*, white robes and turbans, silk and gold-thread silk saris, and floral-pattern painted cottons.

Reinoso's paintings provide the earliest reliable depiction of textiles from coastal south India at the beginning of the seventeenth century known to date. We can now see that changes to the designs occurred through time, as over-all repeat patterns gradually gave way in the eighteenth century to cloths organized to a more regular formula, consisting of a large centrefield, narrow side borders and elaborate end-borders with a series of registers typically featuring a saw-tooth pattern (Malay *tumpal*). This configuration does not have direct Indian prototypes and appears to have been generated in response to Southeast Asian models. Visual sources for textile designs are preserved in south India in the form of sculpture and paintings [24, 33]; they provide a rich vocabulary of patterns but tell us little about the materials, weaving and decorating techniques employed. It is only from surviving cloths that we can begin to reconstruct the early history of India's textile trade.

Meanings and uses

An Indian export textile acquired an acculturated Southeast Asian meaning quite distinct from that intended by the producer. The cultural boundaries in

These paintings, commissioned by the Jesuits of São Roque to enhance Francis Xavier's reputation prior to canonization, provide a rare dated context for textile patterns from south India at the beginning of the seventeenth century. They are also highly indicative of how garments were worn. Women are shown in sari (above, at left and right), lungi – skirt-cloths – *and blouses (left), and shawls; men in* lungi, *coats, and turbans.*

which it operated were very often localized and specific. The importance of the non-utilitarian uses to which Indian textiles were put in Southeast Asian societies is underscored by the sheer volume of the trade, which far exceeded the needs of the region, given that much of the clothing of the people was provided by inexpensive locally woven goods. The demand for imports manifested itself as a two-tier market: high-quality cloths which the élite enjoyed as a means of setting themselves apart from the rest of society, and coarser cloths affordable to the broader population. Both markets were driven by a demand for exotic textiles which could meet specific social, ceremonial and ritual needs.

These cloths were, by virtue of their importation and high value, exotic and desirable. They were clearly understood indicators of rank and therefore served as signifiers of prestige and status. They were used both to enhance the separateness of the ruler from his subjects and to secure loyalty through a system of patronage and rewards. They indicated a ruler's authority and power to attract highly valued commodities from beyond his realm. In Thailand, for example, the restricted distribution of imported Indian cloth played a central role both in the sumptuary laws enforced at court and in the monarch's patronage of members of the nobility [5, 12].

Beyond this role as social barometers of rank, the textiles assumed a spiritual importance unimagined by their makers, as in Indonesia where they entered the realm of sacred heirloom objects (*pusaka*), the very embodiment of a ruler's supernatural authority. Intrinsic to a cloth's value was its particular life history: its power (and hence value) was enhanced by its previous ownership and associations with important people and events, not unlike sacred objects in medieval Europe.[6] Such precious goods were high on the list of booty in traditional Southeast Asian warfare.

In Islamic communities in Southeast Asia textiles were often ascribed protective and healing properties. These talismanic powers were seen as intrinsic to the cloths and were understood to have a transformative effect on the wearer. Thus a green robe (the holy colour of Mohammed) might be worn by a warrior, while the turban of a revered Islamic teacher was believed to transmit his authority.[7] The dissemination of cloths imbued with the spirituality of their owner was seen as a way of sharing in that person's holiness: shrouds from the tombs of Muslim holy men were cut up and distributed with this intent.

Textiles were a central element in the performance of rites of passage ceremonies, such as those surrounding birth, marriage and death [1, 4]. They served as canopies, backdrops, awnings, floor coverings, swaddling cloths for the new-born, robes and head covers for initiates, and shrouds for the dead. When Indian textiles became too expensive for the local economy to bear or were otherwise in short supply, their use was not, as might be expected, abandoned. Rather, such was their established efficacy in the ritual lives of the peoples of Southeast Asia that their motifs and designs were systematically integrated into the pattern repertoire of locally woven cloths, typically using tie-dyeing (*ikat*) or resist-dyeing (*batik*) processes. Indeed, there is a body of evidence to suggest that the technique of batik, and many of its designs, are the result of the stimulus provided by the presence of imported Indian textiles [cf. 6]. The acceptability of local cloths to consumers may thus have been shaped by the belief that the authority of the imported cloths could be appropriated by the imitation of their appearance.[8]

Textiles in Southeast Asian societies have traditionally made up a significant portion of the goods employed in gift exchange, a mechanism used to establish

4 A body lying in state, Singaraja, north Bali, *c.* 1900. A mix of local and imported cloths shroud the coffin: a *patolu* and a painted cotton with an Indian floral design are visible, and another floral cloth, possibly also Indian, serves as a screen, enclosing the space of the dead. Textiles have always played a central role in funerary rites in Southeast Asia, both for wrapping the dead and for shrouding the coffin. The value and prestige of Indian imported cloths meant that they were favoured. Many had acquired heirloom status and they were often regarded as imbued with magical properties, which made them effective objects in mediating with the spirit world. Koninklijk Instituut voor de Tropen, Amsterdam.

5 RIGHT The presentation of the young crown prince Chulalongkorn (the future Rama V) to his father, King Mongkut, at the Royal Palace, Bangkok, possibly on the occasion of the prince's tonsure ceremony, held in 1866. Richly decorated textiles, probably gold brocade, hang from the pillars of the royal pavilion [cf. 195]. Photograph by John Thomson, c. 1866. Private collection.

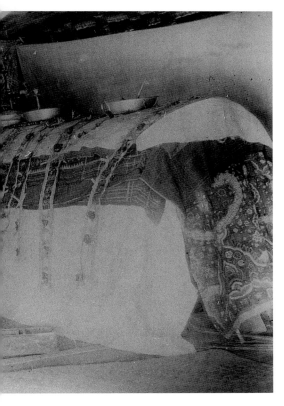

and consolidate social relations and allegiances. At the state level, they formed an integral part of diplomatic and court protocol, most clearly seen in Thailand and the Malay world. Central to their effective use in the political realm was their scarcity: it was only through restricted circulation that their elite status could be protected. The Dutch regulation of the flow of Gujarati silk *patola* cloth to the local rulers of eastern Indonesia is a case in point [7].

At the family level textiles were used widely in securing marriage contracts, forming an important part of the gift exchange process. Here their accumulation was seen as a way of enhancing the status not only of an individual but also of the group. Intrinsic to the ownership of imported cloths was the necessity, even duty, to display them on occasions of importance to the whole community. At such events the benefits of display were collective [10].

Textiles were also a recognized means of storing wealth, a readily convertible form of wealth which could be used in the settlement of business or social debts. This is a feature of Southeast Asian societies in which cloth was a major trade commodity – durable, portable, and above all universally valued. This practice contrasts with that in the Indian subcontinent, where domestic surplus income was traditionally stored in the form of gold and silver jewelry. For most of their history in Southeast Asia, Indian textiles were exchanged through a bartering system, even after monetarization was well-established. This reflected confidence in cloth as a universally accepted medium of exchange.

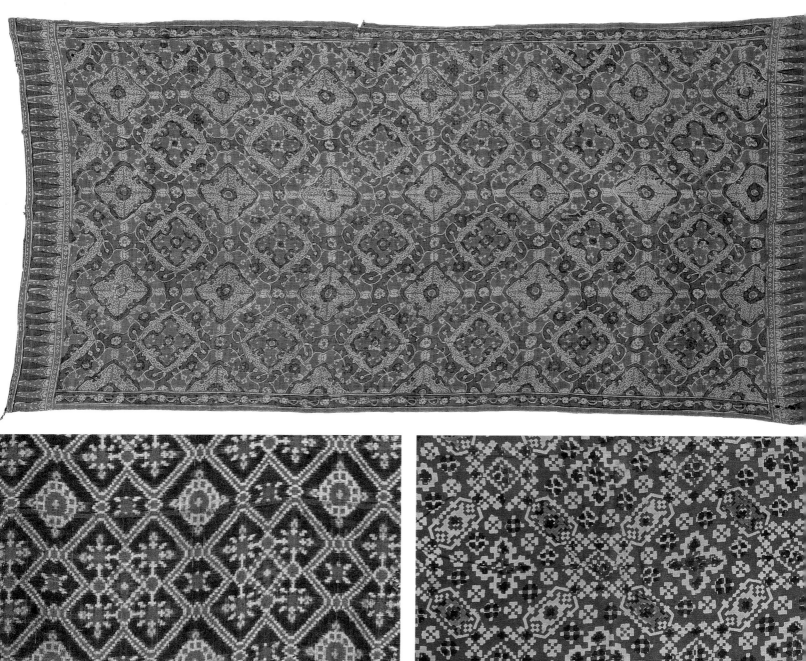

6 OPPOSITE, ABOVE *Kain sembagi*, skirt- or shoulder-cloth. Coromandel Coast, for the south Sumatran market; eighteenth century. Cotton, block-printed and painted mordant-dyed and resist-dyed; 170 x 85 cm. Private collection, London.

7 OPPOSITE, BELOW LEFT *Selendang*, ceremonial shoulder cloth, of *patola* (detail). Gujarat, probably Patan, for the Indonesian market; nineteenth century. Silk, double ikat. Victoria and Albert Museum, London.

8 OPPOSITE, BELOW RIGHT Ceremonial cloth, imitating *patola* (detail). Gujarat, for the Indonesian market; late eighteenth century. The cloth bears a VOC stamp on the reverse. Cotton, block-printed mordant-dyed and resist-dyed. National Gallery of Victoria, Melbourne; gift of Michael and Mary Abbott, 1985.

9 RIGHT *Geringsing pepare*, ritual cloth (detail). Tenganan, Bali; early twentieth century. Cotton, double ikat, in a technique known locally as *geringsing*. Victoria and Albert Museum, London. ◆ The ancestry of Balinese *geringsing* is far from clear, and although some cloths display the unmistakable influence of *patola* [125], others, such as this example, seem to be overlaid with more complex messages. Here intersecting circles and four-pointed stars provide the basic pattern, which is related to *patola* in its elements but not in its structure. Closely similar Indian versions are known [10], all to date found in south Sumatra.

10 BELOW Ceremonial cloth. Coromandel Coast, for the Indonesian market, found in south Sumatra; eighteenth century. Cotton, block-printed mordant-dyed and resist-dyed. Collection Diane Daniel, Los Angeles.

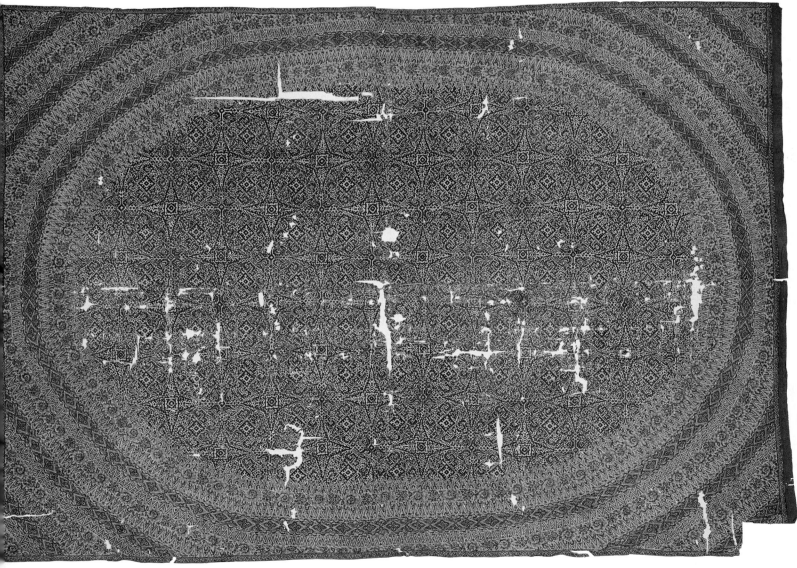

Textiles and spices

Trade to Southeast Asia was motivated by a demand for a variety of exotic goods of which the most important were spices. In the early centuries AD two great markets emerged whose existence was to shape the region's history thereafter: to the West lay the Mediterranean world, unified under the Romans, and to the north lay Han China. Together they generated an almost insatiable appetite for spices, aromatic woods, resins and gold. The wealth created through the gathering and distribution of these goods, and the experience of a broader world opened up through international trade, directly fed the process of state formation in early Southeast Asia. The spread of Islam to India and Southeast Asia was stimulated by the demand for spices. The European search for independent supplies, prompted by the partial closure of the Middle Eastern trade routes after the Ottoman capture of Constantinople in 1453, generated an era of state and privately funded merchant-adventurers. The initial 'discoveries' (as they appeared from Europe) led to over four centuries of European involvement in Asia, which evolved from small-scale commercial adventurism in the sixteenth century to the creation of colonial empires in the nineteenth. At all stages in this process Indian textiles featured as the principal trading commodity.

The spices which were central to this process were surprisingly few in number: pepper, cloves, nutmeg and mace. Their value was determined by their scarcity, a result of the highly restricted and isolated regions in which they were cultivated. Pepper is native to southern India and was introduced early into Sumatra and Java. Cloves, nutmeg and mace were the exclusive products of the islands of Maluku in eastern Indonesia. Cloves – most highly prized of all for their culinary and medicinal applications – are native to a string of tiny islands off the coast of Halmahera, of which Ternate and Tidore were the most important. Nutmeg, and its red bark, mace, were originally the exclusive product of the island of Banda, south of Seram, whose capital Ambon features prominently in the history of the 'Spiceries'.

When the Europeans began their ventures into the waters of eastern Indonesia in the early sixteenth century to secure the prized spices, they were confronted by a well-established Asian exchange system. They quickly discovered that the key to successful participation in this trade was to secure goods in demand in the 'Spice Islands' (Maluku). Indian cotton cloth had long proved its worth as the most acceptable commodity. When James Lancaster, who captained the first English East India Company ship to Southeast Asia, captured a Portuguese carrack in 1601, it was found to be loaded with Indian cotton goods, which he successfully exchanged for pepper in Banten (Bantam), West Java.[9]

Periodic shortages in supply are cited in early European company records as the biggest impediment to procuring spices: in 1617 a Dutch official wrote from the outer islands to his superiors in Banten that there was an abundance of pepper to buy 'as long as cloth is to be had'. The Europeans were learning what the Arab, Indian, Malay and Javanese merchants had known for centuries: that profits were easiest won in Asia through interregional trade, and that a central commodity in the economics of exchange was Indian cloth, bought cheap and traded through a sophisticated bartering system.

A triangular trading system operated, in which capital (silver or gold coinage) was used to buy cloth in India for the express purpose of exchanging it for spices in one of the great emporiums of Southeast Asia [77, 92, 160]. The spices were in turn shipped to other ports in Asia and Europe, where they were sold for the highest profits realizable on any commodity of their day. The communities of merchants who were instrumental in this complex process of exchange ensured the movement of goods around the globe. They formed a diaspora, uniting the realms linked by the Indian Ocean and the seas beyond into an integrated economic sphere. Common to transactions everywhere was the use of Indian cotton textiles [11].

Few early European commentators understood the nature of Asian maritime trade as acutely as Jan Pietersz Coen, Director-General of the newly formed VOC, who wrote from Banten to his directors in Holland in 1619 of the commercial opportunities awaiting the Company in Asian waters:

> Piece goods [cloth] from Gujarat we can barter for pepper and gold on the coast of Sumatra; rials and cottons from the [Coromandel] coast for the pepper in Banten; sandalwood, pepper and rials we can barter for Chinese goods and Chinese gold; we can extract silver from Japan with Chinese goods...and rials from Arabia for spices and various other trifles – one thing leads to another.[10]

A recurrent theme in Coen's report is the central role played by Gujarati and Coromandel Coast cottons in lubricating the wheels of the spice trade. Asian sources are very limited, but it is clear from the complaints in the European correspondences of 'unfair competition' that the Asian merchants operated on much smaller margins than the highly capitalized Western ventures. It was only through coercion and intimidation (frequently including acts of piracy) that the trading companies were able to secure a share. Achieving sustainable profits proved far more difficult than Coen and his successors anticipated. The European reliance on superior weapons and a willingness to use force fractured the laisser-faire nature of Asian commerce. Attempts to win political control of the sources of the spices followed and, as is evident from VOC records, central to that was regulation of the trade in Indian textiles.

The Portuguese seizure of Melaka (Malacca) in 1511 marked the beginning of the Western quest to secure spices at their source. Yet it is a measure of the

11 The Indian Ocean world.

very limited success of the Europeans in Southeast Asia that not until the eighteenth century did they control the major share of the Asian trade. Paradoxically, by that time both the European demand for spices and the vogue for Indian textiles were waning; the VOC, having secured a virtual monopoly of Indonesian spices, was effectively bankrupt and was finally dissolved in 1800.[11] The legacy of the policies of the trading companies and their colonial government successors (the Dutch East Indies and the British Raj) was to generate an impoverishment of the peoples of Asia as forced cash-cropping and regulated piece-work production exposed progressively larger segments of the populations to the deadly fluctuations of the international markets.

The Indian textiles presented in this book are today virtually unknown outside specialist circles, and yet it was as a direct result of these cloths, and the international hunger for spices that they helped satisfy, that much of the history of Asia, and indeed Europe, was shaped. Indian trade textiles can then be seen to have played a central role in a much larger economic and political drama that was being enacted on the Asian stage.

Sources

The sources for such a wide-ranging study as this are extensive. As far as possible I have attempted to root it in the evidence that can be drawn from the textiles themselves. Although dating of the cloths is very problematic, some progress has been made through the combined approaches of scientific analysis (radiocarbon analysis), inscriptional and seal evidence, stylistic analogies with other media, and contextual dating from archaeological finds. The evidence proffered by the textiles is then provided with a historical and anthropological context by drawing on a variety of other sources.

The archaeological evidence comes in several forms. Excavations in the Red Sea and Lower Egypt regions have yielded Indian dyed cotton cloth radiocarbon dated to the late ninth/early tenth century, the earliest date for Indian textiles in

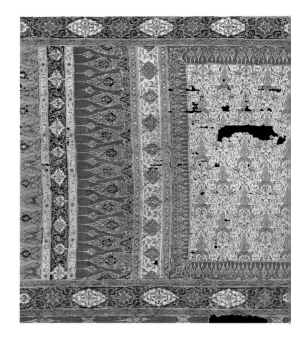

12 *Pha nung*, ceremonial skirt-cloth (detail; see also **180**). Coromandel Coast, for the Thai market; late eighteenth century. Cotton, painted mordant-dyed and drawn resist-dyed, and painted; weft 88 cm. Victoria and Albert Museum, London. ◆ Thai market cloths are among the finest Indian painted cottons produced for the Asian trade, and are comparable in delicacy of drawing and quality of colour to the best chintzes intended for Europe.

the world.[12] There are no actual finds in Southeast Asia which can be dated before the fourteenth century (see 'Radiocarbon-dated Indian textiles', p. 186), but depictions of textile patterns in relief sculptures and mural paintings are plentiful from the tenth century onwards.

The study of Indian trade textiles is endowed with an extensive source literature, which takes a variety of forms. References by early economic geographers and travellers begin with the Greek *Periplus of the Erythraean Sea* in the first century AD. Arabic and Chinese writers become more plentiful from the tenth century on. Isolated European accounts, such as that of Marco Polo (1271–95), provide tantalizing glimpses of the luxury trade of Asia. In the course of the fifteenth century the situation alters dramatically as the trickle of European travellers turns into a flood, all seeking the wealth promised by the 'Spiceries'. The Portuguese, followed by the English, Dutch, French and Danes, left a wealth of contemporary accounts of their voyages, richly detailing the commercial potential of the countries they visited. As the Europeans' presence in Asia became more institutionalized so the data they produced became more detailed and systematic. The English East India Company (1600–1858) and the Dutch VOC (1602–1800) have both bequeathed detailed economic information on products, prices and markets. Indian dyed cottons feature prominently throughout these records. Company edicts and proclamations catalogue attempts to regulate and police the trade.

The present study also examines the decoration of Indian trade textiles in their stylistic context, largely through pictorial and iconographic comparisons with other media. This enhances our understanding of their broader cultural significance as well as providing useful reference points for dating. A related issue is that of local versus foreign designs. Interpreting the process of acculturation requires the disentanglement of the Indian design components from indigenous elements. Such an enquiry opens up a way to understanding the process of commissioning, and the vexed question of the flow of influences. Were Indian designs adapted to foreign taste by Indian designers, or can we assume that where they are self-evidently non-Indian they must have been copied from imported samples? References to samples and pattern books survive from the seventeenth century, but for the earlier periods we can only speculate as to how designs were transmitted. The traffic in imagery between the cultures must have been continuous, creating a melting pot of design elements formed and reformed through time.

A further source is the evidence provided by ethnographic observations of the recent past. Particularly significant are studies of village Indonesia, where Indian trade textiles continue to feature in ceremonial and ritual life. The bulk of these studies belong to the twentieth century and their retrospective application must be handled with care. There are however in earlier travel accounts objective descriptions worthy of the modern anthropologist, which provide details of local dress and customs. Where possible, I have attempted to let the historical commentators and observers of textiles in daily life speak in their own words.

The records give some indication of the volume of cloths in circulation, and it is clear that what survives represents only a small percentage of a huge trade sustained over many centuries. The textiles preserved in Asia are those that were assigned a high social or ritual value by the communities that used them. Of the more mundane cloths destined for everyday use, which formed the staple of the Indian textile trade, little can be seen today.

13 Display textile, possibly intended as a theatrical backdrop. English technology, for the Burmese market; early nineteenth century. Cotton, machine-printed; 40 x 79 cm. Victoria and Albert Museum, London. ◆ The final phase of Indian trade textiles saw the increasing substitution of copies on machine-woven cloth printed by a transfer method from copper plates. This technology had been available in India as early as the 1780s; although primarily intended to undercut English cloth printers in supplying the British market with 'printed Calicos', it appears also to have been used for regional specialist markets such as Burma.

TECHNIQUES AND PRODUCTION CENTRES

These cloths acquire their value and price from their brightness and, if I may say so, from the solidity and fastness of the colours they are dyed with.…[Nature] has granted India ingredients, and above all, certain waters, whose particular qualities have much to do with the beautiful combinations of painting and dyeing represented by Indian cloths.

Father Coeurdoux, 1742[1]

Mastery of the traditional techniques of weaving and decorating textiles in India, like sericulture in China, was a carefully guarded professional secret. Such skills, upon which the livelihood of whole communities depended, were kept within the designated castes and shared only with those who married into that section of society. Even with the arrival of European entrepreneurs in the Asian markets the situation altered little. The new merchants, and the companies they represented, were interested only in securing marketable goods of the desired quality and design and in the appropriate volumes. How they were made, by whom, or in what conditions, concerned them little. Occasional marvellings at the fastness and brilliance of colours did not extend to a scientific curiosity about production processes until nearly a hundred and forty years after the commercial potential of Indian textiles first caught the European imagination.[2]

Techniques of trade cloths

The Indian subcontinent has been blessed with abundant supplies of the materials necessary for the production of cotton and silk textiles and of the dye-stuffs for their decoration.

Dye-stuffs

The patterned cloths were dominated by combinations of red, blue, black, violet, green and yellow [42]. All these colours could be achieved from dyes available in the subcontinent; supplementary sources were obtained from Iran, the Arabian Peninsula and Southeast Asia. Knowledge of the superior properties of particular dye-stuffs resulted in a brisk inter-regional and international trade.

Indigo was the principal dye, together with *chay* and madder red, in the decoration of the vast quantity of Indian cotton goods produced for trade to the Middle-Eastern markets from at least the late ninth century. *Indigofera tinctoria*, introduced to western India from Africa and Iran, produces a remarkable range of hues of blue and was famed for the intensity of its colour.[3] The regions around Agra and Ahmedabad were especially noted for the quality of their indigo, which was widely traded in the form of dried cakes. Marco Polo reported in the thirteenth century that Gujarat was the most prolific centre of production and that Arab traders were instrumental in its distribution.

The other dominant colour for cotton export cloths was red. This was obtained from two main sources, both of which involved the most complex of extractive and dyeing processes. *Chay* (or *chaya*), widely used in southern India, was extracted from the roots of the *chay* plant (*Oldenlandia umbellata*); the finest specimens were known to grow in the lime soils of the Krishna River delta, around Madurai and in the Jaffna district of northern Sri Lanka.[4] Cloths which were first treated with the mordant alum received the *chay* dye as a rich and fast red. The second source of red was the madder plant, the roots of which

14 A cotton-printer at work, using a wooden printing block; large blocks with floral designs are displayed behind. Ahmedabad, Gujarat, 1880s. Victoria and Albert Museum, London.

yielded the colouring agent alizarin (*Morinda citrifolia*). This was the principal red dye source in western India, where it was known as *ail* or *al*. The red achieved from madder was regarded as inferior to that produced from *chay*. A further source of red was sappanwood (also known as brazilwood), a dark red wood imported from Southeast Asia.[5]

Additional dyes from a variety of plant, animal and insect sources ensured that Indian cottons were patterned with the most varied and rich colourings of any dyed textile tradition. The complex methods of preparing the cloth ensured a degree of colour intensity and fastness unrivalled anywhere in the world.

Cotton

Cotton is recorded from the earliest urban civilization of the subcontinent, that of the Indus Valley city of Mohenjo Daro, of the second millennium BC. Its cultivation in India was known to the Greeks, who were in awe of the wool-bearing trees and, according to the *Periplus of the Erythraean Sea* – a first-century AD Greek account of commerce in the western Indian Ocean – imported it as a luxury fabric.[6] Sanskrit literature is silent on the subject, apart from a short discussion of the organization of the weaving industry in the *Arthasastra*.[7] Jain and Buddhist sources refer to its preparation, and the sixth-century Buddhist murals at Ajanta depict some of the stages in its transformation into cloth [15], by processes which are essentially the same as those employed by spinners and hand-loom weavers today [16, 17].

The major cotton-growing regions are in the Deccan and extend across the width of the subcontinent, ensuring supplies to the major production centres in the hinterlands of the east and west coasts. Where local sources were limited or of indifferent quality, as on the northern Coromandel Coast, raw cotton was transported by bullock cart from the central Deccan. This long-distance trade appears to have boomed in the early decades of the seventeenth century in response to an insatiable demand for high-quality cloth for export.

On the whole, the factors determining where the different stages of production took place were closely linked to the availability of raw materials. Typically,

15 Women wearing woven and ikat-dyed skirt-cloths, from a mural painting in Cave 1, Ajanta; sixth century. It appears that the woman on the right, holding a rectangular frame, is spinning yarn from a ball of thread held by the woman in the centre, and threading it onto the frame. The frame also bears some resemblance to those used for binding threads prior to dyeing [cf. 21]. If so, this is the earliest depiction of the ikat or tie-dyeing technique. Copy by J. Griffiths, *c*. 1850. Victoria and Albert Museum, London.

16 Tamil woman twisting spun yarns together to made a strengthened multi-ply yarn suitable for the weaver. Kanchipuram, Tamilnadu, 1995.

17 Tamil weaver at a pit loom, producing a check-patterned *lungi* (skirt-cloth). Kanchipuram, Tamilnadu, 1995. Trading company records describe such a loom in each household in villages engaged in weaving for the export trade. The craftsmen worked to order, having undertaken to supply cloths of the dimensions and quality appropriate for particular markets.

cloth was spun and woven in one place, where there was raw cotton and labour, and then transported for painting and dyeing to an area with abundant supplies of clean water essential to the patterning processes. The finished textile was finally taken to a collection point for grading, stamping and marketing.

Most of the textiles produced for export to Southeast Asia consisted of plain woven cotton which was decorated either by mordant-dyeing alone or, more commonly, where several colours were involved, mordant-dyeing in combination with resist-dyeing. These 'painted cottons' – a term that must be used, though it is potentially confusing since not all were strictly *painted* – were known by a variety of names in trading records. Some were derivations of the Indian term *chitta* ('spotted cloth'), including 'chintz',[8] the most universally recognized word for the painted cotton textiles with which this survey will be chiefly concerned. Other terms also survive into modern usage, such as *sarasa* and *saudagiri*, Gujarati names for painted and printed cottons for the export trade to Japan and Thailand respectively, and *sembagi*, a variant Malay word used for these textiles in western Indonesia.

Mordant-dyeing

Cotton does not readily respond to dyes in the way that silk and wool do. To ensure a degree of colourfastness, an agent must be used to ensure that the dye adheres to the fibre. This fixative agent is a mordant, a metallic oxide which combines with the dye to bond onto the fibre; it also produces a variety of colouring effects, depending on the dye and mordant combinations. Two mordants were favoured in Indian trade textiles: alum, which when used with an alizarin dye (madder) produced a range of reds, and iron, which yielded black when combined with tannin.[9]

The use of mordants is described as a 'positive' process, for the dye adheres only to those areas of the cloth which have been treated. Mordants and dyes were applied by one of two methods, which were sometimes used together: painting and block-printing. In the first, the mordant is painted with a pen or fine-haired brush known as *qalam* (Persian: 'pen') directly onto the washed cloth. *Qalams* were traditionally made of bamboo with tied fibres or hair to act as a reservoir; by the seventeenth century metal applicators were also in use [18]. Cloth decorated by this method is known as *kalamkari*.[10] Fine *kalamkari* is associated most strongly with the cloth-painting workshops of the Coromandel Coast, where the best-quality hand-drawn chintzes were produced for domestic luxury consumption in the Deccani and Mughal courts, and for export. The *qalam* is still employed at Kalahasti, southern Andhra Pradesh, one of the few centres producing *kalamkari* by traditional methods [19].

In the second application technique, the mordant for the design which is to take up the dye is stamped onto the fabric with wooden blocks [14]. A further variation to the process is when a resist (wax or mud) has first been block-printed onto the cloth, adding another level of complexity to the design. The result lacks the finesse and refinement of hand-painted work, and the method was used where considerations of speed and economy prevailed over quality. Nonetheless, the best-designed blocks did produce cloths of considerable

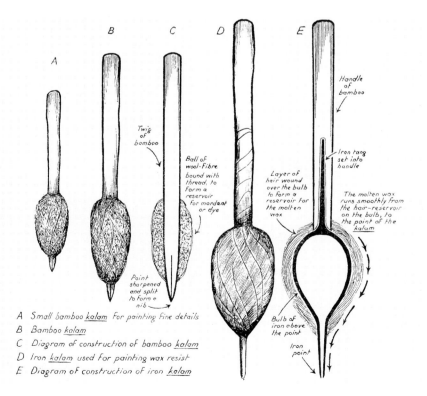

A Small bamboo *kalam* for painting fine details
B Bamboo *kalam*
C Diagram of construction of bamboo *kalam*
D Iron *kalam* used for painting wax resist
E Diagram of construction of iron *kalam*

18 Two types of *qalam*. On the left (A, B, C) is a bamboo and fibre brush, which is used to apply the mordant solution to cloth that is to be dyed; this is the means by which a cloth painter achieves the design, as only areas treated with mordant accept colour in the dye bath. On the right (D, E) is an iron version, which is used to apply molten wax for resist-dyeing; in that technique, the waxed areas resist the dye and the design is revealed by the undyed areas of fabric. The metal *qalam* closely resembles the Javanese *canting*, the wax applicator used in hand-drawn *tulis* batik.

19 A cloth painter using a *qalam* to apply a mordant to a cloth on which the design has been outlined in charcoal. This process will be repeated, and combined with wax-resist dyeing, to achieve a variety of colour combinations [see **38–41**]. The finished cloth is locally known as *kalamkari*. Kalahasti, Andhra Pradesh, 1995.

decorative charm. Wooden block-printing (*chit*) was an innovation of the work-shops of western India. An eyewitness description of the process at Ahmedabad in Gujarat survives from 1678, confirming its presence at that centre of printed cotton production.[11] The desired patterns were transferred to teak printing blocks by woodworkers using an array of iron chisels and die punches to create the design in deep relief. One workshop undertaking this skilled work survives today, at the village of Pethapur, forty kilometres from Ahmedabad.[12] The major printing and dyeing workshops were in Ahmedabad, where the woven cotton was decorated using a mud-resist dyeing technique. The cloth was first dyed in one colour and then block-printed with the remaining colours. In both technique and elements of design the nineteenth-century Gujarati cloths resemble the *arjakh* mud-resist-dyed textiles of Kutch and Sind, cheap printed cottons produced for local consumption and for the Islamic markets of West Asia.[13] Samples of Gujarati block-printed cottons retrieved from sites in the Middle East have yielded radiocarbon dates which establish that this technology was in use from at least the ninth century.

Resist-dyeing
Both painting and block-printing were also employed in the 'negative' process of resist-dyeing. This involves the application of a solution – molten wax or moist mud – to those areas which were *not* intended to take up the dye.

Indigo dyeing was traditionally achieved in Indian cotton cloths by the resist method, although the design was on occasions also applied directly.[14] In the southern states of Andhra Pradesh and Tamilnadu, the resisting agent was wax, applied with the *qalam* to often remarkable effect. In the west, in Gujarat, Rajasthan and Madhya Pradesh, it was customary to use mud. After the elements of the design had been painted or stamped onto the surface of the cloth, it was immersed in a hot dye bath. The depth and intensity of colour depended on the concentration of the dye, the duration of immersion, and the number of dyeings. The colour revealed itself through oxidation upon contact with the air.

A complex procedure involving the resisting of alternative areas, and double-dyeing of others to achieve third colours (such as red on black to produce violet, and yellow on blue to produce green), meant that cloths went through a bewildering series of stages of dyeing to achieve the often spectacular finished result (see below, pp. 34–37).

Silk

The dyes sources are essentially the same as those used for cotton, but the dyeing of silk, an animal fibre, is far less problematic than that of cotton; the fibres take up dyes readily and hold them well. The favoured way of decorating silk in India is by a variety of tie-dye resist techniques. The most relevant in the context of this study is that which involves binding clusters of warp or weft threads to resist the dye, a method widely referred to by the Malay term *ikat*. It requires an exact understanding of the design that the dyer wishes to achieve, which is bound into the prepared but unwoven threads; pattern books were developed to assist in the process [20, 21]. Additional colours required the resisting of other areas of the thread, and of those areas already dyed, to achieve the desired combination. The most common colours were red, blue, green, yellow and black, in combination with white (the undyed threads) [22]. All can be achieved by the use of three dye baths only.[15] This method of decorating results in both sides of the cloth displaying identical colour intensity, a highly desirable indicator of quality.

The technique which produced one of the most prestigious trade cloths in Southeast Asia was that of double ikat, in which both the warp and the weft threads are bound and resist-dyed to create a predetermined design. When the weft threads are woven onto the loom (in a simple tabby or plain weave) they combine with the warp to reveal a pattern of often extraordinary density and complexity, with a more clearly defined sharp geometric character than single ikat. Each 'step' in the design represents one cluster of threads which were bound before dyeing. After the threads have been combined on the loom to

20 Pattern book produced by *patola* (double ikat) weavers, as a guide to the person responsible for the complex binding of the warp and weft threads before immersion in a dye bath. Workshop of Kantilal Lallubhai Salvi, Patan, Gujarat, 1993.

21 LEFT Binding the warp threads of raw silk, to ensure the desired design appears after dyeing. Workshop of Chhotalal Manilal Salvi, Patan, Gujarat, 1993.

22 OPPOSITE, ABOVE *Patolu* with a design of elephant and parrot within a trellis with flowers, known in Gujarati as *popat kunjar bhat* (detail). Silk, double ikat, with gilt metal thread on the end-panel. Victoria and Albert Museum, London. ◆ This design, seen in the pattern book above, is popular in Gujarat among Brahmin communities; while no examples have been found in Southeast Asia, it is recorded from Kerala, where Indonesian-market *patola* [cf. **108**] are known to have been traded en route.

23 OPPOSITE, BELOW Shri Chhotalal Manilal Salvi, master weaver, tightens and aligns threads of a *patolu* on the loom, using iron needles, in his workshop. Patan, Gujarat, 1993. He is adjusting threads on a wedding sari before 'locking' the pattern into the weave. The design is closely related to the frangipani pattern seen on Balinese double-ikat *geringsing* [**125**], for which it is probably the source.

create the cloth, the master weaver uses a metal stylus to correct any slippage in the warp and weft that would distort the pattern. He then tightens the weave on the loom [23]. Such textiles have historically been expensive, a reflection of the laborious and highly skilled process involved: a typical sari length (5–6 metres) takes in excess of six months to produce.

The Gujarati silk-weaving industry was responsible for the famous cloth made by this most intricate and exacting technique, known as *patola*.[16] (The singular form is *patolu*; the plural, *patola*, is used both for the technique and, as a generic term, for cloths produced by that technique.) The word appears in a number of variant spellings in Indian sources as early as the fourteenth century and in the accounts of numerous early sixteenth-century European commentators. Considerable ambiguity surrounds the term, which appears to have encompassed non-silk as well as silk cloths.

Among the Portuguese, Duarte Barbosa (1518) wrote of the demand in the Spice Islands (i.e. Maluku, or the Moluccas) for '*patola*, (that is to say Cambaya cloth), some of cotton, some of silk'. [17] By referring to cotton versions, was Barbosa identifying the *patola* imitations known to have been in circulation a century later, or was he merely careless with terminology? Gaspar Correa (1522) records silk *patola* as part of a gift from Cambay to the Queen of Maluku used in the securing of contracts for cloves.[18] In 1526 Jorge de Albuquerque, Captain-General of Melaka (Malacca), sent 'silks and *patolas* [to the] King of Borneo and to the nobility of that country to compact friendship with them'.[19] The pilot of the Spanish expedition to the southern Philippines led by Villalobos in 1543 described the clothing of the people of Mindanao as consisting of 'sleeveless robes called *patolas*', adding that those of the wealthy were of silk, and those of others were made of cotton cloth.[20] All these sixteenth-century sources are unanimous that *patola* was expressly (and it appears exclusively) the product of Cambay, the great port of the western Indian textile trade. Regrettably, they do not give any clue as to whether the cloths resembled what we know today; it seems likely that that was the case by the beginning of the seventeenth century. What is clear is that *patola* never disappeared from the trade and retained their high position in the hierarchy of cloths as gifts worthy of rulers.

In India, *patola* were favoured for the traditional ceremonial sari of Gujarat and were adapted for other uses; for example in Kerala they assumed a role in temple ritual associated with the dressing and decorating of the deity during worship.[21] The circulation of *patola* in the south is further attested by a large-scale mural painting of a textile with *patola*-inspired design at Tiruppudaimarudur [24]. When exported to Southeast Asia, the cloths took on a broad array of ceremonial, ritual and even magical functions quite unimagined by their Gujarati creators (see Chapters V and VI).

For the classic *patola* imported Chinese yarn had been preferred by the weavers, but increasingly substantial quantities of Bengali silk were also used. By the late seventeenth century Bengal was the main supplier, with Kasimbazar supplying two-thirds of its output to the Gujarati silk-weaving industry.[22] *Patola* is linked to the major textile centres of Gujarat, notably Patan, Ahmedabad, Cambay and Surat. The last two cities frequently appear in trade records and may have served principally as shipment points rather than production centres. Today the necessary skills survive only in Patan, a city whose long and close association with this cloth is reflected in local legends and inscriptions.[23]

The technique of single and double ikat was also practised on the Coromandel Coast, in Orissa and in Andhra Pradesh, where cotton was woven as well as

24 Mural painting in the vestibule of the Sri Narompunadaswami Temple, Tiruppudaimarudur, Tirunellveli district, Tamilnadu; seventeenth century. The mural replicates a textile, with centrefield and border, the latter with a stepped-square pattern, probably a legacy of the circulation of Gujarati *patola* in southern India. The mural also evokes the use of cloths as hangings in temples.

silk.[24] Trade records of ikats from Andhra Pradesh (*telia rumal*) are limited but samples have survived in Japanese collections [226].

Production centres

The location of production centres of textiles for the export trade was determined by accessibility to materials and markets. Whilst certain areas were traditionally known for their weaving and dyeing, others emerged in response to the demands of merchants.

Three regions, all with good harbour facilities and access to well-populated hinterlands, served India's overseas textile markets: western India, especially

25 The Indian subcontinent, showing sites of significance for the textile trade.

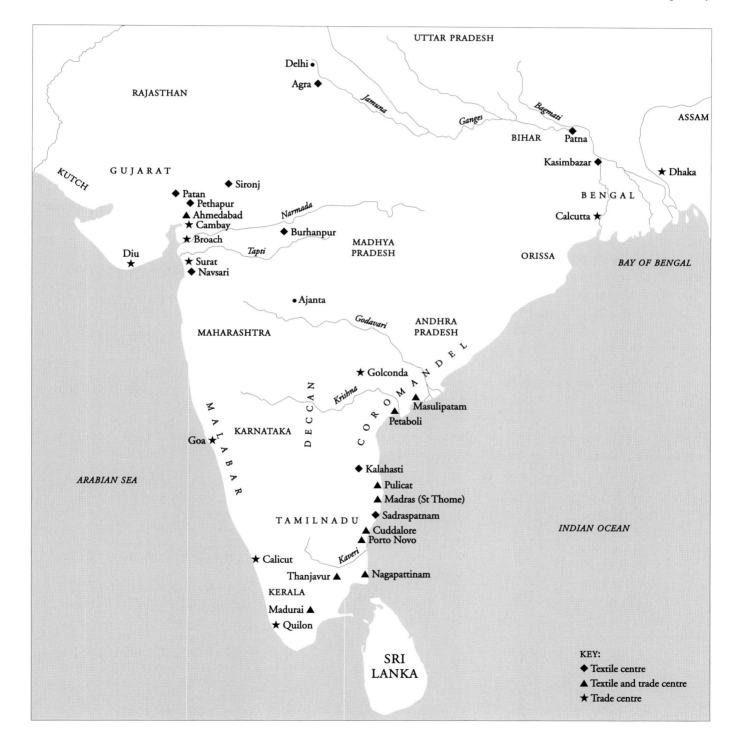

UTTAR PRADESH

RAJASTHAN

Delhi •

Agra ◆

Jamuna

Ganges

Bagmati

ASSAM

BIHAR   Patna ◆

Kasimbazar ◆

★ Dhaka

KUTCH   GUJARAT

B E N G A L

◆ Sironj

◆ Patan

◆ Pethapur

▲ Ahmedabad

Narmada

★ Cambay

◆ Burhanpur

MADHYA PRADESH

Calcutta ★

★ Broach

Tapti

ORISSA

Diu ★

★ Surat

◆ Navsari

BAY OF BENGAL

• Ajanta

Godavari

ANDHRA PRADESH

MAHARASHTRA

Krishna

C O R O M A N D E L

★ Golconda

▲ Masulipatam

▲ Petaboli

M A L A B A R

DECCAN

KARNATAKA

Goa ★

◆ Kalahasti

▲ Pulicat

▲ Madras (St Thome)

◆ Sadraspatnam

ARABIAN SEA

T A M I L N A D U

▲ Cuddalore

▲ Porto Novo

INDIAN OCEAN

Kaveri

★ Calicut

Thanjavur ▲

▲ Nagapattinam

KERALA

Madurai ▲

★ Quilon

SRI LANKA

KEY:
◆ Textile centre
▲ Textile and trade centre
★ Trade centre

Gujarat; the Coromandel Coast in the south-east; and Bengal in the east. The antiquity of their foreign trade is clear from the *Periplus of the Erythraean Sea*, where all are named as cotton-exporting centres.[25]

The importance of Gujarat for silk ikat-dyed cloth has been discussed above. Western India had an equally venerable tradition of cotton dyeing. This well-established export industry was further boosted by the establishment in 1411 of the independent state of Gujarat, with a new capital at Ahmedabad. Together with the rebuilding of naval forces and the refurbishing of the port of Cambay, the political climate stimulated an unprecedented boom in the textile trade. Cambay's rich hinterland was able to support a vast industry, and western India's cloth trade to the Red Sea was virtually monopolized by 'Cambay goods'. Cambay maintained its position as the major western port after the Mughal conquest of Gujarat in 1577. However, a gradual silting of the river estuary resulted in its relegation to second place, as Surat rose to prominence under Mughal administration. Many of the cotton goods and silk *patola* traded to Indonesia are associated by contemporary commentators, or by the seals and stamps they bear, with Surat. Ahmedabad held a dominant position as the largest textile producer in the region, but it is other centres like Burhanpur, Agra and Sironj that are named in seventeenth-century European accounts as the sources of fine-quality painted cottons. Both Peter Mundy (1630) and Thevenot (1666) specifically noted that Sironj was renowned for its painted fabrics.

Types of export textiles:

'Painted' cotton from Gujarat

26 LEFT Ceremonial cloth with a pattern of female figures (detail: see 146). Gujarat, for the Indonesian market, found in the Toraja area of central Sulawesi; radiocarbon-dated 1370 ± 40 years. Cotton, block-printed mordant-dyed and painted resist-dyed. Victoria and Albert Museum, London.

Silk patola *(double ikat) from Gujarat*

27 OPPOSITE, ABOVE LEFT *Patolu*, ceremonial cloth used as a breast-cloth (detail). Gujarat, for the Indonesian market, found in Java; late nineteenth century. Silk, double ikat. Victoria and Albert Museum, London.

Chintz – fine painted cotton – from the Coromandel Coast

28 OPPOSITE, ABOVE RIGHT Fragment of cloth for the European market, found in Japan (detail); late eighteenth century. Cotton, painted mordant-dyed, resist-dyed, and painted, with glued gold leaf. Idemitsu Museum of Art, Tokyo. ◆ Some of the finest Indian painted cloths in circulation in Asia were made for the European market. They were traded east usually to serve as gifts from European traders to local dignitaries. Resist-dyed in the border of this example are a Telegu inscription, probably the maker's name, and cartouches to receive traders' stamps. A similar piece, preserved in the Rijksmuseum, Amsterdam, has a dated Dutch provenance of 1775.

Painted cotton from the Coromandel Coast

29 OPPOSITE, BELOW *Kain sembagi*, skirt-cloth. Tamilnadu, for the Javanese market; late nineteenth century. Cotton, painted mordant-dyed and drawn resist-dyed. Victoria and Albert Museum, London. ◆ According to the Museum's records, this cloth, acquired in 1897, was destined for the Batavia (Jakarta) market.

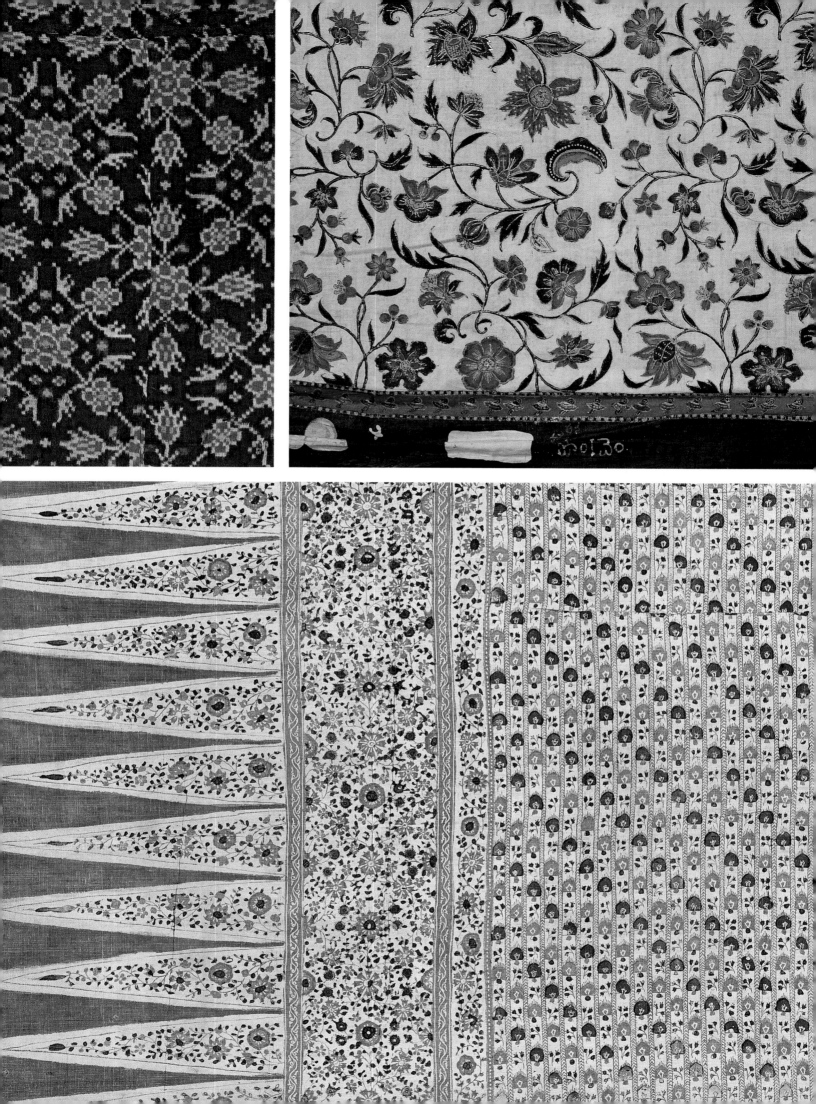

The commentators, however, repeatedly measure the quality of western Indian painted cloth against that of the Coromandel Coast and are unanimous in praising the latter as the most technically refined and aesthetically pleasing of the age. William Methwold's *Relations of the Kingdom of Golconda* (1626) records that a plentiful variety of northern Coromandel cotton cloths ('Callicoes') were available and that they were readily identifiable by the strength of their colours, most notably the red and blue derived from locally grown *chay* and indigo:

> The paintings of this Coast of Choromandel [are] famous throughout India, and are indeed the most exquisite that are seen, the best wrought all with pensil [*qalam*] and with such durable colours that, not withstanding they bee often washed, the colours fade not whilst the cloth lasteth.[26]

The port which emerged in the sixteenth century to serve the cosmopolitan city-state of Golconda and the growing Coromandel Coast export trade was Masulipatam [30].[27] From its rise to prominence in the early decades after 1500, linked to the emergence of Golconda as an independent kingdom, until its dramatic demise in the 1660s following ruinous famines and warfare, Masulipatam dominated much of India's international trade, most notably with Iran and Southeast Asia. The French traveller and jeweller Jean-Baptiste Tavernier, drawn to Golconda by its famous diamonds, visited this great entre-pot just before its decline, and described it as 'the sole place from which vessels sail for Pegu, Siam, Arakan, Bengal, Cochin, China, Mecca and Hormuz and also for the islands of Madagascar and the Manilas'.[28]

Masulipatam's success was due not to its harbour facilities (which were inadequate in many respects) but first to its geographical location, which served as a springboard for the Asian spice trade, and secondly to its vast hinterland [31]. The latter served both to generate goods for export, especially cotton tex-tiles, and to act as a strong market for imported luxury goods. The Golconda élite participated in this trade alongside other leading merchant communities, notably the Telugu-speaking northern Coromandel Coast traders involved in the Malay trade, the Klings (Tamil-speaking traders), Chettiars (Tamil Hindus), and the Chulias (Tamil Muslims), as well as Arab, Persian and European traders. A large ship-building centre nearby, at Narasapurpeta, ensured a supply of sturdy teak vessels to serve the needs of the merchants for both coastal and long-distance trade. Cloth was also imported into Masulipatam from Thanjavur and other southern centres, such as Madurai, as well as from Bengal to the north, to

30 A pattern-drawing, from Masulipatam, Andhra Pradesh; watercolour, dated on the reverse 1810. Victoria and Albert Museum, London. ◆ It may reasonably be assumed that textile orders were prepared on the basis of patterns supplied by the clients or their agents. This drawing is one of the very few to survive, and is linked to a major centre of the painted cotton trade.

supply the Southeast Asian trade with the wide variety of textiles it demanded.

Pulicat, south of Masulipatam, was another centre renowned for the quality of its painted cotton goods. The Dutch had their headquarters there, known as Fort Geldria. Chettiar merchants operated a direct trade from Pulicat to Melaka, exchanging cotton cloth for Malay and Sumatran gold.

After the collapse of Masulipatam the commercial focus progressively shifted further south.[29] The English established themselves at Fort St George (Madras) and in 1690 the Dutch moved their headquarters from Pulicat to Nagapattinam, ensuring the future commercial dominance of the textile export industry by the southern Coromandel Coast. Many weaving and cloth-painting families responded to this reorientation in the international textile trade, migrating from coastal Andhra Pradesh to the Fort St George area and further south along the Tamilnadu coast. This movement of skilled labour may explain the frequent occurrence of inscriptions in Telegu (the language of Andhra Pradesh) on *kalamkari* from Tamil regions. The ports of Nagapattinam and Nagore served Thanjavur district, a major textile-producing region, and continued to function as important embarkation points for the cloth trade to Southeast Asia well into the nineteenth century.

Bengal as a centre for textile production remained important, though its artisans never attained the high reputation of the Coromandel Coast cloth painters. Their skills lay elsewhere, in fine muslins and the famous Kasimbazar

31 Masulipatam. Engraving, first published in Philippus Baldaeus, *Naauwkeurige Beschryvinge van Malabar en Choromandel,* Amsterdam, 1672. This was the most famous port on the Coromandel Coast for securing supplies of high-quality painted cottons, used by European and Asian merchants alike. The view is of the city and the sea beyond; in the foreground is the bridge built to provide efficient passage across river and floodplains to the highway leading to the hinterland of the kingdom of Golconda.

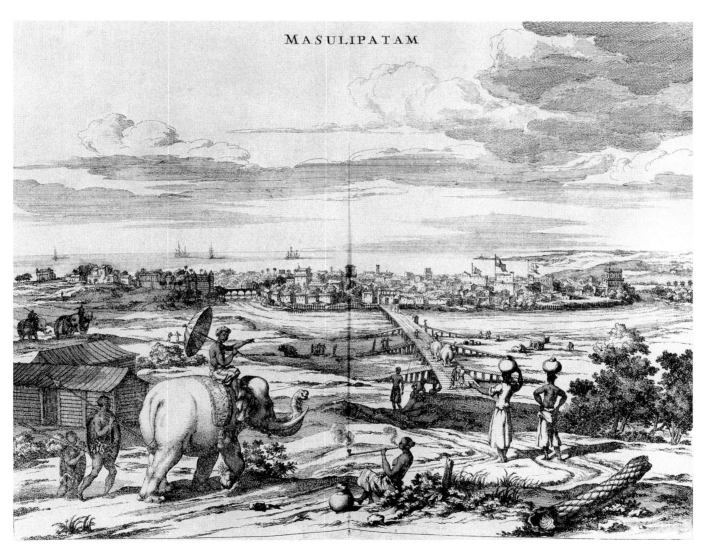

MASULIPATAM

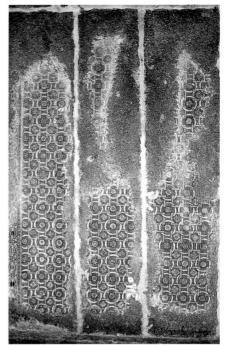

silks.[30] Bengal's textile export received a fillip with the rise to prominence of Calcutta in the late eighteenth century. Through Calcutta and Fort St George the English gradually extended their control over the production of cloth along the length of the coast, excluding other European competition.

When English machine-printed cottons began to challenge the very existence of the Indian handloom industry in the early nineteenth century, it was the weavers of the southern Coromandel Coast who were best equipped to resist this pressure and to continue to compete successfully for the patronage of the Southeast Asian consumer, as witnessed by the great number of weaving centres in the hinterland of Tamilnadu active in the nineteenth century [29, 34–37].

Whilst weaving in western India appears to have been centred in towns, in southern India it was primarily village-based. Weavers combined working their looms with agricultural activity. Some measure of the intensity of the industry can be gauged from Dutch records of the later seventeenth century. Statistics survive recording the output of villages in the eastern Godaveri delta, which supplied the Dutch factory at Draksharama: for the year 1682, 16 villages (comprising 5,960 households) had nearly 7,000 looms actively weaving for the VOC.[31] That is, on average every household in the villages surveyed had at least one loom engaged in producing cloth to order for the Company [cf. 17]. This pattern was probably repeated in villages contracted to other merchant interests operating in the Masulipatam hinterland.

Demand for greater quantities of cotton goods for export grew in the sixteenth century and peaked in the seventeenth. Procuring supplies in the marketplace proved increasingly unreliable, as a Masulipatam-based English Company official lamented in 1630: 'the cloth of these parts is growne very deceitful, as wanting in both lengths and breadths, which will be very prejudiciall to the profit.'[32] Commissioning practices were developed to exert greater control over the commercial life of the weavers, painters and dyers. Weavers worked to Indian agents, supplying agreed quantities in the requested dimensions to the approved standard. Responsibility for the painting of the cloths lay with the commissioning merchants (brokers), which meant that the European

32 ABOVE LEFT A Hindu textile vendor, engaged in a transaction. Thanjavur, Tamilnadu; gouache, Company School, c. 1800. British Library, London. ◆ This view of the interior of a cloth-seller's shop gives a vivid impression of the woven and dyed goods available.

33 ABOVE Painting on the ceiling of the mandapa of Tirupparuttikkunram, a Jain temple near Kanchipuram, Tamilnadu; Nayak period, seventeenth century. The decoration of geometricized circles is imitative of textile designs known today from traded examples and no longer extant in India. Cloths are frequently used in Indian temples as ceiling canopies, to define sacred spaces. Replicating them on painted ceilings was a pan-Indian practice [cf. 64].

34, 35, 37 OPPOSITE, TOP ROW AND LOWER RIGHT Fragments of textiles formerly used as cloth bindings on manuscripts. Thanjavur district, Tamilnadu; early nineteenth century. Cotton, block-printed mordant-dyed. Saraswati Mahal Library, The Palace, Thanjavur. ◆ One of the finest libraries to be formed in British India was assembled by Maharjaja Sarabhoji II (r. 1798–1833) at his palace at Thanjavur. The manuscripts from which these samples were retrieved were most probably bound during his reign with cloths from a number of centres in the region (see pp. 171 ff.).

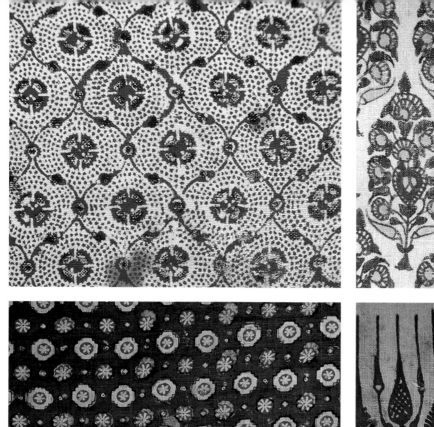

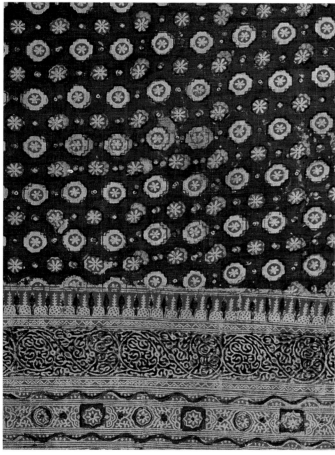

36 ABOVE Ceremonial cloth (detail). Coromandel Coast, for the Indonesian market, found in Sulawesi; early nineteenth century. Cotton, block-printed mordant-dyed and resist-dyed. Victoria and Albert Museum, London.

companies had a degree of direct control over this important stage of production. However, in reality the Company and their agents could not supervise the actual production: methods had to be devised to ensure a degree of quality control [30]. Samples ('musters') were sent to serve both as models for the cloth painters to follow and as standards of quality against which to assess new stock. Consistency became an vital issue when procuring stock for long-distance trade. Quality was traditionally measured by the density of weave, expressed as the number of units of thread in a given width.[33] Density, dimensions and colours were assessed against the agreed muster cloths (following procedures common in the European textile industry). The textiles were sorted for sale in two ways: by quality, into grades priced for different markets, and by variety of designs, according to the tastes and preferences of the intended buyers.

The Painting of Chintz (1688)

H. A. van Rheede

(Translated by Ruurdje Laarhoven[1])

This description of the technique of chintz painting is the earliest known, predating that of M. de Beaulieu (1734) by nearly fifty years.[2] It is extracted from a letter written by the Dutch East India Company's Commissioner-General, Hendrick Adriaan van Rheede tot Drakesteyn, Lord of Mydrecht, from Pulicat, on the Coromandel Coast, received in the Netherlands on 1 December 1688.[3]

The best chintz painters of south Coromandel are found in Sadraspatnam, because of the neatness of their painting, and because of the pure water that is found there, which imparts the highest gloss and the longest durability to all dyes, qualities which cannot be matched in other places. And since this manner of painting is unknown in Europe, and is so admirable, it may not displease Your Honour to learn the way in which this happens, and how it is done.

The colours used to dye or paint the cotton cloths are: red, blue, green, purple, and black. The red colour is made of four, and possibly more, roots and barks, the most beautiful of which is one by the name of chay,[4] being a shrub the size of common heather, which has small, elongated leaves divided into many small branches with small, white flowers, which have four-pointed petals and in which calyxes with many small, oblong-round, flat seeds are enclosed. The shrubs grow on the east and north sides of the island of Ceylon, all over Madura, the neighbouring islands, and also on Coromandel, but those of Mannar[5] are best of all. Only the roots of this little plant, which are not unlike heather roots, are used. These are at times valued at no less than 50 pagodas per bahar of 480 pounds.

A second kind of red is made of the ruynas,[6] also called mandosti and t'sjoli, which comes from Persia and Arabia, the best of which is sold at 60 to 70 pagodas per load of 480 pounds.

The third kind of red is made of sappanwood, which is a kind of brazilwood. The fourth kind is made of the bark of a tree named pattasjaja.[7] Caleaturwood gives a red dye too, but this, and some other kinds, are apt to spoil good dyes and deceive people. Neither is the pattasjaja of any use, nor is it fast.

The first two roots are mashed, and the woody stems discarded; then water is added, the mixture is put over a fire, and heated until it is too hot to be touched, but not to the boiling point. Into this mixture are put the cloths to be dyed, but only after they have been prepared, otherwise they would not take on colour, nor keep it. Since these two [roots] are used in almost the same way, I shall take only the chay. It is remarkable to see how they [the chintz painters] put a piece of white cloth in the dye vat, which, when they take it out, shows nice red flowers and leaves or tendrils, while the rest remains white. When the cloth is washed, the colours are so durable that they never fade.

The cloth they want to paint on, in order to make chintz or something else, is prepared in two ways. In the first instance, they take a fruit, here called carica, while it is unripe, but in other places, they take the ripe fruit for its juice. It is a kind of *Mirabolana citrini*,[8] which looks almost like a gallnut. These [fruits] are pulverized and mixed with water and thus made into a poultice which is strained through a piece of cloth. The [resulting] liquid is mixed with the same quantity of buffalo milk. Into this liquid, the cloth is dipped, two or three times; each time it is wrung out and hung in the wind to dry, after which it is folded and beaten until it becomes smooth, like a piece of canvas that is primed ready for paint. And since all their dyes are water colours and juices, this preparation serves to prevent those liquids from running, and also to prevent the red chay from getting to spots other than those intended, in other words, only to those spots they have dipped in alum water. The cloth prepared in this way acquires a yellowish colour from the carica, which will disappear later.

A second method of preparation is the one with 'cansje',[9] the water poured off boiled rice, and carica, but without milk. It is handled in the same way as described [above], except that those parts of the cloth they want to keep white are coated with hot wax, as the cloth is put into the dye vat.

The instruments they work with are few [18, 19]. They consist of two brushes or rather writing pens, one for the wax, and the other for the water colours, [and] a bench or stand with three movable legs, in length a little more than an ell, a foot or a little more in width, [and] a foot and a half in height from the ground. For the rest, there are small or large pots, in which they keep their wax or dye. The pen they use to paint or draw with [in wax] is made of iron, a span in length, as thick as a writing pen, the bottom part split in two up to the middle, and about two fingers or somewhat more in width below. Those split parts are bent out in a half circle, but meet again, in the way some compasses are made, to enable them to open and close. This iron pen is wrapped around in the middle with human hair,[10] so that its shape and size is like that of a chicken egg, over which a cotton thread is wrapped like a ball of rope-yarn. The pen to be used for the dyes is prepared in the same way, except that this one is made of a piece of bamboo, which is split like a pen, and sharply cut. They hold these pens in their whole fist, with the writing end below their hand, and while moving them, they produce a firm line, with such skill that it is a wonder to behold. When working with wax they sit, seven or eight together, in a circle. In the middle over a small fire to keep it hot stands a wide, flat pot with molten wax. The pot is placed in such a way that they can all reach it with their right hand, in order to fill their pens with wax, which collects in the [ball of] hair, and with pressure from the hand, trickles down to the point of the pen, where it is used to write in the same way we would do with a pen.

All of them have their little stands sitting on the ground in front of them from which their pieces of cloth hang down as from a table. They do it the same way when working with water colours, but in that case, they don't have to sit in a circle, because each one can have dye of their own in a little pot, or even in a potsherd. When they want to paint materials of little consequence, they do it by heart, as their imagination dictates, but if the fabric is of more importance, they have, or design, special patterns, which they sponge through with charcoal onto the cloth, without using forms or moulds [i.e. printing blocks] to print them on, as people in Europe used to think, but everything is inked with the pen. And [if], in our home country, it is found that the painted cloths have spots or stains, then these are caused by the carelessness of the painter, who has dropped dye, or has touched spots which should not have been touched.

I have seen them working to produce a white cloth painted with red, blue, purple, green, black, or yellow flowers, in the following way. After the cloth has been prepared with milk in the way described above, four flowers are drawn by heart with a pen made of bamboo or cane; the drawing is done in a liquid that looked like watery buttermilk; after the outline has been drawn that colour changes into reddish brown and, a moment later, into pitch black. This ink is made of burnt blacksmith's coal mixed with greyish rice vinegar, or fermented sap of the cocospalm called suri[11] to which a piece of iron is sometimes added, but if one should use this on paper, or on ordinary cloth, it will hardly turn black. With this ink, here called kalikan, all black chintzes, and the backgrounds of colourfast cloth which one sees in Europe, are made. After outlining those flowers in ink, the leaves that are to be red are painted with the juice of sappanwood, which is grated, boiled, and mixed with alum. It is done in such a way, that in the places where the flower has to be vivid red, they either cover them entirely, or hatch them in that red dye which in itself does not keep the colour. After that, this cloth is put into a pot. In the pot in which the chay had been prepared and heated over a small fire, the cloth is dipped and raised again many times, and soaked in water, then left for three hours, and after having been taken out, is rinsed, dried and dipped in the juice of the carica without milk. After it is dry again, it is put into the big dye vat for the second time, and left in it for two to three hours, after which it is taken out, looking very unfinished, but it is cleansed with goat or sheep dung and water, the cloth being spread on the ground, covered with [the dung], dried in the sun, every now and then sprinkled with fresh, clean water, for three hours, this being a way of bleaching. And this is done in the same way twice, after which the cloth is washed. Then the white part comes out clearly white, and the red part comes out beautifully, that is, the red of the pot, or the chay, appears in those places where the flower had been moistened with alum, as a light, bright red, and in the places that had been painted [only] with sappanwood, it is a darker red, as if the colour were shaded in, thereby creating a complete red flower on a white background, whereas the other flowers are just outlined in black.

In order to make a blue flower and green leaves, the whole cloth is painted or covered with hot wax, as described before, with the exception of those parts that should be blue. After that, the whole cloth is put in the blue dye vat or pot, immersed, and taken out again three to four times, then rinsed in cold water and dried in the sun. Following that, [it is dipped] several times in and out of hot water to remove all the wax. The cloth is washed and dried, then for the third time rinsed with carica, and dried, in order to start other colours.

All the blue parts that are to become green are covered with the juice of curcuma which is yellow and called majela here, added by juice from the carica flower along with a little alum, after which the covered area becomes green, but the colour is not stable. After this, the purple flower is made, for which brown-red is needed. This dye is made by taking one part alum water, sixty parts ordinary water, a lump of mashed curcuma the size of a hazelnut, and one part of sappanwood water. Divide this in half and add a mixture made of half of the [former quantity] of sappanwood and fourteen parts greyish rice vinegar, made from boiled brown rice. All this is mixed together. The flower to be coloured deep purple is made by taking part of the ink that turns black, thirty parts of vinegar made of starch, and 10 to 12 drops of sappan dye, all mixed together, and after that is done the cloth goes for the last time into the dye vat for half an hour. Rinsed and dried, the cotton cloth turns out snow white, with light red, reddish brown, blue, purple, and columbakel[12] flowers with green leaves and black branches, perfect.

As for all these water colours, none are lasting, unless they have been put into the general dye vat with the chay root, because that is the dye which itself has a vivid red colour, and makes other colours last. In this way, all the painted cloths and chintzes coming from Coromandel and going to Europe are made.

And since Your Honour has spent so many thousands on this, I hope Your Honour will not be displeased to read how this painting is done. It would also not be without profit for the General Company, if her servants would acquire a complete and thorough knowledge of that product, since it is the Company which has to deal with the purchase and the receiving of it, which almost everywhere leaves much to be desired, as if it were embarrassing to be dealing with it. For lack of that necessary knowledge, they [the Company's servants] are ignorant about how much a labourer can earn on a daily basis, how long it takes for someone to work on a known piece of cloth, and what expenses have to be paid for it, in order to know the cost of it, knowledge of which so far has not been shown by Your Honour's servants. Since everything is done on the basis of guesswork, and in the same old way, it is thereby left up to the merchants who enjoy their good luck that the Dutch know so little about the business they conduct for the General Company, while they meanwhile continue to reap the profits.

I have always been surprised about the beautiful colours which are produced here on the cloths with white backgrounds,

38–41 Samplers illustrating stages in the chintz process, produced on the Coromandel Coast; early twentieth century. Victoria and Albert Museum, London.

TOP LEFT The design has been drawn in a mordant solution, and the cloth dyed in an iron-rich black dye bath, the colour adhering to those areas treated with the mordant.

TOP RIGHT Red areas are achieved by mordanting the cloth a second time.

BELOW LEFT Blue areas are achieved by applying a wax resist to all areas that are not to be blue, and dyeing the cloth in indigo.

BELOW RIGHT Finally, additional colours are painted directly onto the cloth: here, these are yellow, and yellow-on-blue to create green.

42 OPPOSITE *Palampore*, bedcover or curtain (detail). Coromandel Coast, for the European market, found in Indonesia; first half of the eighteenth century. Cotton, painted mordant-dyed, resist-dyed, and painted. Collection Cora Ginsberg LLC, New York.
◆ A number of Indian cloths decorated to European taste have been found in Southeast Asia; this example has a red ground, much favoured by the Dutch. Whilst some of these were undoubtedly for European consumption, others appear to have found favour with local consumers, and were preserved as heirloom objects of considerable value. The stages of the complex dyeing process may be traced in this masterly example of mordant- and resist-dyeing: the red ground is mordanted; blue is produced by resist; yellow is painted directly on at the end.

and have often wondered whether this could be done also on silk fabrics, as is done in Japan, where it is doubtlessly done with moulds and casts.[13] Since I had some time available I undertook to have this carried out in Bengal, in Baticalo [east coast of Sri Lanka], and in Negapatnam, but after various attempts to do it in the same way as with the cotton cloth, it proved impossible to keep the colour of the chay on silk. Because, after a silk and a cotton cloth, prepared in the same way, had been put into the dye vat, and had been taken out again together, the cotton showed a bright red colour, and the silk was stained and dirty, looking unsightly, for not only did it have no colour, but it had also lost its silky gloss. Although actually, there are dyes which could impart colour to silk, they require boiling, and this would therefore make them unsuitable [cloths] with reserved white parts, as is done with cotton. And if one should use a cold dye, and would reserve a white background by covering it with wax, then the wax could not be removed from the silk, since that has to be done in boiling water, and it would also dissolve the dye, which would mix with

the water and spoil everything. Finally, after a hundred fruitless attempts, it was successful in Sadraspatnam, where accidentally a way was discovered to produce very beautiful blue, red, and purple or violet backgrounds, with white flowers and foliage on the white armosins [i.e. taffetas]. Also the same flowers and tendrils [were produced] on a white background which are so colourfast that boiling water cannot make the colours run, yes, as fast as the Bengal red armosins. Now I believe that it would, in the first place, be very profitable in our home country, if this invention were used in producing nightwear, similar to that in cotton that has been sent from Negapatnam; [then] to find out if it would be desired for any other purposes; and, later yet, if many other colours might be discovered. As examples and specimens six morning coats will be sent to Your Honour, leaving on two ships from Ceylon, so that, if they please Your Honour, and if they can be of profit, whether as morning coats or for other uses, they can be ordered quickly, because I am afraid that, if they are successful in Europe, they can't be kept a secret for long or the English and the French will imitate them.

INDIAN CLOTH AND
INTERNATIONAL TRADE

Cambay chiefly stretches out her two arms, with her right arm she reaches out towards Aden and with the other towards Malacca...the trade of Cambay is extensive and comprises cloths of many kinds and of a fair quality.

Tomé Pires, 1515[1]

43 Merchants sailing to India; folio from al Wasiti, *Muqamat al-Harini*, 1237. Bibliothèque Nationale, Paris. ◆ Arab and Persian merchants made regular sailings from ports in the Persian Gulf to trade with India and ventured, by at least the ninth century, as far as China. Great wealth could be secured from such expeditions (witness the 'Tales of Sinbad', which have their origins in this trade), but at considerable risk. The Arab lateen-rigged stitched boat, the dhow, displayed remarkable resilience making such journeys, carrying merchants and their cargoes of Middle-Eastern, Indian and Southeast Asian luxury goods.

It was with remarkable clarity that the Portuguese observer Tomé Pire described the international nature of the Indian textile trade. Cambay was the crucial link in a chain of exchange that stretched from the Mediterranean to Southeast Asia and beyond. It is not surprising to discover that the earliest surviving examples of Indian trade cloths have been excavated from the dry sands of Egypt rather than from the humid tropics of Indonesia. They appear in archaeological contexts from the late ninth century onwards [46], some five hundred years before the earliest surviving examples in Southeast Asia (see p. 98). It is therefore useful to make an excursion westward, to gain a deeper sense of historical perspective than would be possible from the Southeast Asian evidence alone. We shall also look at the visual context of the textile designs at their source, Gujarat.

At Bhadesvar, on the Kutch peninsula of Gujarat, is to be found the Shrine of Ibrahim, dated to the middle of the twelfth century. This monument has the distinction of being the oldest Islamic structure in northern India.[2] Its style, and more especially features of the mosque built at the site a few decades later, point to Arabic inspiration.[3] The Arabic character is a significant indication of the origins of the local patrons, or at least of the contacts enjoyed by local converts to Islam. Western India had long-established maritime contacts with the Arabian Peninsula and the Red Sea area, stimulated by the combined forces of commerce and pilgrimage, the two intimately linked in the annual pilgrimage to Mecca or *hajj* which was served by the port of Jedda. The discovery of Indian textile remains in the Red Sea area underlines the significance of the Arabic-style mosque in Gujarat, namely that the arrival of Islam in India was inextricably linked with commerce and the role of the Arab merchant. Twelfth-century business letters preserved in Egypt at Fustat (Old Cairo) show that both Hindu and Muslim Indian merchants were active in that city at the time.[4] Later, fifteenth-century Arabic sources frequently refer to the activities of Arab merchants trading with India and to the presence of Indian merchants in the Yemen.[5]

The historic Indian textiles found in Egypt span from the ninth to seventeenth centuries; they were excavated at the metropolitan centre of Fustat, at the transhipment site of Quseir al-Qadim bordering the Red Sea, and at the regional outposts of Qasr Ibrim and Gebel Adda in Nubia, indicating a significant degree of dispersal. Study of these fragments has established beyond doubt their place of manufacture as Gujarat.[6] Arab and Gujarati merchants dominated the Red Sea–Cambay trade and were major players on the Cambay–Melaka (Malacca) route to Southeast Asia. As we have seen, the major ports linking the Gujarati hinterlands to the western Indian Ocean trade were Cambay, east of Bhadesvar, and its successor port in the seventeenth century, Surat. They served in turn as the principal entrepots for the gathering and exchange of products along the international trade routes of Asia. A great variety of goods travelled those routes, but the premier items were spices, especially cloves and pepper, and cotton cloth and dye-stuffs employed in textile production. Gujarat

and its cotton goods thus had a key role in a trading system that linked Egypt and the Mediterranean to the lands of spices.

Arabic, Chinese and European sources all speak of western India as the principal source of various and splendid silks and cottons, all much sought-after and valued for their quality and durability of colour. The earliest Arabic text describing the economic geography of the Indian Ocean world contains a reference to the demand for Indian cloths: in *Al-Masalik wa' l-Mamalik* ([The Book of] Roads and Kingdoms), *c.* 846–47, the Persian scholar Ibn Khurdadhbih, who served as chief of post and information in Iraq, lists the products imported from India, most notably cotton and silk textiles, and a variety of aromatic woods and spices.[7] The most valuable early Chinese account of foreign trade is the *Zhufanzhi* (1225). It was compiled by Zhao Rukua, an inspector of maritime commerce at the port of Quanzhou, Fujian, from earlier Chinese sources and from Arab and Indian informants who visited the great south China port. Of Gujarat he wrote:

> The inhabitants of this country…wear close fitting cloths with a cotton sarong wrapped around them.…The native products comprise great quantities of indigo, red kino [a dye-stuff], myrobolans [a black dye-stuff] and foreign cotton stuffs of every colour. Every year these goods are transported to the Ta-shi [Arab] countries for sale.

Zhao Rukua also mentions the role of hinterland states of Gujarat: from Malwa every year 'two thousand oxen or more, laden with cotton stuffs [were] sent over the roads to barter'.[8] His description is closely echoed at the close of the century in Marco Polo's account of the kingdom of Cambay as 'the centre of an active commerce. Indigo is plentiful.…Buckram [coarse stiffened cotton cloth] and cotton are produced in abundance for export to many provinces and kingdoms…[and] many merchant ships call here.'[9]

It is apparent from these sources that Gujarat, through its premier port of Cambay and supported by hinterland states, was the major source of cotton goods and dye-stuffs for the Arab trade. Yet great as that commerce was, there is numismatic evidence that suggests India experienced a deficit with its western Indian Ocean markets, caused largely by the insatiable appetite in the subcontinent for war-horses and other military equipment.[10] Depictions of war-elephants and horses are a feature of Gujarati export cloths.

Indian cotton in the Arab world

The remains of Gujarati cotton cloths recovered from Egypt are significant on three counts. Firstly, they confirm the antiquity of the Indian textile trade; indeed they are the earliest Indian cloths recorded in an archaeologically documented context. Secondly, they provide a rich if fragmentary glimpse of the place of those textiles in the context of medieval Islamic society and illuminate the social and economic documents of the age analysed by Goitein.[11] Thirdly, and most significantly of all for this study, the surviving fragments clearly establish the genealogy of many of the Indian textiles recovered from Southeast Asia, especially Indonesia. Each of these points deserves elaboration.

One of the earliest records of the trade in Indian textiles appears in the first-century AD Greek *Periplus of the Erythraean Sea*, where they are expressly mentioned as exports to the West.[12] The Roman conquest of Egypt opened up direct contacts between the Indian subcontinent and the Mediterranean via the Red Sea route, to such effect that Pliny was moved to record that Indian muslin

It is clear from the evidence provided by these two nearly identical cloths that the Gujarati textile industry was supplying a market in the medieval period which stretched from Egypt to eastern Indonesia.

44 OPPOSITE, ABOVE Ceremonial banner (detail: see 137). Gujarat, for the Indonesian market, found in the Toraja area of central Sulawesi; radiocarbon-dated 1340 ± 40 years. Cotton, block-printed mordant-dyed, block-printed and painted resist-dyed. Victoria and Albert Museum, London.

45 OPPOSITE, BELOW Fragment of Indian cloth, recovered from Fustat, Lower Egypt. Gujarat, for the Red Sea trade; radiocarbon-dated 1340 ± 40 years. Cotton, block-printed mordant-dyed and resist-dyed. Ashmolean Museum, Oxford.

was impoverishing Rome.[13] With the collapse of the Roman Empire trade shifted to the overland routes and to the Persian Gulf. The Arab tradition of travel and navigational literature reveals that Arabic-speaking mariners and merchants were trading in Southeast Asian waters from around the sixth century. The earliest surviving sources are compilations of travellers' accounts, of which the *Akhar al-Sin* is believed to be the oldest: although published in 851 (AH 237), it contains information clearly much earlier. Ports such as Basra (serving Baghdad) and Siraf (serving Shiraz) were active at this time; a merchant from Basra is recorded visiting China around 775, and the perilous journey, trading and collecting goods en route in India and Southeast Asia, was to be a regular occurrence for Gulf merchants throughout the next two centuries [43].

The archaeological textiles and Gujarati design

Indian cloths were widely distributed within the Arab world. The textile samples retrieved to date from widely scattered sites in Egypt are closely comparable to one another. A resist-dyed blue-and-white panel with alternating elephant and tree designs found at Fustat is matched by another fragment excavated at Quseir al-Qadim in 1982.[14] Both examples may be dated by comparison with an Ashmolean Museum example radiocarbon-dated to *c.* 895 AD [46]. No doubt other sites will emerge as archaeological investigations are undertaken, particularly at the historic port cities of the Arabian peninsula.

Excavations at Fustat in 1980 yielded some three thousand fragments associated with the upper range of a stratigraphy dated between 750 and 1100. One sample appears to be Z-spun thread characteristic of Indian cotton, with a resist-dyed blue-and-white pattern.[15] The earliest cluster of results for radiocarbon analysis, undertaken at Oxford between 1994 and 1996 (see p. 178), revealed dates spanning the period from the late ninth to the eleventh centuries. Other Egyptian-provenanced fragments of Indian cotton textiles which were analysed produced radiocarbon dates between the mid-thirteenth and the late seventeenth centuries, with a cluster in the fifteenth and sixteenth centuries.[16] Controlled excavations at Quseir al-Qadim associated this class of Indian imports with the port's revival under the Mamluks in the fourteenth century.[17]

Some of the samples have designs and fabric weights closely comparable to cloths recovered from Indonesia. For example, two Ashmolean Museum fragments depicting wooded landscapes are dated *c.*1265 ± 40 years and 1390 ± 75 years respectively [47]. The former is especially close in pattern, drawing quality and colour range to a cloth from Indonesia [44, 137] which has yielded a radiocarbon date of 1340 ± 40 years All are decorated in strong red and blue by a combination of mordant- and resist-dyeing. The dating concurs with stylistic comparisons which may be drawn with western Indian sculpture and painting, especially in the conventions used to depict landscape and tree varieties in these textiles and in Gujarati tombstones and manuscript and cloth paintings of the fourteenth and fifteenth centuries [48].

A shared visual vocabulary operated across the arts of western India. In Jain manuscript painting a variety of designs are depicted which also appear on textiles from excavated contexts in the Middle East [57, 58]. Another parallel is with the decoration of Ahmedabad's fifteenth-century mosques. Ahmedabad served as the capital of the Sultanate of Gujarat between 1408 and 1573, and its finest Islamic architecture dates from the beginning of that period. A striking feature of the mosques of Sayyid 'Alam (1412) and Jami Masjid (1424) is the reliefs and the pierced stonework windows which, when backlit

46 Fragment of Indian cloth, recovered from Fustat, Lower Egypt. Gujarat, for the Red Sea trade; radiocarbon-dated to 895 ± 75 years. Cotton, block-printed resist-dyed; 33 x 8.5 cm. Ashmolean Museum, Oxford. ◆ This fragment, with bands of elephants and horse and rider between floral meanders, has been radiocarbon-dated to a period spanning the early ninth to late tenth century, the earliest date established for an Indian export textile. It, and others variously dated up to the sixteenth century, securely establish the antiquity of the Gujarati textile trade to the Middle East, and throw light on the nature and longevity of cotton textile production in western India.

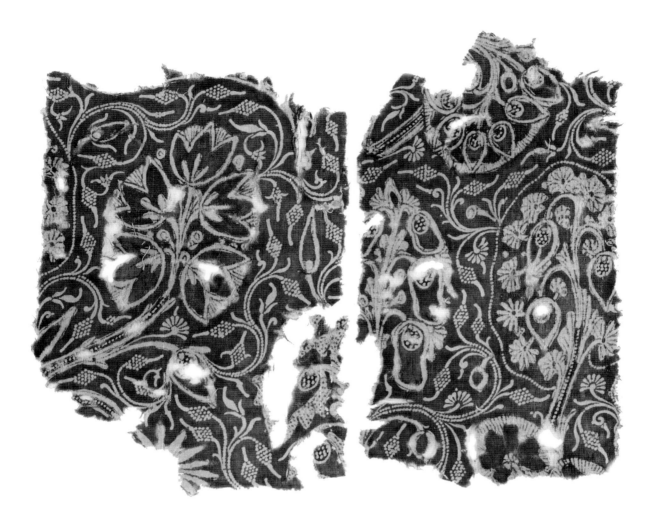

47 Fragment of Indian cloth, recovered
from Fustat, Lower Egypt. Gujarat, for
the Red Sea trade; radiocarbon-dated to
1265 ± 40 years. Cotton, painted mordant-
dyed and resist-dyed; 33 x 31 cm. Ashmolean
Museum, Oxford.

48 *Jayatra yantra*, victory banner (detail).
Gujarat, probably Ahmedabad, dated by
inscription to 1447. Gouache on cloth.
Victoria and Albert Museum, London.

*The fragmentary cloth with a wooded landscape
design reflects mannerisms of the Gujarati
painting style of the medieval period, seen
especially in the differentiation of tree types and
the stylization of floral elements [cf. 44, 45].
The painters responsible for textiles were
evidently aware of the stylistic conventions
prevailing in studios producing illustrated
manuscripts and gouache paintings on cloth for
temple use, as seen right. Indeed, manuscript
painters may have applied their skills to dyed
cloth painting, or at least trained those who did.*

by brilliant daylight, provide a decorative screen that gently illuminates the interior. All their patterns feature also in Gujarati textile designs [54, 116]; the motifs can in fact be traced to much earlier Hindu structures such as the Raniki Vav, Queen Udayamati's stepwell, built in the last quarter of the eleventh century, which pushes back the dating possibilities for their appearance in textiles considerably further than previously suggested and concords with the recent evidence from the Egyptian-provenanced fragments cited above.

The stonework screens are a veritable catalogue of Gujarati designs. They include a variety of radiating star and petalled flower motifs, the endless knot, and stepped patterns which evoke the *patola* woven in Ahmedabad and nearby Patan. The carved blind door of Ahmad Shah's tomb in Ahmedabad [51], dated 1442, has a grid of stepped crosses that has direct parallels in textiles, for instance an Egyptian-provenanced fragment [52]. Many of the patterns appear on cloths with an Indonesian provenance, including both silk *patola* and resist-dyed cottons [55]. Characteristic Gujarati trees, with flamboyant and dense foliage, feature prominently on the Jami Masjid in Ahmedabad [50], and are also a familiar motif on cloths for both the Arab and Indonesian markets – a tangible verification of Pires' claim that the cloths of Gujarat circulated from Aden to Melaka in a single integrated trading system.

49 OPPOSITE, ABOVE Two bays of the Mosque of Sayyid 'Alam, Ahmedabad, built in 1412, photographed in the 1880s. The pierced stone screens provide an anthology of medieval Gujarati designs which were also translated into silk *patola* and painted and printed cottons. Victoria and Albert Museum, London.

50 OPPOSITE, BELOW Relief of a flowering tree, on a pier at the entrance to the Jami Masjid, Ahmedabad's most revered mosque, 1424.

51 RIGHT, ABOVE Carved blind door to the tomb of Ahmad Shah, Ahmedabad, 1442. Victoria and Albert Museum, London.

52 RIGHT Fragment of Indian cloth (detail), recovered from Fustat, Lower Egypt. Gujarat, for the Red Sea trade; radiocarbon-dated 1690 ± 90 years. Cotton, block-printed mordant-dyed and resist-dyed. Ashmolean Museum, Oxford.

The close correspondence between the patterned cloth and the blind door underscores the shared vocabulary among the arts in medieval western India.

Trade textiles in medieval Islamic society

The trade in Indian cloths to the Middle East provides a window into the social and economic life of the people of medieval Egypt, and allows a backward glance into India's own textile history. The Arab lands, including Egypt, were minor cotton producers, whereas both in the cultivation of cotton and in weaving India was highly developed. India's greatest commercial advantage, however, lay in her mastery of complex dyeing processes. Her cloths were renowned for their vividness of colour and fastness of dyes, losing little through repeated washings. The trade records indicate that, in addition to finished cloths, dye-stuffs – especially indigo for blue, and for red sappanwood, also known as brazilwood (itself an import from Southeast Asia), and lac – were regular exports from India to the Middle-Eastern ports, to feed the indigenous cloth-making industry. These dyes were expensive, representing around 25 per cent of the total cost of locally made cloths, which were typically silk or linen.[18]

A remarkable set of documents exists for the study of the Indian textile trade to the Middle East, most notably the Jewish Geniza archives from Fustat, together with a number of Arabic commentaries on the social and commercial life of the port cities of West Asia. The Geniza records consist of the contents of an archival storehouse (*geniza*) attached to a synagogue; they include a wealth of documents belonging largely to the eleventh to thirteenth centuries.[19] Fustat was the capital of Abbasid Egypt (750–969) until the Fatimids (969–1171) invaded from north Africa and established their capital a short distance to the north at Cairo. Fustat nonetheless retained its commercial importance under the Fatimids and into the following Ayyubid (1169–1250) and Mamluk (1250–1380) eras, as witnessed by the vivid descriptions of commercial life the Geniza hoard provides. Some of the earliest references to the long-distance trade later noted by European commentators occur here: in 1085 a Tunisian merchant made a 150 per cent profit in Palestine selling sappanwood, which must have been traded from Southeast Asia.[20]

It emerges from Goitein's masterful study of the Geniza documents that in medieval Middle-Eastern society Indian cotton textiles were relatively inexpensive utilitarian items, for use as garments and as household furnishings by the lower levels of society. Little or no religious or magical character was ascribed to them; they rarely appear in dowry lists, presumably because of their relatively low value.[21] An alternative explanation may, however, be that such records do not accurately record the situation, as cloths were generally classified by function and colour rather than fabric type.

Certainly the archaeological evidence suggests that Indian cotton goods were widespread in Arab society. The situation contrasts dramatically with the reception that Indian cloths received in Southeast Asia, where they were the objects of conspicuous consumption, serving as the preferred attire of the elite, from the sultan and raja to the village headman (see Chapters V and VI).

Clothes in medieval Islamic society were a major item of expenditure. Representing as they did a serious investment of family wealth, it was expected that such goods should be robust and long-lasting, to be inherited or passed on as dowry or gift. They also functioned as a form of stored wealth realizable in times of need, as witnessed by the record of a merchant who used robes as payment of customs duty on a large consignment of pepper.[22] Most prized of all for clothing was silk, a commodity in which India had to compete in metropolitan Fustat with the Byzantine world, Iran, Iraq and China.

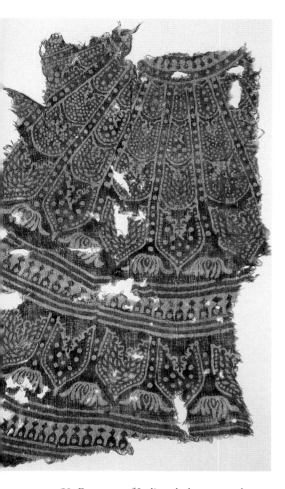

53 Fragment of Indian cloth, recovered from Fustat, Lower Egypt. Gujarat, for the Red Sea trade; fourteenth–fifteenth century. Cotton, block-printed mordant-dyed and resist-dyed; 51 x 31 cm. Victoria and Albert Museum, London. ◆ Part of a large lotus-petal design cloth, which may have formed a canopy or curtaining for domestic use. It was found in the burial grounds of Fustat, and had probably finally been used as a shroud, the most likely fate of all the Fustat-provenanced textiles.

Study of the Indian cotton fragments from Egypt reveals that they usually formed part of tailored items, either costume or furnishings, notably floor and cushion coverings, bedding, curtains and canopies [53]. That they were tailored locally is clear from the consistent evidence of stitching not in cotton but in flax, the ubiquitous fibre of the Egyptian textile industry.

The extravagant consumption of textiles was such that they were singled out by one of the founders of the pious Sufi sect, Ibrahim Adham, when he lamented the wastefulness of his times: 'Sinful luxury, *israf,* is not perpetuated in eating; [but] it is in furnishings and clothing.'[23] Fine linens and silks were highly valued by the wealthy (including some *mullahs*), although for comfort cotton must have been widely used for undergarments and linings. Cotton was the fabric of the lower social classes who farmed and practised the numerous trades (of which local cloth-making represented a major part). An act of charity regularly referred to in the Geniza records was the donation of clothing to the poor, a practice vividly illustrated by the case of the eleventh-century Jewish merchant Nahray ben Nissim who received a letter from a colleague in Alexandria requesting such support: 'here in the house in which I live there is a poor woman who has nothing to wear in the hard winter....Perhaps you will collect among your friends half a *dinar,* for which a piece of cotton cloth could be bought here to serve her as a cover. By doing so you will acquire great religious merit.'[24] The commonest garment distributed in this way was the *jukaniyya,* a *futa* or sari-like untailored cloth worn by both sexes. It is referred to in commercial correspondence as '*mahabis*' (wrappers). Sari lengths of Indian cotton were well suited to the purpose. Headcovers were a required item of attire, with larger turbans worn as a signifier of wealth and position. The volume of cloth used in this way must have been considerable: the records tell us that turbans could require more fabric than a robe.[25]

For Muslims, the pilgrimage to Mecca also stimulated demand for Indian cloth in the form of religious souvenirs, as it was customary for pilgrims to bring away with them a shroud of fine linen or cotton dipped in holy water.[26] The ports of Mocha and Jedda, which served as transhipment points for the pilgrims, did a brisk trade in such items. The popularity of shrouds is demonstrated by the great quantities of fragments retrieved from the burial grounds of Fustat.

Indian textiles served a broad market in the Arab world, and although there is little direct evidence that they captured the attention of the elite, that impression may be erroneous. While Indian cottons do not feature by name in the dowry lists of the wealthy, they were undoubtedly among the fabrics used for less prestigious purposes, such as domestic furnishings.

The mechanisms of trade

Indian merchants regularly feature as members of the expatriate merchant communities, and as seasonal traders, in the Arab port cities. The volume of goods carried on a single ship was sufficient to cause movement in market prices, even at the larger frontier ports such as Aden or Alexandria. Information on the activities of customs officers, import agents (*wakil tujjar*),[27] warehousing facilities, and the systems of credit in operation all points to a highly organized commercial infrastructure.

The goods traded were recorded by weight as well as in terms of individual items: the standard measure for transporting textiles was an *'idl* or ship's bale of 500 pounds (*c.* 227 kg), which was identical with a camel load, clearly a convenience for the transfer of goods from sea to land transport. The Indian textiles destined for Fustat were shipped from Gujarat to Aden or Jedda, where they would have been sold to local Arab merchants who in turn shipped them on to small ports like Quseir al-Qadim and Suez for land transport by caravan to the metropolitan markets of Lower Egypt.

Throughout the history of trade in both the pre-Islamic and Islamic periods, the Persian Gulf had always been the main rival to the Red Sea, at times surpassing it in importance. The fluctuating fortunes of the ports of each region were determined by shifts in the centres of political power and the resulting changes in Middle-Eastern trading patterns. The port of Siraf on the Persian side of the Gulf was at its height in the ninth and tenth centuries, deriving much of its wealth from the China trade.[28] A tenth-century Persian shipmaster based there, Buzurg ibn Shahriyar, wrote a collection of sailors' tales that he titled *Kitab 'Aja'ib al-Hind* (Book of the Wonders of India) which contains colourful and doubtless exaggerated accounts of the India and China trade.[29] The achievements of a prominent twelfth-century Persian merchant, Abu'l Qasim Ramisht, emerge from the Geniza documents. His ships operated on the India route but his immense wealth was associated with his trading ventures to China. Ramisht is most remembered for his donations to Mecca – a cover of Chinese cloth for the Ka'ba in 1137–38, and on his death a gold water-spout (*mizab*).[30] More prestigious acts of endowment in the Muslim world are difficult to imagine. He was buried at Mecca where his tombstone described him as 'the ship-owner' (*nakhuda*). A painting of an Arab dhow from a manuscript edition of *Muqamat al-Hariri*, dated 1237, provides a wonderfully detailed and evocative depiction of merchants en route from the Persian Gulf to India in the type of vessel owned by Ramisht [43].

Iran and the later textile trade

The dominance of the Red Sea ports continued until the beginning of the sixteenth century. Duarte Barbosa (1518) was still able to describe Aden as the distribution centre for markets of which he observed: 'it seems an impossible thing that they should use so much cotton cloth as these ships bring from Cambaya'.[31] In the course of the century, however, the Red Sea trade was overshadowed by the rise of Iran and of the Persian Gulf ports of Hormuz and Bandar Abbas which served Isfahan and Shiraz. A peace concluded between the Persians and Turks in 1638 revived the port of Basra, which served Baghdad and, by land, the Turkish and Mediterranean markets. By the late seventeenth century Indian cloth was the leading commodity at Bandar Abbas,[32] a pattern repeated at other Persian Gulf and Red Sea ports.

On India's west coast, the port of Cambay was abandoned in preference for Surat, which then served as the premier port for the western Indian textile trade throughout the seventeenth century until its own sharp decline in the early eighteenth century. Surat's commercial importance was enhanced by the establishment there of trading factories by the English, French and Dutch companies and by its role as the principal western port of the Mughal Empire. Trade was dominated by Hindu merchants (*banias*). Muslims also played a significant role, especially in the Arab trade, and other members of their community were active in the weaving industry. The Governor of Surat and other leading officials owned ships on the Iran trade route, as did even the rulers of Banten (Bantam) in Java and Pegu in Burma. The Dutch were the largest of the European

These two cloths, recovered from Egypt and Indonesia respectively, vividly illustrate the words of Tomé Pires (1515), who wrote that the trade of Cambay, Gujarat's premier port, in 'cloths of many kinds and of fair quality' extended from Aden to Melaka. This highly stylized floral design is strongly evocative of some Gujarati patola.

54 BELOW Fragment of Indian cloth (detail), recovered from Fustat, Lower Egypt, fifteenth–sixteenth century. Cotton, block-printed mordant-dyed and resist-dyed. Museum der Kulturen, Basel.

55 OPPOSITE Ceremonial cloth (detail). Gujarat, for the Indonesian market; sixteenth century. Cotton, block-printed mordant-dyed and resist-dyed. National Gallery of Australia, Canberra; gift of Michael and Mary Abbott, 1988.

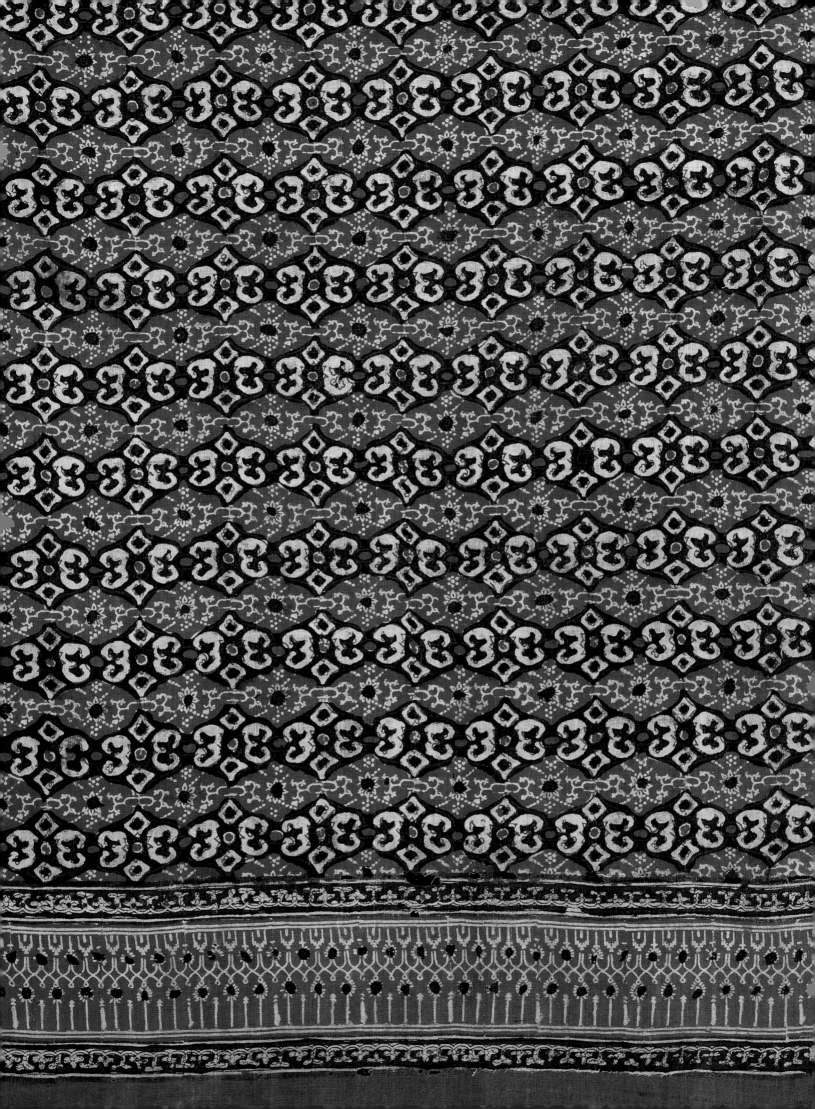

companies trading with Iran, linking their factory in Hormuz with that at Surat and those to the east at Batavia (Jakarta) in Java, Ayutthaya in Thailand, and Deshima in Japan in a carefully integrated commercial system [11].

The chief export from Surat was the cotton cloth most commonly referred to as 'bafta' in contemporary sources, a coarse to fine-quality undecorated textile, typically dyed red or blue. Surat was supplied from numerous production centres in western and northern India, of which Broach, Burhanpur, Navsari and Baroda were most highly renowned for their quality. Ahmedabad and Agra were the premier centres for indigo dyeing. According to the French entrepreneur Jean-Baptiste Tavernier (1676) Sironj 'chites' – i.e. chintz – was highly regarded for its brilliance and fastness of colour. Lesser grades were evidently produced there as well, 'with which the common people of Persia and Turkey are clad'.[33] As we have seen, turban cloths were also a favoured line for the Middle Eastern market.

The seventeenth century also saw the introduction of Indian textiles from other sources, most significantly the Coromandel Coast. The principal region supplying this trade was the kingdom of Golconda, which maintained close commercial ties with Iran through the port of Masulipatam. Tavernier, who visited Golconda several times in the mid-seventeenth century, reported that the ruler of the kingdom sent a ship each year to Iran, laden with chintz and calicoes; he adds that the cloths with flowered designs achieved high prices.[34]

56 *Palampore*, intended as a ceremonial hanging. Coromandel Coast, Masulipatam, for the Persian market. It bears a verse in Persian, 'May this place be ever blessed with wealth', and a date year equivalent to AD 1815. Cotton, block-printed mordant-dyed and resist-dyed, 203 x 137 cm. Victoria and Albert Museum, London.
◆ Cloths such as this evolved from the earlier *palampores* [cf. 143]: the flowering tree has assumed a more subdued form as a cypress, and the overall treatment is more in keeping with Persian taste. Although produced primarily for the export trade to Iran, they also found a ready market in southern India and Southeast Asia.

A steady trade in Persian-market *palampores* with flowering tree designs and in prayer mats continued from Masulipatam, and subsequently from other Coromandel ports, right up until the beginning of the twentieth century [56].

Parallels with Southeast Asian market textiles

It is clear from a comparative study of the Indian cloths traded to the Middle East and to Southeast Asia that they belong to a single continuum and are parts of a larger picture. The merchants who handled textiles from the Gujarati ports of Cambay and Surat serviced a system which, as Pires stated, linked Aden with Southeast Asia through the medium of Gujarati cloth. Such contacts continued into the modern era, strengthened by the *hajj*.[35] The shared origins can be demonstrated through a series of provenanced examples, which all display the same physical characteristics: they are coarse Z-spun cottons, coloured by mordant- and resist-dyeing, predominantly in red and varying hues of blue from light aqua to a near-black.

The most striking feature of the Southeast Asian provenanced textiles is that they are generally complete cloths, often several metres in length, in marked contrast to the Middle-Eastern examples which are small fragments. This is clearly related to differences in age and in circumstances of preservation; and behind that, a further explanation must lie in their differing function in each society. As noted above, the Middle-Eastern consumers viewed the textiles as essentially utilitarian, whereas in Indonesia they assumed ritual and symbolic functions which ensured their careful storage and preservation.

From the Geniza documents, dowry lists for example, it emerges that the favoured colours were white, blue, red, 'black' (i.e. dark indigo blue) and green. Indigo was the largest dye import, followed by sappanwood and lac for red.[36] Blue and resist-dyed blue-and-white cloth is the most common among the excavated finds in Egypt. Resist-dyed blue cloths may also have formed part of the earliest textile trade to Indonesia, where it could be argued their memory is preserved in Javanese batik, the earliest of which is predominantly blue-and-white.

Red-and-blue dyed cloths are the next most common type found in the Middle East. An example from Fustat has a dramatic interlocking floral design centrefield with a lappet border [73]. It can be related to another fragment from Fustat, dated to 1555.[37] A complete cloth nearly 5 metres in length found in Indonesia [55] has a related red-and-blue centrefield design and differs only in its border decoration, an interlocking line pattern which finds its analogy in other Fustat fragments.

The grid or trellis as a means of structuring a design was popular in the Middle East, to judge from the Egypt-provenanced fragments, many of which display a repeat cartouche framed by an interlocking trellis with medallions. Again, numerous examples have been found in Southeast Asia, in both the Malay–Sumatra region [86] and in Thailand.

A finely drawn pattern consisting of an eight-pointed flower encircled in a vine tendril with a four-pointed star at the intersections of the trellis appears on a Fustat fragment dated to the late sixteenth century. Similar patterns occur on a number of Southeast Asian trade cloths, including Gujarati silk *patola* of the type widely exported to Southeast Asia [116]. The device is known in Gujarat as the basket design (*chhabdi bhat*); in Java it is called *jlamprang*, be it in *patola* or a batik version, while in eastern Indonesia, where it appears on cotton ikats, it has a variety of local names.

From radiocarbon analysis results and dated visual evidence, a clear picture has emerged of the perseverence of the hamsa *or sacred goose design in Gujarati export trade, both to the Middle East [58] and to Southeast Asia [59].*

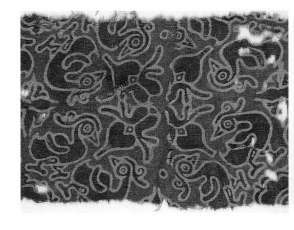

Textiles using the *hamsa* or sacred goose as their principal motif are also found in both areas. They are known in India from at least the Gupta period (*c.* 320–600); the mural in Cave No. 1 at Ajanta in the western Deccan depicts a male figure wearing a garment with such a pattern, and the fifth-century court poet and dramatist Kalidasa refers in his *Raghuvamsa* to a silk wedding dress woven with figures of geese.[38] Jain manuscript painting of the later fourteenth and fifteenth centuries documents the presence of this motif in Indian courtly dress [57] at the time such textiles were being traded to Egypt [58]. Several complete cloths have emerged from Indonesia; all display the geese arranged around stylized flowers and flower buds [59]. A variant composition exists from Egypt: with a frieze of alternating geese and flowers framed by pearl border,[39] it was probably used to decorate a canopy or hanging.

Three summary conclusions can be drawn from this brief account of the Indian textile trade to the Middle East. Firstly, Indian cotton goods were an important commodity in the region from at least the ninth century. Secondly, the commerce was dominated by western Indian cloths obtained through the ports of Cambay and Surat. Thirdly, it is clear that these goods were thoroughly integrated into a trading system that ensured that the spices of the remotest islands of eastern Indonesia found their way to the markets of the Middle East and the Mediterranean world through the medium of textile exchange.

THE ASIAN TRADE BEFORE EUROPEAN INTERVENTION

'Step on the spread cloth'

A Tamil stone inscription dated 1082 was discovered late last century at Lubo Tuo, Barus, an important coastal centre for the gathering of camphor and benzoin from the interior of Sumatra for the international trade. It was recently fully translated and found to record the decision of the Indian merchant community resident there (members of the South Indian *ainnurruvar* guild) to require all merchants to pay a charitable fee before being permitted to 'step on the spread cloth', that is, to engage in trade.[1] One can envisage that such transactions would have taken place in a open marketplace or pavilion, as they do today, where the vendor invited his client to sit on his cloth floorcovering and engage in the business of exchanging goods [61].

The primary objective of Indian merchants in Southeast Asia in the first millennium AD was to acquire the forest and sea products and mineral wealth of the region for sale in China, India and the Middle East. These exotic goods included such rarities as rhinocerous horn, ivory, tortoiseshell and kingfisher feathers, as well as a range of aromatic woods and spices. The biggest market driving this process was China, whose legendary wealth had attracted merchants from the earliest period of international trade. China demanded great quantities of cotton and did not produce much herself until around the twelfth century. The cultivation of cotton in insular Southeast Asia was also very limited, and local weaving and dyeing were no match for the sophisticated techniques of Indian craftsmen.

The antiquity of the Indian textile trade to the east is difficult to measure, but there is evidence that it was established practice by at least the first century AD, when Indian merchants were establishing themselves in the region.[2] Contacts were established first through both overland routes and coastal shipping, as witnessed by Indian trade items discovered by archaeologists in central Burma and the Thai Peninsula. The fine muslins for which Bengal was famous in the late Roman world (evocatively described as 'woven air') found their way east to China and the emerging states of Southeast Asia. The evidence is scarce but the presence of Arabic- and Tamil-speaking merchants in the port cities of Southeast Asia and China, commemorated by Muslim tombstones and Tamil inscriptions, points to the means by which such goods circulated.[3]

These cross-currents of commerce helped to stimulate the emergence of trading centres in Southeast Asia. The kingdom of Srivijaya, centred around Palembang in southern Sumatra, was the single most important commercial centre in maritime Southeast Asia from the late seventh century until its collapse in the second half of the fourteenth. Its economic *raison d'être* lay in the great and growing east-west traffic in exotic commodities between the Middle East and India on the one hand, and China on the other; it was known to the Arabs as 'Sribuza', and to the Chinese first as 'Shih-li-fo-shih' and later as 'San-fo-chi'. Srivijaya's prosperity was built not only on serving this commerce, but on

60 OPPOSITE Ceiling painting depicting the Buddha's footprints (*Buddhapada*), in Temple No. 437, Pagan, Burma; early thirteenth century. The configuration of the composition, complete with a flame-like design prefiguring the *tumpal* motif of later textiles [cf. 67 and 29] on two end-panels, strongly suggests that the painting is imitative of a textile canopy (see p. 56).

61 BELOW The Governor of Banten in discussion with a Muslim elder from Mecca. Engraving based on observations of the port of Banten in 1596 by Willem Lodewycksz, published in Amsterdam in 1598.

supplying many of the forest products and spices in demand at both ends of the trade route. The South Indian merchants who left their inscription at Barus regularly visited Sumatra to exchange cotton goods for camphor to be sold on to the Chinese market.

The wealth generated by this activity directly contributed to the process of state formation already under way in Southeast Asia. Local rulers progressively consolidated their authority, largely through the marshalling of the economic power resulting from control of international trade. One way in which these rulers sought to express their authority was to acquire exotic goods, which tangibly demonstrated their wealth and their access to international sources. Indian culture informed most aspects of elite society in early Southeast Asia, shaping concepts of kingship, religion, language and scripts. It is therefore not surprising to witness Indian textiles assuming a prestigious position in the local hierarchy of cloth.

A review of the premier states in Southeast Asia prior to the sixteenth century illustrates the extent to which Indian cloth was central to ceremonial and state dress. Depictions of textiles whose designs strongly suggest that they were Indian imports are to be found in sculptures and wall-paintings in temples in Southeast Asia. That pictorial evidence is supported by inscriptions and travellers' commentaries on local dress.

Burma

The Buddhist temples of Pagan, the capital of the Burmans (1044–1287), are endowed with richly detailed mural paintings, which are widely accepted as following Indian models of the late Pala era of the eleventh–twelfth centuries. They show a variety of textiles in use, both as clothing and as decor. In the Lokahteikpan Temple, we see the figure of a ruler (his status indicated by the presence of an umbrella), wearing a cloak with an interlocking circle pattern [62]. Fabrics featuring that design were in use in India from at least the Sunga period (first century BC–first century AD) [63]; that they circulated throughout the Buddhist world can be deduced from the pattern's appearance in Central Asian and Chinese textiles. Some of the garments worn by princely figures show the additional use of gold. A fine diaphanous white fabric is presumably the much-prized Bengali muslin; Pagan had extensive contacts with Bengal and undoubtedly acquired prestige textiles from that ancient Indian centre of production.

The paintings also record the practice of decorating the interiors of temples – and no doubt palaces too, although for that there is less evidence – with large hangings [60]; iron hooks that are still visible high on the walls were in all probability intended for securing them. Nothing of the sort survives, so we are dependent on the murals to inform our understanding: a beautifully executed floral pattern within interwoven vines seen in the Thetkyamuni Temple, for instance, is a standard Indian design which persisted into the nineteenth century in printed cottons [64, 65]. Painted versions occur most frequently on the barrel-vaulted ceilings of the temples, surfaces not suitable for the placing of actual fabrics.

The murals provide information not only on use but also on the structure of the designs, most clearly seen when decorative hangings are depicted in their entirety. The overall composition is familiar from known Indian examples (all, of course, later than the Pagan murals): they display elaborate repeat-patterned centrefields framed within carefully proportioned borders and end-panels, the

62 OPPOSITE, ABOVE The King of Vesali, after a mural painting in the Lokahteikpan Temple, Pagan, Burma, built during the reign of Alaungsithu (1113–c.1155). He wears a cloak with an interlocking circle design, a motif that appears in early Indian ornamentation from at least the first century BC [cf. 63].

63 OPPOSITE, BELOW Detail of a doorjamb with two patterns known from the textile repertoire carved in its central section: interlocking circles [cf. 73], and an interlocking S-weave pattern. Sandstone, from north India; Sunga–Kushan periods, *c.* first century BC–second century AD. Collection of Rossi and Rossi, London.

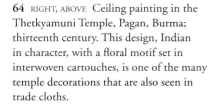

64 RIGHT, ABOVE Ceiling painting in the Thetkyamuni Temple, Pagan, Burma; thirteenth century. This design, Indian in character, with a floral motif set in interwoven cartouches, is one of the many temple decorations that are also seen in trade cloths.

65 *Kain sembagi*, skirt-cloth (detail). Coromandel Coast, for the south Sumatran market; nineteenth century. Cotton, mordant- and resist-dyed, with block-printing in the borders. Victoria and Albert Museum, London. ◆ This piece is typical of the Indian trade cloth entering western Indonesia in the later nineteenth century. The design is firmly rooted in an Indian painting tradition; it has been embellished with filigree detail to instil an Islamic flavour appropriate for a Sumatran clientele.

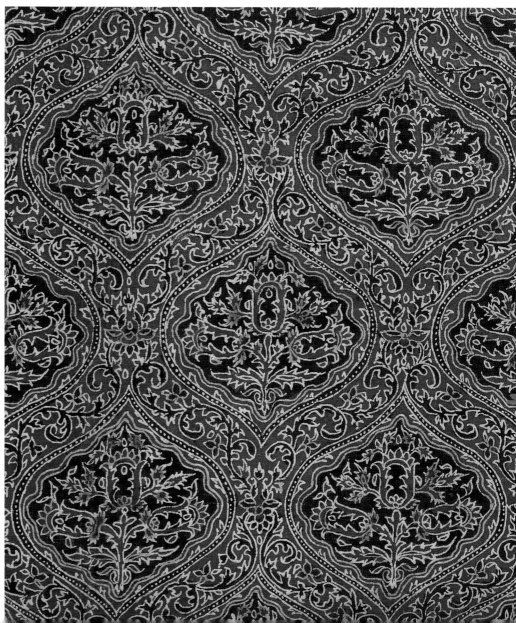

latter with multiple registers that include the distinctive saw-tooth or *tumpal* motif, a ubiquitous element in the trade cloths as well as in Southeast Asian products. The colour schemes are chiefly red, blue and white, the standard colour range of early Indian textiles. The depiction of imported Indian cloths at Pagan makes clear the prestige that they carried among the ruling élite of the first Burmese capital.

Cambodia

At Angkor, the capital of the Khmer people's kingdom, Indian textiles are known to have enjoyed the highest status. A late thirteenth-century Chinese source provides a revealing description of life and customs at this political and religious centre. Zhou Daguan, a member of a Chinese diplomatic mission to the court of the Khmer king Indravarman III, was resident at the Cambodian capital in 1296–97. He was an astute observer both of the details of daily life (he lived with a Khmer family during his stay) and of the broader social forces at work. His comments on Khmer costume provide a unique description of the textiles in circulation:

> Every man and woman, from the sovereign down…leaves the shoulders bare. Round the waist they wear a strip of cloth, over which a larger piece is drawn when they leave the houses.…Among the fabrics worn by the sovereign are some, very rich and sheer, which are valued at three or four ounces of gold. Although certain fabrics are woven in Cambodia, many are imported from Siam [Thailand] or Champa [Central Vietnam], preference being given to the Indian weaving for its skill and delicacy.[4]

In addition to describing the simple manner in which the untailored garments of the Khmer were worn, the Chinese observer indicates that cloths for royal use, which included Indian imports, were valued in gold, an indicator of their high status. Less prestigious textiles were bartered in the marketplace, a hundred pieces of cloth, we are told, being required to secure a healthy slave.[5]

In the king's palace much use was made of 'double-woven silks spangled with gold, all of which are gifts of foreign merchants'.[6] These could have been Indian silks made by the double ikat process, cloths later referred to in trade sources as *patola*. However, they could also have been Chinese: Zhou Daguan states that Chinese figured silks and other textiles were readily available at Angkor and that his country's trading community had growing influence in Cambodia, stimulating the demand for such goods as porcelain, furniture and silk. Chinese silk brocades with gold threads (*zhijin jin*) were favoured in the Yuan and Ming periods as diplomatic gifts to rulers of foreign states, including those of the kingdom of Zhenla (Cambodia).

It is clear that the elite preferred imported cloth. Social distinctions could also be actively enforced through sumptuary laws restricting the wearing of particular designs, and it is evident from Zhou Daguan's account that such laws were in force in thirteenth-century Cambodia:

> Many rules, based on rank, govern the choice of materials.…Only the ruler may wear fabrics woven in an all-over pattern.…The wearing of fabrics patterned with recurring groups of flowers is permitted to high officers and princes. Ordinary mandarins are allowed to wear only material with two groups of flowers, and women of the people may do likewise.'[7]

Zhou Daguan's description of the use of repeat patterns and floral designs may be compared to the costumes depicted in the reliefs of Angkorian monuments, which provide a rich inventory of textiles and fashions of the Khmer kingdom

66 Relief of a temple dancer, from the inner wall of the upper terrace, Angkor Wat, Cambodia; first half of the twelfth century. She is dressed in a fine diaphanous skirt with a floral pattern, combined with an extravagant waist-sash and an abundance of jewelry, and is set against a background almost certainly inspired by textiles of the time.

[66]. The garments worn by celestial and human figures are decorated with a variety of flower, star, vine-leaf and wave motifs, arranged as a repeat in a grid or trellis structure. The patterns include stripes and checks, four-petalled flowers, diamonds, radiating suns and interlocking flower and vine. The motifs are generally depicted as a weft design, running across the width of the cloth. The borders are finely detailed and the ends richly elaborated with a series of decorative registers. Backgrounds, too, sometimes suggest textiles, like the flower-and-trellis pattern behind what are variously identified as celestial maidens (*apsaras*) or temple dancers at Angkor Wat. Many of these elements recur in later Khmer textiles, most notably the multi-banded end-panels and the stepped square centrefield, features which are common to Indian cottons for the Thai market [cf. 12, 168]. A long line of designs can be traced from the Angkorian period through to recent times: the patterns in the sculptural reliefs are not so far removed from those that were still in production in nineteenth-century Gujarat for the Thai and Cambodian markets. These continuities, spanning nearly a millennium, are a recurring characteristic of Indian trade textiles.

The Khmer legacy in Thailand

The Thai kingdom of Sukhothai (*c.* thirteenth century–1458), and Ayutthaya (1351–1767) which absorbed it, were in many respects the inheritors of the Khmer tradition. The Thai decorative repertoire is to a surprising degree informed by Khmer art, be it in architectural ornament, sculpture or regalia. The crowned divinity or *deva* (*thepanom*) rising from a lotus with hands held in veneration became one of the most pervasive motifs in Thai art. A favourite subject for depiction in Sukhothai architectural ceramics, such as roof end-tiles and gable finials [69], it recurred in a variety of media, including Indian textiles specifically produced for the Thai market, a phenomenon that will be discussed in detail in Chapter VII. The use of the floral vine roundel as a compositional device, sometimes encircling a human figure as seen in reliefs at Angkor Wat, was given renewed life in the applied arts of the Ayutthaya period, and appears in cloths ordered from the Coromandel Coast in the seventeenth and eighteenth centuries [cf. 70, 71]. Khmer architectural ornament provides a catalogue of motifs which appear later in decorative arts in Thailand. The sandstone carving on the Khmer temple of Prasat Hin, Pimai, in northeast Thailand, is a classic example [67]: one register, for instance, displays a pointed-leaf motif with serrated flame-like border above a row of flower-bud bosses which is a regular feature of textiles in Thailand, both locally made and of Indian manufacture.

Indian cloths designed to Thai taste formed an important part of textile consumption among the elite. The enhanced status attaching to imported cloths evidently extended to locally woven pieces employing imported thread: a fourteenth-century literary source, the *Traibhumikatha* (*c.* 1345), stresses of a textile intended as a royal gift that it was woven of imported silk, 'without any admixture of Thai thread'.[8]

Early Java

Old Javanese inscriptions provide a valuable if fragmentary source of information on Indian textiles in early western Indonesia. The tax-grant (*sima*) inscriptions of central and eastern Java, which appear in the late ninth century and continue until the end of the fifteenth century,[9] record gifts to those of rank. They catalogue the commodities in circulation, including a variety of local and imported textiles; pieces from India feature regularly, indicating the high

67 Leaf pattern and flower-bud bosses decorating a sandstone plinth moulding, Prasat Hin Temple, Korat, north-east Thailand; late eleventh–twelfth century. This vigorous flaming-leaf motif, closely related to the *tumpal*, originated in the Khmer period and was perpetuated in later Thai arts, including mural painting and textile design, where it was widely favoured as an end-panel motif [cf. 68].

69 ABOVE Glazed stoneware roof finial ornamented with a deity or *thepanom* – of Khmer inspiration – emerging from a lotus bud. Sukhothai, north-central Thailand; fifteenth century. Asian Art Museum of San Francisco, gift of James and Elaine Connell.

68 LEFT Border of a *pha nung*, skirt-cloth (detail: see 174). Coromandel Coast, for the Thai market; eighteenth century. Cotton, painted mordant-dyed and painted resist-dyed, and painted. Victoria and Albert Museum, London. ◆ This shows the *thepanom* absorbed into textile design, in a distinctively Thai *tumpal* end-panel.

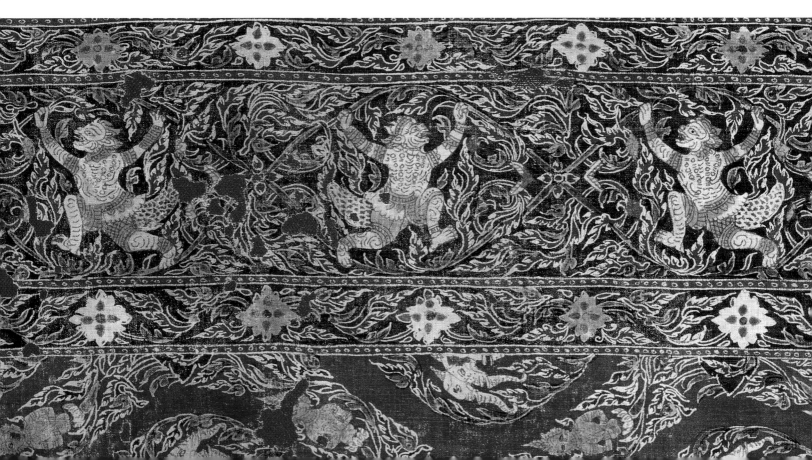

72 The Bodhisattva Manjusri. From Ngemplak, Semarang, central Java; early tenth century. Solid cast silver. Museum Nasional, Jakarta. ◆ This superb example of Javanese metal-casting depicts the Buddhist saviour wearing a skirt-cloth with a design of flowers and circles in alternating horizontal registers, a configuration very different from later elite textiles in use in Java, which favoured trellis or overall repeat patterns. The textile techniques employed are unknown.

70 OPPOSITE, BELOW *Pha nung*, skirt-cloth (detail). Coromandel Coast, for the Thai market; eighteenth century. Cotton, painted mordant-dyed, drawn resist-dyed, and painted. Private collection, London. ◆ The borders of this cloth [se also **161**] are dominated by monkey-warrior figures with scaled marine monster tails struggling with flaming vine roundels. The composition has direct antecedents in Khmer reliefs of the twelfth century [**71**], underscoring the continuities in Khmer–Thai art.

71 BELOW Relief of warriors in vine roundels from Angkor Wat, Cambodia; first half of the twelfth century.

status they enjoyed. Over fifty types of men's cloths and fifteen types of women's cloths are distinguished, coloured predominantly in red and blue.[10] The Polengan III copperplate inscription of AD 876 lists ten textiles which constituted gifts. Among them are *buat inghulu* (a cloth made upstream or inland), *buat waitan inmas* (a gilded fabric made in the east – possibly Chinese silk brocade), and *buat kling putih*, a white cloth made in India.[11] 'Kling' is a term variously associated with the northern part of the Coromandel Coast (Kalinga) and with that coast as a whole. One gift list included, together with gold artefacts, *yu wdihan buat kling putih* (a pair of white Indian cloths for male dress). *Yu* is an abbreviation of the Sanskrit *yugala*, meaning 'pair': the use of an Indian unit of measurement for textiles in Java is an indication of the influential role that imports from the subcontinent must have acquired there by the ninth century.

Textiles are also differentiated in the texts on the basis of use. Cloths for dress are distinguished from those intended as decorative hangings and screens in buildings, as seating covers or as ceremonial wrappings for ritual utensils. Indian white cloth is described as part of the gift lists. Patterned cloths of unspecified origin are mentioned – *nagapuspa* ('white flower of the nagasari tree'), *siwapatra* ('Siva's flower' = red lotus), and *tuwuh-tuwuhan* ('vegetal pattern') – but we can only surmise about their origin and the techniques employed.

The word '*tulis*' makes its appearance in *sima* inscriptions of the late twelfth century. The term is today used to describe batik which has been hand-drawn with a wax-pen (*canting*), in distinction to that which is stamped (*cap*). In the inscriptions it is associated with techniques of decorating finished cloth, suggesting a link with its modern meaning.[12] An text in Old Javanese, the *Arjunawiwaha kakawin*, refers to a red cloth with *tulis* decoration (*randi tinulis*), which may imply a resist-dyeing process. We know that such techniques were in regular use in Gujarat for the decoration of export cottons to Egypt from at least the late ninth century (see Chapter III), and there is strong contextual evidence that such cloths were also traded East.

The only record of the appearance of textiles in the Central Javanese Period comes from Hindu and Buddhist sculpture of the ninth to eleventh centuries. Similarities with patterns seen in Indian art give some clues to the regional origins of the cloths themselves. The most common design is of flowers and circles floating on an open ground or set in bands. Pan-Indian in its distribution, it could have reached Java either as fabric or depicted on portable metal sculptures. Bronze images imported from Bengal provided one important prototype for Central Javanese sculptures,[13] such as a superb early tenth-century silver image of Manjusri [72]. The Buddhist deity is wearing a cloth decorated with parallel bands of four- and six-petalled flowers, separated by narrower bands of evenly spaced double rings. Comparisons with contemporary depictions of deities in eastern Indian illustrated manuscripts suggest that the cloth is diaphanous, perhaps the fine muslin for which Bengal had long been famous. On such a garment the flowers, woven or embroidered, would appear to float, as if wind-borne.

Other patterns that feature prominently on the garments depicted in Javanese sculpture consist of schematic floral motifs in trellis patterns and interlocking circles with floral infill. As discussed above, the latter design appears throughout Asia and its antecedents can be traced to first-century north India. The earliest surviving Indian textiles to display it were found in Egypt and may be dated around the mid-thirteenth century, contemporary with a Javanese Ganesa sculpture which is inscribed with a date equivalent to AD 1239 [73, 74]. The similarities between the pattern seen on the sculpture and that on the Gujarati textiles from Egypt deserve scrutiny: the interlocking circle with a central flower is closely followed in the pattern worn by the Ganesa, as are the lappets with 'pearl' border. It is highly probable that the Ganesa was represented wearing a prestigious imported Indian cloth. This design became an important pattern in the later Javanese batik repertoire, where it was known as *kawung*.

A unique first-hand description of the dress of a fifteenth-century Javanese king is provided by the Chinese observer Ma Huan, who visited the realm of Majapahit in eastern Java in 1432: 'He wears a crown of gold leaves and flowers [Javanese *sekar*]; he has no robe on his person; around the lower part he has one or two embroidered kerchiefs of silk. In addition, he uses a figured silk-gauze or hemp-silk to bind [the kerchiefs] around his waist…[and in it] he thrusts one or two short knives.'[14] A comparison with Javanese court literature (*kidung*) confirms the accuracy of Ma Huan's account: here we find references to the use of two lower garments, known as *wastra*, *kampuh* or *dodot*, worn

73 OPPOSITE Fragment of Indian cloth found in Egypt. Gujarat, for the Red Sea trade; mid-thirteenth century (closely comparable with another cloth in the same collection radiocarbon-dated to 1255 ± 55 years). Cotton, block-printed mordant-dyed and resist-dyed. Ashmolean Museum, Oxford.
◆ The pattern of the field, and the lappet border, are very close to those of the skirt-cloth and waist sash on the Javanese sculpture of Ganesa [74].

together with a waist-sash (*sabuk*). According to another Javanese text, *Wangbang Wideya*, these could be from a number of sources, including fine *puru* of Kling manufacture and *'patawala'*, *patola* of Gujarati origin.[15] Cloth names appearing in the Javanese and Balinese literature of the fifteenth century suggest that members of the nobility wore a mix of imported and local fabrics.[16] It is clear, however, that imported Indian cottons and silks retained their prestigious position in the period leading up to the arrival of the first European merchant ships at the beginning of the sixteenth century. Thereafter a growing body of European written sources enhances the picture, adding a new level of detail and a catalogue of shifting consumption patterns and market preferences.

74 RIGHT Rear view of a seated figure of Ganesa (with a large protective *kala* mask carved on the back of the head). Stone, found at Bara, near Blitar, eastern Java; dated equivalent to AD 1239, Singhasari period.
◆ The Hindu divine remover of obstacles wears a *kain panjang* decorated with an interlocking circle design, secured by a waist sash with lappets and pendant pearls. The technique is impossible to know, but parallels may be drawn with Gujarati cotton textiles known from Egyptian excavations (below).

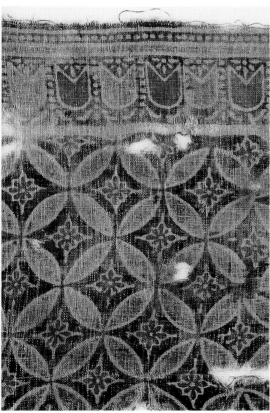

THE MALAY WORLD

75 OPPOSITE *Kain sembagi*, skirt- or shoulder-cloth (detail). Coromandel Coast, for the Sumatran market; nineteenth century. Cotton, block-printed mordant-dyed, with glued gold leaf. Collection Dr J. Luth, Hanover. ◆ Many imported South Indian cloths were embellished locally with applied gold leaf, in the technique known as *prada mas*, reflecting the Malay disposition for gilded cloth and its display; the gilding is restricted to the area visible when worn.

76 BELOW *Tapis*, a woman's skirt, from Lampung, south Sumatra. Its central panel is Indian printed cotton imitating double-ikat silk *patola* [cf. 121, 123]; this is bordered with local cotton warp ikat and silk-embroidered panels; 115 x 61cm. Asian Civilisations Museum, Singapore.

This chapter focuses on the role of Melaka (Malacca) in the Asian textile trade and on the regions which came within that entrepot's economic and cultural sway. For much of its history Sumatra's orientation has been to the Straits of Melaka and its neigbours on the Malay Peninsula , rather than the islands to the east with which it is now united as part of Indonesia.

The textile trade: Melaka and Sumatra

Melaka

Just as the Gujaratis traded great quantities of western Indian textiles to Egypt, so they were well positioned to trade eastward to the regions where they could procure profitable spices. The fourteenth century witnessed their rise to prominence in Southeast Asia, a position only seriously eroded by the Dutch in the later seventeenth century. Through their principal port of Cambay they controlled the bulk of the east–west trade, supplying Middle-Eastern ports such as Hormuz with products taken on at Melaka, a strategically situated entrepot on the Malay Peninsula. Both within India and in Southeast Asia they were renowned for their enterprise.

Tomé Pires' observations about the role of Gujarati merchants in Southeast Asian waters are the most revealing of the period, based on first-hand experience of Goa (the Portuguese base on India's west coast), Melaka and Java. Pires was sent from Goa in 1512 by Afonso de Albuquerque, conqueror of Melaka and Governor of Portuguese India, to serve as accountant at the Portuguese trading centre or factory at Melaka. He stayed until 1514 and during that period accompanied a Portuguese fleet to Java as its factor (commercial controller). He describes the Gujaratis as actively engaged in trade from the kingdoms of the Deccan, Goa and Malabar in South India, and noted that they 'have factors everywhere, who live and set up business...in places like Bengal, Pegu, Siam,

Pedir, Kedah...there is no place where you do not see Gujarati merchants. Gujarati ships come to these kingdoms every year, one ship straight to each place.'[2] Pires estimated that a thousand Gujarati merchants resided at Melaka and some four or five thousand Gujarati seamen visited each season.

The city-state of Melaka had become the axial point through which Indian textiles were disseminated in the Southeast Asian and East Asian trading networks. Strategically positioned at the equatorial meeting point of the Indian Ocean, South China Sea and Java Sea, it could take full advantage of the seasonal sailings dictated by the monsoons [11]. It was the successor to the kingdom of Srivijaya (see pp. 55–56) in Sumatra, and to Kalah and other ports on the Malay Peninsula which feature prominently in the early Arabic sources. Its position was assured in 1409 when the Chinese Emperor Yongle extended recognition to it as a sovereign kingdom and guaranteed protection from a predatory Thailand. Ma Huan, the Chinese Muslim who accompanied Admiral Zheng He on three of the Ming 'treasure-ship' (*bao chuan*) expeditions between 1413 and 1433, records that the city was frequented by many foreign merchants and that the king had constructed over the river more than twenty bridge-pavilions from which 'all the trading in every article takes place' [77].[3] Brick godowns (secure storerooms) were built to protect the precious stocks of Indian cloths and other commodities from fire, an ever-present risk in markets constructed principally of wood, bamboo and rattan. The fragile and transient nature of those structures partly explains the difficulty of locating the lost coastal cities of Southeast Asia. The search for Srivijaya is a classic example, where temporary building materials and the shifting geomorphology of the coast have all but obliterated evidence of what was a major entrepot [78].

Melaka consolidated its control over the spice and textile trade in the course of the fifteenth century, working in concert with other Asian and Arab merchants upon whom its prosperity depended, and its paramount position remained unchallenged throughout the century. It cultivated close relations with regions which would ensure its supply of spices, most notably northern Sumatra for pepper and the north coast ports of Java through which the cloves, nutmeg and mace of eastern Indonesia were channelled. The commercial dominance of Melaka was reflected in the widespread adoption of the Malay language as the *lingua franca* of the archipelago. The conversion to Islam in 1430 of the ruler, Raja Kecil Besar, served to strengthen the commercial advantage Melaka enjoyed geographically, by forming a religious alliance which linked his entrepot with the greater Muslim world. This apparently unassailable position, skilfully underpinned by political and religious alliances, was rudely shattered by the Portuguese attack and capture in 1511.

The seizure of Melaka did not mean the end of its commercial dominance in Southeast Asia. Rather, the Portuguese sought to usurp control of this hub of the Asian trade as a platform for expanding their own commercial interests. Tome Pires remarked on the city's cosmopolitan character, claiming that some 84 languages could be heard spoken in the port and that the foreign merchants and factors numbered some four thousand. After the Gujaratis the next most important group were the Kling traders of the Coromandel Coast.

Some of these merchants were immensely rich, able to raise the capital necessary for each voyage without the customary spreading of risk through a consortium. The Portuguese Duarte Barbosa (1518) described 'a certain merchant there who alone will discharge three or four ships laden with every kind of valuable goods and re-lade them alone from his own stock'.[4] The success of

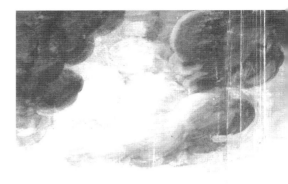

77 View of Melaka from the sea. The fortified enclosure on the right, crowned by St Paul's church, was built, like the fort, by the Portuguese. Seized by the Dutch in 1641, it is shown housing the Dutch factory, with flag flying. Beyond it to the left, over an enclosed bridge, are the wooden and bamboo structures used for trading by the numerous foreign communities attracted to Asia's leading entrepot. Algemeen Rijksarchief, The Hague.

78 View of Batang Hari, Jambi, south Sumatra. This photograph of 1879 makes clear the fragile nature of coastal urban settlement in Southeast Asia: most of the housing is built over water, in perishable materials. Such communities could relocate in times of danger or economic hardship, leaving little trace of their presence. Koninklijk Instituut voor Taal-, Land- en Volkenkunde, Leiden.

the Indian merchants is witnessed by their rise to prominence as leaders of the foreign communities at port cities, where they frequently held the post of *shahbandar* or controller of maritime trade: significantly, of the *shahbandars* at Melaka the Gujaratis were ranked the most senior, indicating their pre-eminent role in the port's commercial life.

The trading system which linked Melaka to the Coromandel Coast, to Malabar (at Calicut), to Gujarat (at Cambay) and to the Arabian ports of the Indian Ocean at the beginning of the sixteenth century is vividly described by Pires. The merchants of the Red Sea, Arabian Peninsula and Persian Gulf would gather in Cambay each year, bringing with them goods in demand in India and the east. They would form companies and hire Gujarati ships for the journey to Melaka. During Pires' stay up to four ships arrived annually from Gujarat, carrying in the merchandise up to thirty varieties of cloth.[5] Pires placed great importance on the interdependence of Melaka and Cambay for their common prosperity, which was built on the exchange of Gujarati goods for Indonesian spices. At the heart of this exchange was Gujarati cloth: 'All the cloths and things from Gujarat have trading value in Malacca and in the kingdoms which trade with Malacca.'[6]

Other Indian merchants' ships from Malabar carried Gujarati merchandise to Southeast Asia, taking on 'coarse Kling cloth' at Pulicat on the Coromandel Coast before sailing direct to Melaka. Kling merchants (Tamil-speakers from Coromandel) sailed direct from Pulicat and traded some thirty varieties of 'rich cloths of great value'. Assuming that the types of cloth carried by the Gujarati traders and the Coromandel merchants were not identical, then Pires' account alone indicates that up to sixty varieties of Indian cloths would have been available in the markets of Melaka at the beginning of the sixteenth century. He does not describe them in full but he does give an indication of the markets they were intended for. Notable are the Kling cloths expressly commissioned for the Thai market (see Chapter VII) and those from Cambay, the Coromandel Coast and Bengal destined for Java (see Chapter VI).

There was a hierarchy of Indian cloths in Southeast Asian markets in the early sixteenth century. Pires noted that in Melaka those from Gujarat were the most highly valued, followed by Bengali white cloths and all those from Coromandel.[7] The European merchants who first ventured into the Malay trading world were surprised by the level of product discrimination exercised by the consumers. The Dutchman Peter Floris, who served as the chief merchant on the voyage of the English East India Company vessel the *Globe* to India and Southeast Asia in 1611–15, recorded the problems encountered when he attempted to sell cloths from Petaboli, a major production centre for painted cotton on the Coromandel Coast. He had understood that the cloths were intended for the Malay market, when they were in fact designed expressly for Thailand, Floris having confused them with the cloth of Pulicat, another Coromandel Coast textile centre:

> a great oversight hath bene committed…for [all the Petaboli cloths have] a little narrowe white edge, and the upright [i.e. correct] Maleys cl[o]ath muste bee withoute it, as the cl[o]ath of Paleacatte [Pulicat] was…yf I had not nowe founde it by experience I had never believed it, that so small a faulte shoulde cause so great an abatement in the pryce.…Those of Maleys saye they bee Siams sortes, so that I shal bee compelled to sende them thether, as also the red yarne, which will no kynde of waye vente [sell] heere.'[8]

Indian textile traders supplied Melaka with a great range of both styles and qualities to satisfy the demands of different sectors of the region's markets. The year 1641 saw a dramatic shift in the power-relations of Southeast Asian trade, with the Dutch capture of Melaka. In 1665 the English shifted their policy to market higher quality textiles, partly in an attempt to circumvent the growing Dutch control of supplies.[9] In the Sumatran kingdoms of Jambi and Palembang, the Dutch in turn were criticized for failing to offer to the rulers the 'richer and more fashionable cloth' available from the English.[10]

Sumatra

The interior of Sumatra was a major source of the forest products supplied to Melaka for international trade. The prosperity of the kingdoms there was thus linked to that of Melaka and its successor states in the Malay Peninsula. The Sumatran courts which had adopted the religious and – it may be assumed – cultural trappings of Indianized rulership in the Srivijayan period were, by the fifteenth century, increasingly under the cultural sway of the Malay realm, a bond strengthened by the adoption of Islam by the local rajas.

The small kingdom of Barus on the west coast of Sumatra illustrates the place of trade in shaping cultural identity in these coastal states. Barus was a port of some significance in the sixteenth century; according to Pires it was frequented by merchants from Gujarat, the Coromandel Coast, Bengal, Iran and Arabia.[11] Its prosperity was generated by the trade in resins, notably the camphor and benzoin gathered by the Batak people in the mountainous interior. John Crawford, who explored the east coast of Sumatra as a potential market for textiles on behalf of the English East India Company in the early nineteenth century, observed that 'the best camphor is purchased at Barus...always the emporium of the commodity'.[12] Historically, the principal product traded in exchange was Indian cloth. It appealed equally to the upland Bataks and to the coastal population who were, in the words of Crawford's contemporary John Anderson, 'properly a Malayan establishment', that is, they followed Malay dress conventions rather than those of the upland communities.

The diverse peoples of Sumatra had a seemingly insatiable appetite for new textiles and modes of dress. In exchange for the wealth of the interior they avidly acquired cloths from across the archipelago and beyond. William Marsden, resident of Bencoolen (Bengkulu) in south Sumatra from 1771 to 1779 as an employee of the East India Company, provided in his encyclopaedic *History of Sumatra* (1811) a detailed list of the variety in circulation: the major centres of Indian textile production – Surat and the Malabar and Coromandel coasts – supplied chintzes and blue and white cloths; Makassar, Java, Ceram and Bali a variety of sarongs (skirt-lengths); China coarse silks and metallic thread; and Europe imitation chintzes;[13] The latter became increasingly popular in the course of the nineteenth century,[14] though the overwhelming bulk of cloth imports were Indian cottons.

Textiles in Malay culture

This appetite for Indian cloth cannot be accounted for merely by the desire of the population to dress in the cotton goods India could supply, superior though those might be, for the volume imported far exceeded what was required for clothing. The explanation lies in the other roles that textiles took on in the cultural life of the consumers.

79 A bridegroom of Padang, west Sumatra, dressed in formal attire, photographed *c.* 1900. He is wearing a distinctive rigid cloth turban, gold-thread-brocaded skirt over trousers, and a jacket or *baju*. Koninklijk Instituut voor Taal-, Land- en Volkenkunde, Leiden.

81 *Baju*, jacket (shortened, probably after damage), tailored from Coromandel Coast cloth in Sumatra; late eighteenth century. Cotton, painted mordant-dyed, resist-dyed, and painted; width 151 cm. Victoria and Albert Museum, London.

The style of jacket seen here belongs to the Malay world, where its introduction is linked to the spread of Islam and the influence of Arabic and Indian modes of dress. The popularity of the baju, *combined with trousers for both sexes, rather than the traditional skirt-cloth, represented a radical change in dress etiquette in Islamic Southeast Asia. The earlier jacket [81] is tailored in a finely painted floral design in European taste, typical of the late eighteenth century; the other [80] is printed with a design more obviously suited to a Muslim client.*

80 LEFT *Baju*, jacket, tailored from Coromandel Coast cloth in Sumatra; second half of the nineteenth century. Cotton, block-printed mordant-dyed, resist-dyed, and painted; height 112 cm. Victoria and Albert Museum, London.

Dress

Indigenous accounts of contemporary dress are rare in Southeast Asia. Rather we have to rely on the observations of foreign travellers. Ma Huan in 1433 provides the most comprehensive and earliest description of royal and commoners' dress in fifteenth-century Melaka:

> [the king] uses a fine white foreign cloth to wind round his head; on his body he wears a long garment of fine-patterned blue cloth, fashioned like a robe….The men of the country wrap the head with a square kerchief…round the lower part they wrap a white cloth kerchief; [and] on the upper part they wear a short jacket of coloured cloth.[15]

We have here the essential elements of traditional Malay male dress [79]: the wrapped skirth-cloth or skirt (*kain*), the jacket (*baju*), and the head-cloth. The 'fine white foreign cloth' and the 'fine-patterned blue cloth' are almost certainly of Indian origin, probably Bengali and Coromandel respectively.[16]

The dress of the people of the interior (*orang ulu*), isolated from the cosmopolitan influences of the urban coastal dwellers, was less refined. As Marsden

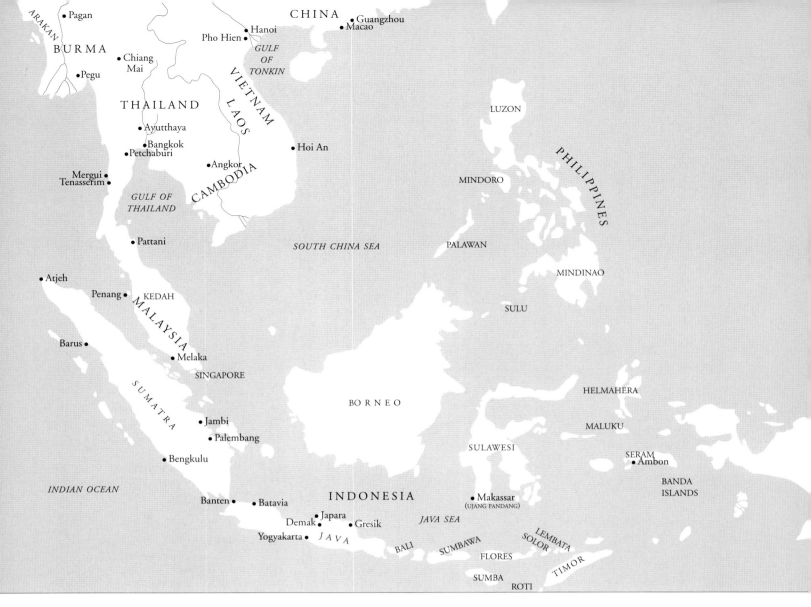

Map labels, reading across the map:

PAGAN · Pagan
ARAKAN
CHINA
Guangzhou
Macao
Hanoi
Pho Hien
GULF OF TONKIN
BURMA
Chiang Mai
Pegu
VIETNAM
LAOS
THAILAND
LUZON
Ayutthaya
Bangkok
Petchaburi
Hoi An
Angkor
CAMBODIA
PHILIPPINES
Mergui
Tenasserim
MINDORO
GULF OF THAILAND
Pattani
SOUTH CHINA SEA
PALAWAN
MINDINAO
Atjeh
Penang · KEDAH
MALAYSIA
SULU
Barus
Melaka
SINGAPORE
HELMAHERA
SUMATRA
BORNEO
MALUKU
Jambi
Palembang
SERAM
Ambon
Bengkulu
SULAWESI
INDIAN OCEAN
BANDA ISLANDS
Banten · Batavia
INDONESIA
Makassar (UJANG PANDANG)
Demak · Japara · Gresik
JAVA SEA
Yogyakarta · JAVA
BALI
SUMBAWA
SOLOR
LEMBATA
FLORES
TIMOR
SUMBA
ROTI

82 Southeast Asia.

observed, whilst the commoners dressed in local cloth (cotton or bark), 'the superior class wear a strip of foreign blue cloth…and a few have *bajus* [jackets] of chintz' [**80, 81**].[17] His description of men's attire in the Jambi district of southern Sumatra reveals the same elements of dress as described by Ma Huan nearly four hundred years earlier, apart from the adoption of short breeches (*serawal*) in preference to a skirth-cloth: 'The men are fantastical in their dress. Their bajus have the sleeves blue, perhaps, whilst the body is white with stripes of red or any other colour over the shoulders and their short breeches are generally one half blue and the other white, just as the fancy leads them.'[18] Marsden omits to specify the origins of the cloth employed in the tailoring of these colourful garments. By his time domestic weaving had regenerated in response to the higher prices commanded by Indian imports, suggesting the possibility of substitution of either locally woven cloth or cloth acquired by intra-regional trade, possibly from Java. John Anderson, however, observed a few years later that the Karo people dressed principally in blue cloth from Madras or Bengal.[19]

A number of Malay texts do exist which throw some light on the traditional uses of textiles, including dress codes. These are in the form of the *hikayat* literature which records the royal genealogies of the sultans of the Malay kingdoms. From a chronicle of Palembang we learn that in the eighteenth century a decree of the local raja required men to adopt as their standard dress the tubular sarong and to discontinue wearing the traditional wrapped skirt (*kain*). The latter was

83 A Minangkabau headman in traditional dress (*adat*), Sumatra, photographed *c.* 1915. Koninklijk Instituut voor de Tropen, Amsterdam. ◆ The display of rich textiles was central to social and ceremonial etiquette in the Malay world, and communities invested heavily in them. Embellished cloths were used to decorate interiors, as curtaining, cushioning and floor coverings.

to be the exclusive attire of women.[20] Such decrees would have required a swift response from the merchants responsible for ordering imported cottons from India to ensure that cloths of the appropriate dimensions were supplied.

Indian printed cottons, direct descendants of the Coromandel Coast painted cottons, are still part of traditional Malay dress, as seen in weddings and theatrical performances.

Social, ceremonial and ritual uses

For both the sophisticated and cosmopolitan coastal Malay and the isolated interior-living Batak, exotic textiles assumed a significance which transcended their utilitarian role. Textiles were a widely accepted form of storing wealth in Southeast Asian societies [83]. The practice was intimately linked with their central role in gift exchange, which was a mechanism for establishing and affirming reciprocal social relationships. Ritual exchanges occurred at all levels, from the individual to the state, with the aim of securing allegiances and loyalties.

Malay court protocol dictated that a ruler should present important guests with sets of clothing (*peralinan*) – as was also the custom at the Thai court. The guest of course reciprocated in kind, often with Indian textiles, so generating a discrete form of trade. Similarly, the exchange of letters with Malay rulers was accompanied by an exchange of gifts, which were carefully itemized to insure

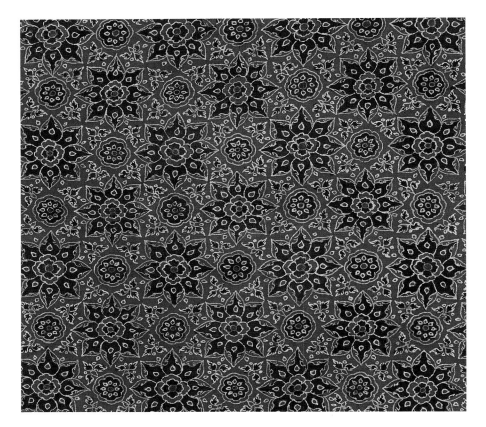

against theft and to guarantee an equivalent return. Indian silk *patola* and cotton both feature in the gift lists in royal correspondence surviving from the eighteenth and nineteenth centuries.[21] Imported Indian textiles also featured as envelopes for diplomatic correspondence and, on occasion, served as the binding of revered texts. Sir Thomas Stamford Raffles, serving as the East India Company's principal agent in Southeast Asia in the early nineteenth century, regularly presented high-quality Indian cloths to local rulers to consolidate British trading interests, together with those 'fancy goods' which the rulers often specifically requested.[22] The account of a German medical doctor who travelled into Karo territory in eastern Sumatra in 1883 records that etiquette required him to present each local ruler he met with a jacket and head-cloth, together with a measure of gold, as a gesture of respect appropriate to the raja's status.[23]

The convertibility of cloth also meant that it could be used in barter. It appears from the explicit nature of the requests and gift lists in correspondence between VOC officials and local rulers that imported textiles had well-understood value equivalents. Why else would the Sultan of Palembang demand of the Dutch five hundred *patola* cloths as part of a single presentation if not to use them to consolidate relations with his subjects and neighbouring rulers through various forms of gift exchange and trade? The role of these cloths in a complex system of allegiance-buying among the upland communities, upon whom the reliable supply of forest products and cash crops depended, would have ensured that they penetrated deep into the interior. The impact of such exotic arrivals is witnessed by *patola*-inspired designs in locally woven cloths, as seen in Lampung, south Sumatra [76].

Stockpiles of cloth would also have served as a portable form of wealth which could be easily transported in the event of political upheaval. In 1808 the King of Jambi reported to the Dutch Resident that a deposed ruler had fled to the interior taking supplies of Indian cloth with him,[24] presumably to use as a

86, 87 ABOVE RIGHT AND RIGHT *Selendang*, shoulder-cloth (detail). Tamilnadu, southern Coromandel Coast, for the Malay market; acquired between 1855 and 1879. Cotton, mordant-dyed, drawn resist-dyed, and painted; weft 127cm. Victoria and Albert Museum, London. ◆ This cloth, with a small repeated double-headed eagle motif in the centrefield and complex borders and *tumpal* end-panel, makes it clear that high-quality work was still being produced well into the nineteenth century. The attached label states that it was bought for 5 rupees from the Madras Bazaar, where it was described as 'chintz' for use by 'Malay women for covering their heads'.

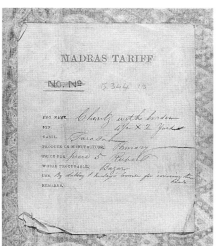

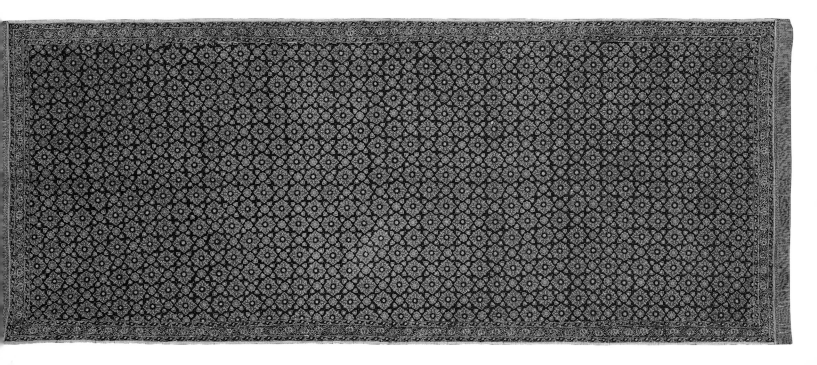

89 Bride and bridegroom receiving guests, Jambi, Sumatra. The central importance of cloths in key events such as marriage is shown by this scene of a couple in their bridal room: they are seated on a pile of woven fibre mats and surrounded by textiles, both locally made and imported, which have formed part of an elaborate system of gift exchange. The display serves to underscore the social status of the couple. Photograph by Tassilo Adam, c. 1920. Koninklijk Instituut voor de Tropen, Amsterdam.

ready form of currency in barter. Even today among the Kudu, forest dwellers of Sumatra, trade textiles retain a central place, with fines being expressed in units of cloth.[25]

Textiles also played important roles in secular and religious ceremonial. Through the wearing and displaying of prestigious cloths, a ruler could demonstrate his wealth on appropriate ritual and festive occasions. Imported textiles, including large pictorial *palampores*, especially those decorated with the flowering tree, were prized as canopies for the elite on formal occasions. A European observer writing of Barus in the eighteenth century noted that on the most formal occasions a large cloth sunshade was used to accompany chiefs and statesmen.[26] Ceremonial umbrellas (*pajung*) as a feature of state regalia were part of the trappings of the Indian concept of kingship absorbed early into Southeast Asia. They were quickly adopted by the Dutch, not merely as a necessary protection from the oppressive tropical sun, but also as a public statement of authority. Any VOC official above the rank of junior merchant was entitled to be attended by a slave holding a *sambreel* [214].[27] Canopies also provided dignity for those temporarily elevated socially, such as a bridal couple [1].

According to the *Hikayat Raja Madu*, textiles had an important function in the rite-of-passage ceremonies associated with birth, circumcision, marriage and death. A recurrent feature is their ritual use in the exchange of gifts between families that formed part of the marriage contract. During a Malay prince's wedding the finest textiles were displayed on silver trays, including decorated Indian cloth (*kain telepuk*).[28] In Jambi, cloths were hung to enrich the wedding setting; in a 1920 photograph they are seen used as the major element of decor [89]. Equally, cloths form an important part of the funeral ritual, as a description of a Muslim funeral in Jambi in 1996 well illustrates:

> the body is prepared at home…a piece of cloth is held above…by four people, one at each corner, while the body is washed in a solution of camphor. The body is wrapped, in the Muslim way, in a 15 metre long white shroud.…On the mattress are placed seven cloths, which must be of different designs.…Over the top of the [portable bed] frame three kain panjang [long skirt-cloths,

typically batik] are placed, and then two white cloths, which are usually embroidered. Finally, on top of it all, a heavy green velvet cloth embroidered with holy texts from the Qur'an. The batiks, the green cloth and the two top cloths are not buried.[29]

The provision of a ceiling canopy (*legangit*) above the corpse reflects the persistence of a widespread belief in the potency of valued cloths to provide a bridge between the mortal and spiritual realms. Although the origin of some of the cloths used has clearly changed, this description illustrates vividly the ritually and symbolically powerful position that imported textiles continue to play in Jambi society.

One aspect of the culture of cloth which appears to be associated with the diffusion of Islam in Southeast Asia is the widespread belief in the talismanic function of textiles. The Javanese *antakusuma* patchwork jacket [136], which is credited with magical powers of protection for the wearer, belongs to this tradition. The protective powers of cloth and of colour are themes stressed in Malay literature. Red cloth was particularly esteemed: the *Hikayat Ali Hannaffiah* exhorts warriors of Islam to wear it tied around their heads to ensure immunity from harm during battle, and red cloth was draped over the cannon during the defense of Palembang against the Dutch in 1659.[30]

The Indian cotton trade to the Malay world, especially from the hand-loom weavers of the southern Coromandel Coast, experienced a boom in the nineteenth century. Many of the textiles which survive date from this period of activity and are known locally as *kain sembagi* and *kain lahore* [84–86].

Imports and local substitution

Indian textiles did not enjoy a monopoly in Southeast Asia. Thailand, Cambodia and Java were also actively engaged in sending their own cloth to Melaka and elsewhere for sale. Pires observed in Melaka that traders from Thailand brought 'a large quantity of cheap coarse Siamese cloth for the poor people' and from Java came 'countless Javanese cloths'.[31] This trade continued to grow through the seventeenth and eighteenth centuries, with coarse Javanese cottons filling the gap left in the lower end of the market created by fluctuations in the supply of Indian cloths [88]. Locally produced cloths were also used to satisfy the needs of those who could not afford the Indian products, which were becoming steadily more expensive, especially in the eighteenth century. Similarly, they were employed for trade with upland communities, where they could be exchanged alongside Indian imports for forest products, spices and foodstuffs. The evidence of Pires, gathered from merchants he met in Melaka and Gresik (East Java), explains how the system worked: Malay and Javanese traders would sail from Melaka with a small stock of Indian cloth which they would sell at profit in Java, then buy cheap Javanese items with the proceeds and travel on to Sumbawa where they exchanged them for a coarse local cloth known to be acceptable to the people of Banda. That cloth was duly exchanged for the cloves, nutmeg and mace of Banda. The Bandanese then utilized it to trade east for foodstuffs, especially sago from as far afield as Papua.[32]

Extensive regional trade in indigenous Southeast Asian textiles underlines the complexity of the traditional trading system. A degree of regional specialization and the emergence of an element of cash-cropping in local economies, notably pepper in Sumatra, rice and salt in Java and spices in eastern Indonesia, resulted in considerable regional movement of textiles.

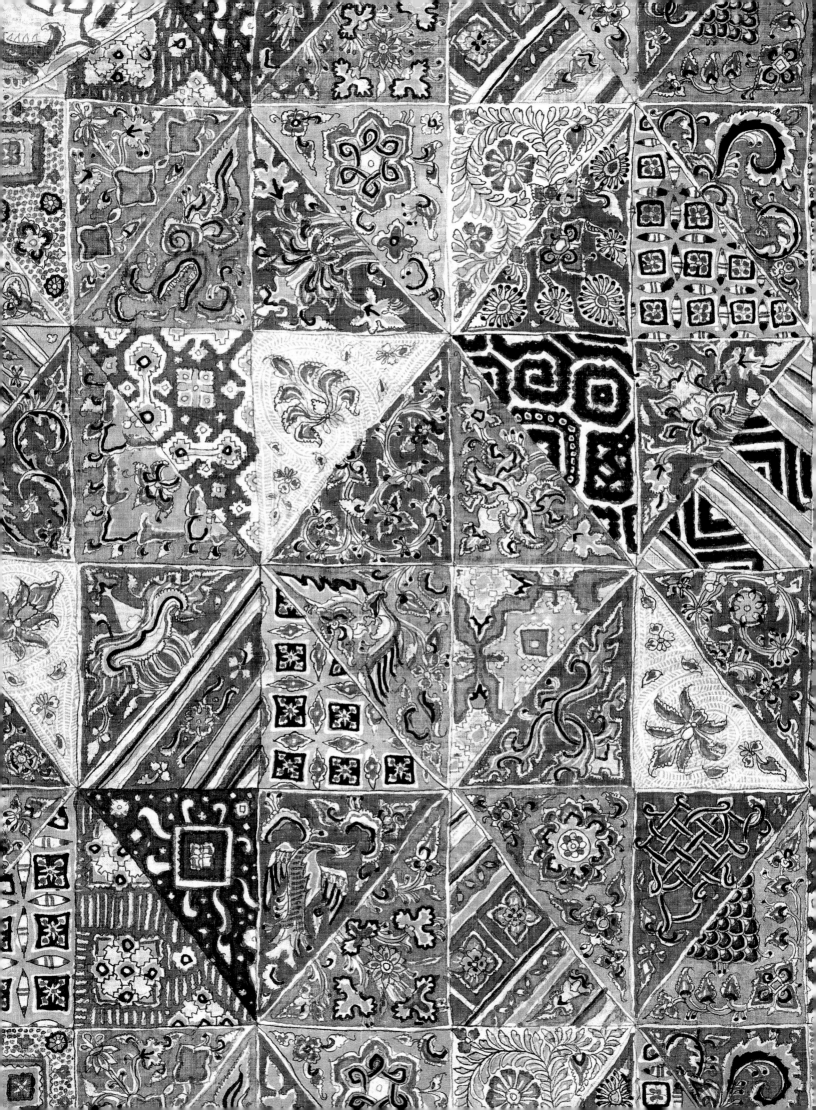

VI

INDONESIA

All Cambay cloth[s]…are of value
in Java [as are] Kling [Coromandel
cloths] and other kinds of cloths from
Bengal…note should be taken of the
large number used by so great a people.

Tomé Pires, 1515[1]

The natives of Java are in general
better dressed than those of Western
India.…They are for the most part
clothed from the produce of their own
soil and labour; but there are parts of
their dress which they willingly derive
from foreign countries. Blue cloths and
chintzes, in particular, have always
formed an extensive article of
importation from Western India.

Sir Thomas Stamford Raffles, 1817[2]

The culturally diverse archipelago of islands that makes up Indonesia has long provided a major market for Indian textiles. The earliest evidence for the trade, and the status of these imports in the early court culture of Java, is outlined in Chapter IV. The rapid expansion of demand for Indonesian spices led to a greater volume and variety of Indian cloths entering insular Southeast Asia.

The fifteenth century witnessed the growth of the ports of the Javanese north coast, known as the Pasisir. Their rise is intimately linked to two forces, the spread of Islam in Southeast Asia and the large-scale influx of Chinese settlers; both served to strengthen the trading diaspora of the region. The port cities of Gresik and Demak became the centres from which the authority of Majapahit, the Hindu kingdom of east Java, was successfully challenged, transforming the power base of the kingdom from inland agrarian to coastal trading. This reorientation reflected both the ascendant importance of trade and its international character, and was mirrored elsewhere in Indonesia, for example in Sulawesi where the inland kingdoms of Wajo and Soppeng faded with the rise of the coastal states of Makassar (today known as Ujang Pandang) and Bone. Imported Islamic tombstones in the distinctive Gujarati style indicate the prominent social positions attained by foreign merchants;[3] the memory of Malik Ibrahim is preserved in his tombstone dated 1419 at Gresik, the port through which many of the spices of Maluku (the Moluccas) were traded in exchange for Indian textiles and other goods demanded by the peoples of eastern Indonesia. Indian merchants continued to hold office into the early seventeenth century, as witnessed by the appointment of a Gujarati governor at Japara, another important Javanese port city.

90, 91 *Dodot*, ceremonial skirt-cloth (details) [cf. 138]. Coromandel Coast, for the Javanese market; eighteenth century. Cotton, painted mordant- and resist-dyed. Victoria and Albert Museum, London. ◆ The centrefield (OPPOSITE) is dominated by a patchwork design containing a remarkably comprehensive selection of Indian trade cloth patterns. This design probably has its ancestry in the talismanic jackets of Islamic culture, which were made up from pieces of revered cloths [cf. 136]. It was in turn perpetuated in central Javanese batik, where it is known as *tambal*. The border (RIGHT) depicts fabulous animals – lion-elephants (*gajasimha*) and dragon-headed creatures – in a flowering landscape.

Spices, cloth and the VOC

The group of islands known as Maluku had been visited by the Italian traveller Ludovico di Varthema in 1505 and the publication of his *Itinerary* in 1510[4] stimulated a flood of adventurers, amongst the earliest the Portuguese and the English, followed by the Dutch. This small archipelago was the unique source of cloves, nutmeg and mace. European navigators called it the Spiceries, or the Spice Islands. It was a measure of Dutch business acumen and ruthlessness that having arrived in Indonesian waters only in 1596, they had within thirty years imposed their exclusive control over the whole of Maluku. Their monopoly necessitated control of the principal medium exchanged for spices, Indian textiles.

Banten (Bantam), the major port of west Java, served as the great clearing house for this regional spice trade. Its community of merchants included a variety of Europeans, all of whom competed for a share of the spice business alongside the Asian traders [94]. Textiles were handled in complete loom lengths ('piece-goods') which were cut to order either by the wholesaler or by the retailer. Peter Floris, a Dutchman in the service of the English East India Company between 1611 and 1615, describes the mechanism of the indigenous commerce in cloth which he witnessed upon his arrival in Southeast Asian waters – small local sailing craft (*prau*), manned by eight to ten 'Indians', each with a bundle of different cloth, selling lengths at low prices.[5] The textile vendors who appear in a 1598 engraving of Banten [92] and in a nineteenth-century lithograph [98] are reminders of the small traders who acted as retailers, representing an important element in the long and complex system of exchange that operated in Southeast Asia.

The English East India Company, founded in 1600, made concerted efforts to secure trading concessions at Banten and in 1603 Captain James Lancaster established the first English factory in all of Southeast Asia here. In the course of the century further factories were opened at Jambi and Bengkulu (Bencoolen) in Sumatra, Makassar in Sulawesi, and Ambon and the Banda Islands in Maluku, though none of these, except Bengkulu, survived for long the commercial and military pressure applied by the Dutch.

92 BELOW Market at Banten, west Java. This engraving, first published in the account of Jan van Linschoten's voyage to Indonesia (1598), depicts the great market where Asian and European merchants congregated to exchange goods. In the left foreground are Dutch merchants, and in the centre, beyond the second row of vendors' stalls, are women holding rolls of cloth offered for sale. Outside the palisade is a mosque, reflecting the growing role of Muslims in Asian trade.

93 OPPOSITE, ABOVE Vessels known as *kora-kora*. Such boats, from Gebe, northern Maluku, were used for intra-regional trade; in the seventeenth century they had been hired by the Dutch East India Company as punitive war ships to enforce the spice monopoly. Those shown here carry a miscellaneous cargo of travellers, itinerant merchants (including a cloth-seller holding up his wares), and soldiers. Watercolour by Alphonse Pellion, 1818. Collection Yu-chee Chong Fine Art, London.

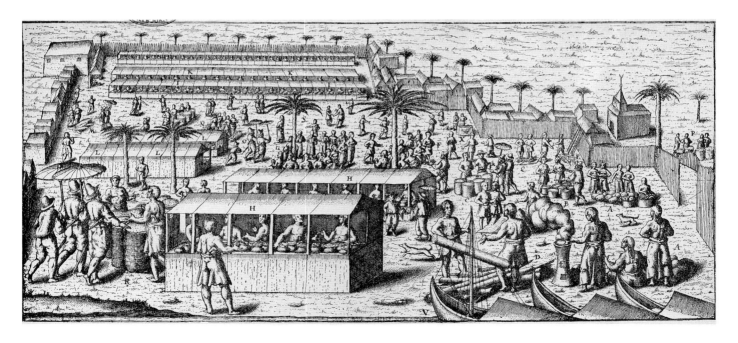

94 BELOW Merchants gathered at Banten –
an Arab, a Javanese and a Chinese – as
observed by the Dutch merchant
J. P. Cortemunde in 1673. The distinctive
character of the national dress of each
merchant underscores the cosmopolitan
nature of Asian ports in the seventeenth
century.

In 1619 the Dutch moved their commercial centre to the small harbour town of Jakarta on the western tip of Java. They renamed it Batavia and built it into the financial hub of their Asian trading interests. Batavia was made the rendezvous point for all VOC shipping traffic and from there the Dutch sought to impose their vision of a spice and textile monopoly throughout Indonesia. In 1628 Governor-General Jan Pietersz Coen imposed a complete ban on non-VOC textile trade in Maluku and nearby Solor[6] and instituted annual *hongi* (war canoe) expeditions to enforce the embargo [93]. The peace treaty imposed by the Dutch on the Sultan of Goa, in southern Sulawesi, at the end of the Makassar War in 1667 gave the VOC exclusive rights to the textile trade of the region. Makassar was a key port in the cloth-for-spices exchange, and its submission to Dutch control a major loss to free movement of goods. Nowhere would this restriction on trade have been more acutely felt than in Makassar itself: only twenty-three years earlier its prince, Pattingaloang, had ordered from the VOC two world globes and two atlases, a clear expression of both intellectual curiosity and an awareness of the economic empowerment that such knowledge brings.[7]

Beyond Makassar lay Maluku, the source of precious spices. It was therefore the region to be most fiercely guarded and the Dutch enforced their restrictions rigorously. Foremost among the region's local traders, however, were the seafaring Bugis, who operated out of Makassar and provided a direct link with the Malay world, bypassing Batavia.[8] Undoubtedly many Indian and other textiles found their way into the islands of eastern Indonesia by this means.

Diplomatic exchanges were encouraged by the European companies as a way of strengthening their competitive position. In 1682 the Sultan of Banten, Abulfath Abdulfatah, accepted an invitation to send two ambassadors to the court of Charles II of England. However, that initiative did little to advance English interests, for in the same year a dynastic struggle was resolved, with

Dutch backing, in favour of the Sultan's son, who granted the VOC exclusive trading privileges in his territories. With the closure of Banten as a free port, the English, along with other nationalities, found themselves cut off from the pepper and other spice markets of this entrepot and were obliged for a time to buy their spices from Dutch Batavia at exorbitant prices.

By 1700 the Dutch had consolidated their control of the spice trade throughout Indonesia at the expense of both Asian merchants, especially the Gujaratis, and the rival European companies. For much of the seventeenth and eighteenth centuries they struggled to maintain their monopoly, but it was continuously menaced both from without and from within.

The first threat to the Dutch monopoly was the activities of the 'country traders', private European merchants and ship-owners who operated in defiance of the embargo: the English Company at Bengkulu had to rely on them for its spices, other than the pepper which was bought locally.

The greater threat, however, to the VOC's success was internal competition. The records indicate extensive private dealing by Company officials. Suppression proved impossible, and the VOC resorted to a series of edicts in an attempt to control the problem. As early as 1617 a proclamation (*plakaatboek*) was issued stating that the free trade in textiles was permitted provided the cloths were purchased from the Company and were not sold to rival European merchants, notably the Portuguese, French or English. Cloths so acquired could be bartered with local traders for the highly profitable spices. Other regulations, such as those issued in 1642 and 1677, directed that the monthly salaries of employees, including soldiers, were to be paid partly in goods, of which textiles made up a sizable portion. That system got out of control to such an extent that an edict was passed in 1687 instructing Company officials in Timor to pay staff salaries only half in cloth rather than wholly, as had clearly become the practice.[9]

Textile distribution

In the decades leading up to the 1750s the VOC was warehousing a textile stock at Castle Batavia (the factory headquarters) which fluctuated between 500,000 and 1,000,000 pieces.[10] Goods were regularly sold at auction to licensed traders, as well as consigned with Company officials for re-sale in eastern Indonesia. Periodically public auctions were held in order to clear inferior-quality, surplus or damaged textiles. Almost without exception the buyers for these 'seconds' were Chinese, who retailed them in licensed shops. An engraving published by Johan Nieuhof depicts the hall used for this purpose in 1662 [99]. Nieuhof describes it and its precise function in Batavian cloth retailing:

> [a] spacious place…in which are sold all sorts of cloaths ready made, as also stuffs and calicos, white and painted…by the Chinese. The whole building is of wood, being divided into five walks or galleries…these little shops have this conveniency, that you may furnish your self here at an easier rate…[than] at the great shops where they will not be satisfied with a small gain.[11]

The sale lists are very informative as they provide details of the textiles, their colour and the quantities involved. At one auction, held in Batavia on 24 and 25 July 1721, the following goods were sold:[12]

> 33 bales of Coromandel textiles
> 15 bales of Surat *baftas* (plain cloth, typically dyed red or blue)
> 24 bales of chintz
> 10 bales of *Tape Kankenia* (possibly from Tapti river area, Gujarat)
> 2,470 *pathoolen* of silk (*patola*?)

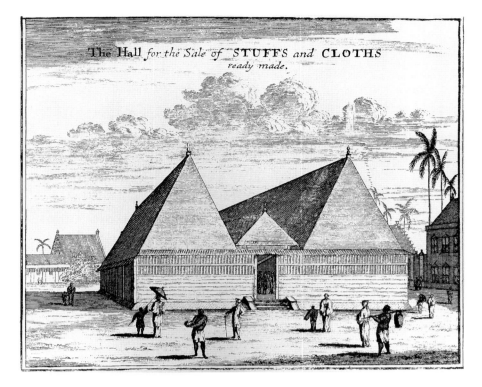

The Hall for the Sale of STUFFS and CLOTHS ready made.

99 'The Hall for the Sale of Stuffs and Cloths ready made', on the square facing the Town Hall in Batavia; engraving from Johan Nieuhof, *Travels in the East-Indies*, 1662. This building was used as a major outlet for imported Indian textiles. The trade was dominated by Chinese retailers, who leased their stalls from the Dutch East India Company.

The auctions contributed to the wider social dissemination of Indian textiles in Indonesian society. The extent to which imported textiles were current lower down the social order emerges in criminal records from Batavia, notably those concerning cases of theft. In one case, a 'free Malay' who was a sergeant in the VOC's regiment of local troops was accused of stealing the following items from a Javanese female resident of east Batavia:

> 1 red *kabaai* (Malay *kebaja*, jacket) from Surat
> 2 green *kabaai* from Japan
> 1 new Javanese dress
> 1 long white ikat *pinjang* (*kain panjang* or skirt-cloth)[13]

This inventory of the possessions of a woman living on the fringes of Dutch Batavia reveals that a person of modest means could dress herself in garments made from Indian and Japanese imports as well as local cloth. One is tempted to speculate that she would have been a customer of those Chinese entrepreneurs who regularly bought the 'seconds' at the VOC warehouse auctions. They came to dominate imported textile sales along Java's north coast, and so effective were they at retailing that the VOC withdrew from direct selling in this region after 1685, relying instead on the Chinese middle-men.[14]

Stamping

The Dutch efforts to control the trade in cloths were based on a system of licences and passes, as a means of reducing the loss of business to itinerant peddlers. The Company attempted to ensure that all textiles entered the local and regional markets only after passing through Batavia. Central to this was the stamping of cloths as a means of monitoring their movement and so ensuring that the appropriate dues were collected and that the marketing accorded with Company policy [100, 101]. The right to tax was also granted to district offices for a time. In an attempt to enforce these regulations the Company introduced the practice of stamping textiles with the VOC seal or *cap*. It is the presence of such stamps that enables us to date cloths prior to 1800, when the VOC ceased

100 NEAR RIGHT Ink stamp of the Dutch East India Company (VOC), on the reverse of a Coromandel Coast block-printed cotton textile produced for the Indonesian market; seventeenth–eighteenth century. National Gallery of Australia, Canberra; gift of Michael and Mary Abbott, 1988.

101 FAR RIGHT Ink stamp of the English United East India Company (UEIC), on the reverse of a Coromandel Coast block-printed cotton textile produced for the Sumatran market; datable to the first half of the nineteenth century. Collection G. Nishimura, Kyoto. ◆ The English Company used a variety of stamps throughout its history (1600–1858), the earliest recorded example dating from 1616. The stamp illustrated was in use on textiles of the 1820s and was still current in the 1850s, shortly before the Company's dissolution.

102 Ink stamp with a Persian inscription suggesting that the cloth on which it appears was made in Surat, Gujarat's premier port in the later sixteenth and seventeenth centuries. A nearly identical cloth [59] has been radiocarbon-dated to 1510 ± 40 years.

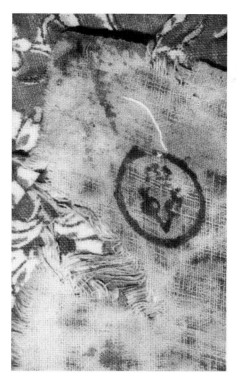

trading. Under a regulation of 1746 cloths sold, or given by the Company as official gifts (*schenkagie*), had to have the VOC stamp and a letter indicating the location of the office releasing them. When cut into marketable lengths, each length required a stamp. When these lengths were sold into another district a further stamp was required. Unstamped or improperly marked goods belonging to the Company's reserve categories found for sale could be confiscated.

A number of Indian textiles in Indonesia display both the VOC stamp and what appears to be a regional office stamp (usually an initial), which is integral to the VOC design; a 'B', for example, indicates that the cloth was cut and released for sale at the Batavia factory [128]. Some cloths also bear another stamp, usually a single letter or numerals in a circle, and it is very likely that these denote a system of classification according to quality or some other aspect of stock control. It is useful to note in this regard that in the eighteenth-century announcements of VOC textile sales the different bales of cloth were marked by the letters A, B or C according to quality.[15] Stamps recording the year are extremely rare, but examples have been found in Indonesia; one carries integral to the VOC mark the year 1763, another 1766.[16]

Significantly, the majority of the Indian cloths recovered from Indonesia do not display VOC stamps. While many post-date the demise of the Company in 1800, others are clearly earlier and must either pre-date Dutch regulation or have escaped Dutch control. Many of the latter are large-scale pieces intended by the maker for cutting into lengths defined by the design to produce garments such as sashes or shoulder-cloths (*selendang*). Two regions which have proved to be storehouses of such textiles are the highlands of central Sulawesi and the islands of eastern Indonesia, major centres for the supply and distribution of spices.

Information on production and distribution of cloths is also revealed by ink stamps applied by makers and Asian distributors. A cloth decorated with *hamsa* (sacred geese) can be taken as an example. It has one seal inscription in north Indian Devanagari script, another in Arabic Nasta'liq script [102]. The

Devanagari inscription begins with the Hindu honorific prefix '*Sri*', but is otherwise illegible. It probably contains the name of the maker or wholesaler. The second stamp is in Persian and can be read as '*Raugrisi* [dyeing material] *Riza Surat yak* [?] *Dallallan 88*'.[17] The reading is by no means clear but appears to suggest that the cloth was dyed by one Risa in Surat. As we have seen, Surat was one of the principal ports serving western India's extensive maritime trade and was noted by many early European writers for its central role in the movement of Indian textiles, particularly in the late sixteenth and seventeenth centuries when this cloth was probably shipped to Indonesia. A nearly identical cloth, also collected in Indonesia, gave a radiocarbon date of 1400 ± 40 years [59],[18] suggesting a considerable lifespan for this textile design in Indian Ocean trade.

Indian trade cloths: function and meaning

Indian textiles in Indonesia had three primary functions: as clothing, both daily and ceremonial, as items of decoration on festive and ritual occasions, and as stored wealth and valued objects of inheritance (*pustaka*).

Dress

Descriptions and illustrations of dress are provided from the seventeenth century onwards. The diarist John Evelyn tells us of the two Javanese ambassadors of the Sultan of Banten who visited England in 1682: 'their garments were rich Indian silks, flower'd with gold, viz, a close wastcoate to their knees, drawers, naked legs, and on their heads capps made like fruit baskets'.[19] A mezzotint after a drawing from life by Edward Luttrell confirms the accuracy of Evelyn's description [103].

At the beginning of the nineteenth century Raffles observed, in his *History of Java* (1817), that the population was well dressed, and he provides the most detailed description of traditional costume current in Java [95, 96]:[20]

> The principal article of dress, common to all classes in the Archipelago, is the cloth or *sarong*....With the *Malayus* [i.e. Malays], the *sarong* is either worn slung over the

103 *Keay Nabee Naia-wi-praia & Keay Abi jaya Sedana, Ambassadors from the Sultan of Bantam to his Ma[jesty] of Great Britain, 1682.* Mezzotint by Edward Luttrell, after a drawing he made of them when they were attending the Dukes Theatre in London. British Museum, London.

shoulders as a sash, or tucked round the waist and descending to the ankles, so as to enclose the legs like a petticoat. The patterns in use among the *Malayus* or *Bugis* [of Makassar] are universally Tartan…the Javans pride themselves in a great variety of others, the common people only wearing the Tartan pattern, while others prefer the Javan *batek* or painted cloths. On occasions of state they wear, in lieu of the *sarong* or *jarit* [*kain panjang*] (the ordinary cloth of the country, which differs from the *sarong* in not being united at the ends), a cloth termed *dodot*, which is made either of cotton or silk and much larger. This is worn in the same way, but from its size, and the manner of its being tucked up, it falls in a kind of drapery, which is peculiar to Java [127, 136].

The men of the lower class generally wear a pair of coarse short drawers, reaching towards the knee, with the *jarit* or cloth folded round the waist, and descending below the knees. …It is fastened round the waist by a narrow waistband or belt (*sabuk*)…[also] a jacket (*kalambi*), having short sleeves reaching to the elbows [95]. This is either white, or more frequently of light and dark blue stripes.

104 A woman of Batavia dressed in checked sarong, striped blouse, and patterned shawl or *selendang*, the latter an Indian painted cotton or batik imitation [cf. 6, 88]. Lithograph after a drawing by F. Hardouin, published by Lemercier, Paris.

A handkerchief…is folded round the head. With the *Malayus* this handkerchief is generally of the Tartan pattern, but among the Javans it is of the *batek* cloth.

The women, in like manner, wear the cloth tucked round the loins, and descending in the form of a petticoat as low as the ankles. It is folded somewhat differently from the cloth worn by the men. …The waistband or girdle by which they fasten it, is termed *udat*. Round the body, passed above the bosom and close under the arms, descending to the waistband, is rolled a body cloth called *kemban*. They also wear a loose gown reaching to the knees, with long sleeves buttoning at the wrists…almost invariably blue, never being of any variegated pattern [96].

Both clothing types and textile designs were traditionally codified according to social class:

by the institutions of the country, a particular kind of dress is assigned to each different rank. …There are some patterns of cloth, the use of which is prohibited, except to the royal family: but these sumptuary laws are for the most part obsolete in the European provinces, and gradually becoming so in those of the native princes.

Textiles and status

As in the Malay world, Indian textiles served widely for display, in both the domestic and public arenas, on occasions of temporal and spiritual importance. The use of a canopy or valance of western Indian chintz was, according to Raffles, a universal practice.[21] Valances were hung over seating places, tables and beds. The extravagant show at a wedding illustrates one such context [89], and their use as processional banners and house decorations by the Sa'dan Toraja people of Sulawesi another.

Indian imported textiles are known in Sulawesi as *maa'*, a term referring to a variety of old cloths, mostly imported from India, the origins of which have become absorbed into local beliefs; they are described as having 'come from across the sea' in mythical times [137].[22] *Maa'* cloths acquired a central place in Toraja beliefs, featuring in the local creation myths which centre around deified ancestors who are screened in heaven by a curtain of *maa'* .[23] At ceremonies to

105 Treasured old textiles, known locally as *maa'* and preserved as heirloom objects, are prominently displayed as banners during religious festivals in Sulawesi. A large *dodot-*type cloth [cf. 139] is seen here top centre, while a locally made banner cloth blows in the wind. Tana Toraja, central Sulawesi, 1976. Koninklijk Instituut voor de Tropen, Amsterdam.

ensure their community's welfare, the Tana Toraja also draped what are locally described as 'old magical cloths' from tall bamboo tree-like structures as protective talismans to ward off evil [105, 139]; priests officiating at life-passage rituals have been known to wear them as head-cloths.[24] The upland communities would have acquired their *maa'* via the port of Makassar. In the recent past a mix of imported and locally produced *maa'* have been in use. It may be assumed that the latter were created in direct imitation of the imported cloths which had become scarce or excessively expensive. *Maa'* are still highly prized, the finest having an exchange value of about twenty buffaloes, those of lesser quality eight to twelve.[25] Today little or no distinction is drawn between the Indian import and the local version in the realms of cultural significance or ritual efficacy.

The textiles

Patola

Patola and *patola*-inspired designs became the most prized of Indian trade cloths in Indonesia. *Patola* is a unique class of Gujarati silk textile produced by the complex process of double ikat, that is, resist-dyeing of both the warp and the weft threads before weaving (see pp. 24–26). The taste for it was undoubtedly established by the Gujaratis, who dominated much of the textile trade. *Patola* cloths for Gujarati domestic consumption were produced to a high standard. Those for the Indonesian market were not generally of the same quality; they were more loosely woven and on occasions employed a mixture of silk and cotton, a blend unacceptable to Indian clients. Dutch Company officials observed that the Javanese, major buyers of both *patola* and fine-quality painted cottons, were more interested in the degree to which the designs conformed to local taste than in the fineness of thread and tightness of weave.[26] This may explain the wide gap in the quality of Gujarati home-market and export *patola*.

The Dutch were quick to recognize the commercial potential of *patola* in the spice trade. A VOC memorandum of November 1603 provides the earliest specific description: 'Tjinden [*chinde* =*patola*] are colourful silk dresses, 8 hasta [*c.* 5.5 metres] long they are used for turbans and belts…in Banda [islands in the Maluku archipelago] they are worth 40–50 catti.'[27] Both in the use of silk and in the dimensions given the cloths resemble the modern *patola* sari. It is reasonable to assume that the standard *patola* as recognized today by that name was established by the beginning of the seventeenth century. The comment that the cloths were worn in Maluku as turbans and belts is supported by modern ethnographic observation.

By the middle of the seventeenth century the Dutch had forcibly secured much of the *patola* trade, distributing the prized silk cloths to local rulers in exchange for commercial concessions. The VOC valued its near monopoly highly and periodically passed regulations specifically prohibiting private dealing in Surat silk 'chindos', as for example in 1680 and 1683.[28]

Patola assumed a paramount position in the authority system of Indonesia, where trade concessions and alliances to ensure regular supplies of spices were critical to the success of the VOC. For the local rulers, the receipt of such prestigious gifts enhanced their authority by demonstrating their ability to command respect from afar. The size of the gift may be taken as a measure of the political importance the VOC attached to winning the allegiance of a particular ruler.

The presence and ceremonial use of Indian *patola* are well documented beyond Java, especially among the clan communities of eastern Indonesia [120].

The right to wear *patola* came to be widely claimed as a prerogative of the nobility throughout Indonesia; in the eastern island of Roti, for example, it was the exclusive preserve of the regent.[29] In some contexts this symbolism went full circle so that the very word '*patola*' was absorbed into the local nomenclature denoting members of the nobility, as in east Sumba, where nobles are known as *hundarangga, ru patola*.[30] Elsewhere in eastern Indonesia, in Lamalera on Lembata, a *patolu* was kept in each clan house as a protective talisman; some clans prided themselves on having designs which they believed to be unique, and integrated elements from them into the most prestigious of their own ikat cloths, most notably the bridewealth cloth known as *kewatek nai telo*.[31]

Patola designs and their uses

Three broad types of *patola* design were produced in Gujarat for the Indonesian market: those featuring one or more caparisoned elephants, those in which the elephant alternates with a tiger, and those with a range of geometric patterns, based on flower motifs of varying degrees of abstraction.

The elephant design

The most spectacular *patolas* are those with the caparisoned elephant pattern [pp. 4–5; 107, 110]. They are the largest, and also of the highest quality, as measured by the density of weave and the complexity and accuracy of dyeing. The classic design has two pairs of confronting elephants with richly decorated canopied *howdah*. The *howdah* has a *mahout* positioned above the elephant's head and two princely figures, holding fans, seated behind. A chariot, standard-bearer, footman and soldiers on horse and camel provide escort. The landscape

107 OPPOSITE, ABOVE *Patolu* ceremonial cloth with processional elephant design (detail). Gujarat, for the Indonesian market; nineteenth century. Silk, double ikat. Collection A.E.D.T.A., Paris.

108 OPPOSITE, BELOW *Patolu* ceremonial cloth with elephant-and-tiger design (detail). Gujarat, for the Indonesian market; late nineteenth century. Silk, double ikat. Victoria and Albert Museum, London.

These two patola *were destined for royal use in Indonesia, as stately backdrops [cf.* 106*], or to be worn by members of the nobility. The triple-register cloth was found in the Solor archipelago, eastern Indonesia, an important region for the spice trade. Such cloths were traditionally highly prized, and preserved as heirlooms by the local elite. Both designs are organized in a diamond lattice grid, a common feature of eastern Indonesian cotton ikat cloths.*

106 BELOW The Prince of Surakarta and his family, formally seated with an elephant-and-tiger Gujarati *patolu* as ceremonial backdrop in the Mangkaunagaran Palace, Surakarta, c. 1924. Mangkaunagaran Palace archive, Surakarta.

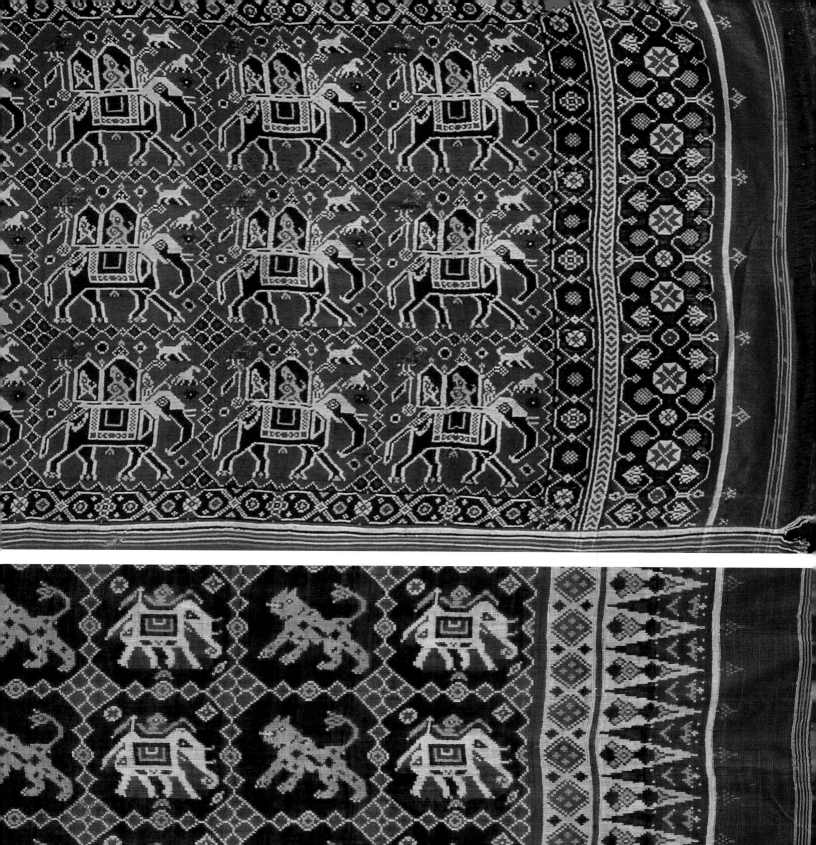

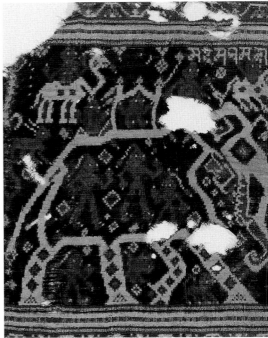

is further populated with peacocks and ducks, and the presence of deer and tiger suggests that the scene is a royal hunt. Decorative upper and lower borders are provided either by a continuous floral pattern or by alternating flowers and elephants. The white reserved area which defines the design, the resist-dyed deep blue and crimson red, and hand-painted touches of yellow and green, combine to create a sumptuous effect. Variant and rarer types contain a double or even triple register of elephants [107].

These are majestic textiles, worthy of the royalty and nobility for whom they were intended. The configuration of the design renders them unsuitable for clothing. Rather, they were in all probability reserved for prestigious display, as their careful storage as prized heirloom objects suggests. The elephant as a symbol of martial power and ceremonial authority has a long tradition which was well understood in Indonesia, even in the eastern islands where the animal itself was unknown but where tusks assumed a central role in marital gift exchange and in the cementing of clan alliances.[32]

The elephant design as a decorative theme has an early ancestry in the textiles of India and the Middle East. As early as the tenth century it appears in a rare samite silk textile from eastern Iran, known as the Shroud of St Josse [109]. It is striking how many elements in the Shroud bear close comparison with the much later Gujarati *patola* – most obviously the confronting elephants, the bands of a 'heart' motif and double chevrons, and the border frieze with geometric and floral decoration. Even the colour scheme – cream, yellow, blue and brown against a red ground – is remarkably similar. The line of (Kufic) script in the Shroud, another distinctive feature, is echoed in a unique elephant-design *patola* found in eastern Indonesia, which has lines of text (in this case north Indian Devanagari script) integral to its design [110].[33] The resemblance further strengthens the case for Indian elephant-design cloths (not necessarily of *patola* technique) existing as early as the tenth century and serving as a prototype for the Persian silk.[34] Resist-dyed Indian cottons decorated with more naturalistic elephants do survive from later centuries, from Fustat in Lower Egypt [46] and Quseir al-Qadim on the Red Sea.[35]

109 ABOVE LEFT The Shroud of St Josse (detail). Khorasan, Iran; Samanid period, datable to before 961. Silk, samite weave. Louvre, Paris.

110 ABOVE *Patolu* ceremonial cloth with processional elephant design and Devanagari inscriptions (detail). Gujarat, for the Indonesian market; date uncertain. Silk, double ikat. Collection Anita Spertus and Robert J. Holmgren, New York.

The parallels between the Iranian and the Gujarati silks are striking, in their composition, subject-matter, and use of scripts, and point to elephant-design cloths having an early ancestry, most probably in western India. The design of the patolu *is highly unusual in that human figures appear on the elephant's body, in a way that recalls the convention in Indian painting where figures are used to construct other composite forms. The presence of an inscription is rare but not unique; other elephant* patola *with resist-dyed inscriptions exist, as do Gujarati export cloths in painted cotton [cf. 149].*

The elephant-and-tiger design

The second major *patola* type, the elephant-and-tiger design, is probably a relatively late development. Known examples are of the loose-weave variety, which appears to have dominated the eastern Indonesian trade in the nineteenth and early twentieth centuries [108]. The pattern seems to have been made exclusively for export to Indonesia, where its distribution and use were strictly controlled. In central Java it was accorded the highest status and restricted to princely houses, as at the court of Mangkunagaran, Surakarta [106].

Geometric patterns

The third category of *patola* design consists of a variety of geometric patterns which echo elements from the natural world, especially flowers and leaves. One of the rarest surviving textiles from Southeast Asia belongs to this family: a shawl or shoulder-cloth *patola* with a geometric patterned centrefield and symmetrical borders [121]. The limited number known and their poor condition suggest that they may be the earliest genre to have been exported. The argument is strengthened by the fact that the largest number of printed cotton *patola* imitations are of this type [123].

Much favoured is a pattern based on the eight-pointed encircled flower, known in Java as *jlamprang*. The structure is reserved in white against a red ground with the flower medallions re-dyed a deep red and other details highlighted in painted yellow and green [116]. The same composition also occurs with a deep blue ground, the flower medallions in a contrasting red [113, 114]. A variant pattern has a stemmed flower set in a saw-tooth grid or trellis. Both were popular in court circles in Java where the cloths were adapted for a variety of uses. Some were worn as *dodot*-style waist-sashes by the Sultan and members of his court, including the palace guard [115]. Nineteenth-century portraits of the sultans of Yogyakarta show them wearing trousers made from a range of *patola*, one pattern being reserved for each day of the Javanese week [112]. A surviving set, believed to have belonged to the grandson of Hamengku Buwono VII, was in use in the *kraton* in the 1900s [111]. Court dancers also wore *patola*, as trousers, sashes, breast-cloths and skirts. Two breast-cloths with a stemmed-flower-in-trellis design display colour combinations rarely seen in the *patola* repertoire: one has a light blue design against a dark blue ground [113], another uses yellow against a dark red ground [114].

This genre may have been permitted a wider circulation than the 'royal' elephant cloths. Many of the cotton imitations of these designs bear a VOC stamp, establishing that both they and the *patola* originals were in circulation before the end of the eighteenth century.

Cotton *patola* imitations

Patola have always been among the more expensive of the Indian trade cloths. To satisfy the less wealthy end of the Indonesian market block-printed mordant-dyed cotton imitations were produced, also in India. Their dating is not firmly established: some carry the stamp of the VOC [123]. Others, judging from the weave and colours employed, are of more recent manufacture. They vary considerably in quality, from designs of great clarity on fine cotton to crudely registered printing on coarsely woven cloth. Most commonly they take the form of a shoulder-cloth (*selendang*) of typically Indonesian proportions (250 x 80 cm). The stepped geometric treatment of the motifs, echoing the binding technique used to make the silk originals, is carefully replicated in the

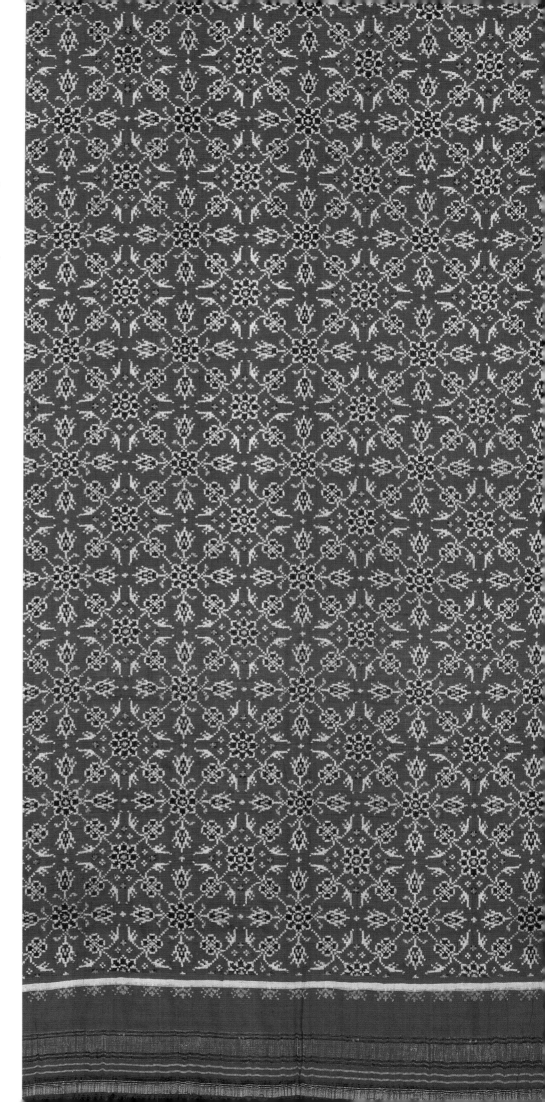

111 OPPOSITE, TOP LEFT A set of *patola* trousers, one for each day of the Javanese week, reportedly in the possession of the grandson of Sultan Hamengku Buwono VII; early 1900s. Yogyakarta Palace, central Java. Collection Irwan Holmes, Jakarta.

112 OPPOSITE, TOP RIGHT The Javanese prince Pangeran Ngabehi (later Sultan Hamengku Buwono VII: see **136**) dressed in his robes of office, Yogyakarta Palace, *c.* 1860. He is wearing trousers made from *patola* and a *dodot* skirt-cloth, combined with a European-style jacket. Koninklijk Instituut voor Taal-, Land- en Volkenkunde, Leiden.

113, 114 OPPOSITE, LEFT CENTRE AND BOTTOM Two *patola*, cut to form breast-cloths (details). Gujarat, for the Indonesian market, found in central Java; nineteenth century. Silk, double ikat. Victoria and Albert Museum, London.

115 OPPOSITE, BELOW RIGHT A member of the palace guard of the Sultan of Yogyakarta, holding a regimental flag. Watercolour, central Java; late nineteenth century. Koninklijk Instituut voor Taal-, Land- en Volkenkunde, Leiden.

The two breast-cloths [113, 144] are high-quality patola *and display colour combinations rarely seen in export examples; the light blue on dark blue ground is especially rare. A closely related version of this pattern was worn as a waist sash by members of the Yogyakarta palace guard [115].*

116 RIGHT *Patolu* ceremonial cloth (detail). Gujarat, probably Patan, for the Indonesian market, found in central Java; twentieth century. Silk with cotton borders, double ikat with painted dyes. Victoria and Albert Museum, London. ◆ This pattern, with its main motif of the eight-pointed flower (Gujarati *chhabadi bhat*, 'flowering basket'; Javanese *jlamrang*, 'eight-pointed star'), was highly regarded in the courts of Java. Elements of the design were carried over into Indonesian cotton ikats [cf. **119**]. In an edict of 1784 the Sultan of Surakarta expressly decreed that its use be restricted to himself and his brothers, as curtains to their sedan chairs. *Patola* continued to be sent to Indonesia up to the 1930s, the probable date of this example. Woven cotton borders appear to be exclusively a feature of export examples, presumably to make them more robust; cotton is never found in home market *patola* in Gujarat.

117 LEFT A priestess or shaman in the Mindahasa region of northern Sulawesi, early twentieth century, wearing *patola* as a skirt-cloth and as a waist sash. In many Indonesian societies *patola* assumed magical as well as prestigious attributes, including the power of healing. Koninklijk Instituut voor de Tropen, Amsterdam.

block-printed version, and mimicked in local double ikat [122, 124, 126]. The printed cotton versions usually have unfinished ends, indicating that the design was repeated on a long length of cloth and cut up for sale, usually in Batavia where most of the VOC stamps were applied. Such production methods are a further indication that the cotton versions were intended for wider circulation than the silk originals.

The considerable quantities of imitation *patola* with geometric floral designs suggest that these were in strongest demand in Southeast Asia. Two versions emerge as the most popular, a diamond-and-flower motif, and the eight-pointed flower medallion [cf. 116]. The richness of the latter design, in strong red and blue, has much in common with many Indonesian batiks and ikats. Printed cotton examples also appear among the textiles from Fustat, indicating that imitation *patola* was not supplied exclusively to the Southeast Asian market.[36]

Printed versions continued to be made into the late nineteenth century when they were displaced by a second generation of *patola* imitation, made by machine. Cloths produced by this technology can be distinguished by their

118 Village elders, Siulu, Bawomataluwo, Nias. The clan leader, on the left, wears a cotton imitation *patolu*. Photograph by Schröder, *c.* 1910. Koninklijk Instituut voor Taal-, Land- en Volkenkunde, Leiden.

uniformity of printing, lacking the interruptions to the design caused by the irregular registration of hand-applied blocks. They were first manufactured in the early nineteenth century in the Netherlands, at factories in Rotterdam and later at Helmond, where they were produced for the Indonesian market up until the 1950s. The result was a growing number of 'Indian-style' cotton cloths entering the Indonesian market which were difficult to distinguish from the originals.

The influence of *patola* on local textile design

The impact both on the design organization and on the repertoire of motifs employed in local textiles is perhaps the most profound legacy of the *patola* trade to Indonesia [119]. The fact that most Indonesian cloths were executed in the ikat technique ensured that the similarity with *patola* was further strengthened. In composition, the influence is chiefly reflected in the movement from an overall repeat pattern to a scheme with a centrefield, geometric borders, and

119 The Raja of Ternate's daughters, Roti, 1926. They are dressed in superb quality cotton ikat skirts and *kabaya* (jackets), decorated in radiating flower motifs which betray the influence of Indian *patola* design [cf. **116**]. Koninklijk Instituut voor Taal-, Land- en Volkenkunde, Leiden.

The relationship between imported Indian textiles and indigenous Indonesian cloths is vividly demonstrated in the three examples illustrated here: the pattern can be traced from the Gujarati patolu *original through an Indian imitation printed on cotton to its echo in a local cotton cloth.*

121, 122 OPPOSITE, LEFT *Patolu* ceremonial cloth, and a detail of its end-panel. Gujarat, for the Indonesian market; eighteenth century or earlier. Silk, double ikat. Collection I. Hirayama, Kamakura.
◆ This design may well represent the oldest type of Indian *patola* in circulation in Southeast Asia, judging from its influence on local dyeing traditions, such as those in Bali, Borneo, and throughout eastern Indonesia. Most imitation *patola* cloths also follow this specific type [123], further supporting the view that it was the most widely available in early Southeast Asian trade.

123, 124 OPPOSITE, CENTRE Imitation *patolu* ceremonial cloth, and a detail of its end-panel. Gujarat, for the Indonesian market, mid-seventeenth–eighteenth century. Cotton, dyed with block-printed mordants. Collection I. Hirayama, Kamakura.
◆ This cloth is a copy of what seems to have been the most popular type of silk *patolu*. It bears the stamp of the Dutch East India Company, indicating that it was in circulation before 1800, and possibly as early as the mid-seventeenth century.

125, 126 OPPOSITE, RIGHT *Geringsing petang desa cecempatkan*, ritual breast-cloth, and a detail of its end-panel. Tenganan, Bali; *c.* nineteenth century. Cotton, double ikat. Collection I. Hirayama, Kamakura.
◆ *Geringsing* are regarded by the Balinese as sacred cloths, and are widely ascribed supernatural properties, especially to assist in forms of healing, including exorcism. They are woven only in the village of Tenganan, but are revered across the island. This design, known locally as the frangipani flower (*cempaka*), is clearly inspired by *patola*.

end-panels consisting of multiple bands terminating with a *tumpal* or saw-tooth element. Prestigious motifs were, as we have seen, absorbed into local ikat traditions. The floral patterns could be directly translated, most dramatically in the Balinese *geringsing* double ikat [9, 125]. In the cotton ikat cloths of eastern Indonesia, *patola* designs were incorporated into the warp bands: in Flores, a woman's skirt made in Ende displays a design closely modelled on the *patola* flower medallion, as does a woman's red cloth (*'utang merang*) from Sikka.[37] Instances can be cited for most of the textile-producing communities in eastern Indonesia, from Bali[38] to Sumba, Lembata,[39] Savu, Roti and Timor. In Sumba certain motifs were adapted from *patola* into the local ikat tradition specifically as status indicators: a superb nobleman's blanket (*hinggi*) from East Sumba has a *patola*-derived four-pointed flower as its centrefield.[40]

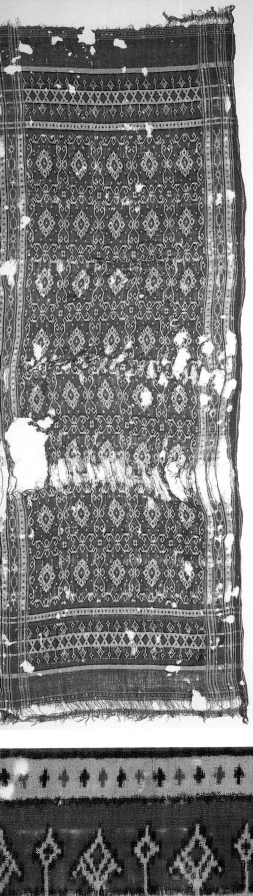

Painted cottons

While *patola* occupied a place of unique significance in Indonesia, the vast majority of Indian textiles in circulation there were cotton, either plain or colourfully decorated through a combination of mordant- and resist-dyeing techniques with patterns of which the most common were simple stripes and floral repeats.

Floral patterns

Typically, these consist of flowers of unpretentious charm set in a continuous meander or a medallion [128, 130]. The dominant decorating technique was mordanting. In the case of the floral meander designs, the outline was block-printed in a black mordant and the ground mordanted in red; the flowers and their stems were reserved in white by the use of a resist, and further details were hand-coloured in green. Seventeenth- and eighteenth-century floral-patterned textiles were typically around 80 cm in width and produced as a single uncut length of 10 or even 15 metres, generally without borders or end panels. Their nineteenth-century equivalents were made to a fixed length and finished with borders and *tumpal* end-panels [132]. The preparation of the cotton warps, stretching down a street or strung between trees, is a characteristic sight even today in the weaving villages of India. The early cloths were exported and sold as loom-pieces ('piece-goods'), from which the desired lengths were cut to order. Many found in Indonesia have been cut to around 6.5 metres, which would be excessive for a sarong and more akin to the standard dimensions of a sari: they were probably intended not for attire but as wall hangings and banners.

A spectacular example of such a cloth was found in Indonesia [137]. The dimensions make clear that it was produced expressly for display, as does its decoration, a landscape thickly populated with flowering trees. The stylization of the trees, and the differentiation of varieties, link this cloth directly to medieval Gujarati architecture [50] and the western Indian painting tradition [48], as seen in Chapter III. Radiocarbon analysis produced a date range of the late thirteenth to early fifteenth centuries, which is compatible with the dates for related fragments excavated in Egypt [cf. 47].[41]

Some cloths were produced in continuous lengths but with a recurrent end-panel which dictated the intervals at which cutting was to be done. An early example identified in an Indonesian context has a variant floral pattern, incorporating the *hamsa* or sacred goose [59]. The design is highly standardized: four *hamsa* encircle a round bud, and stemmed floral motifs fill the intervening spaces. There are no reported sightings of *hamsa* design cloths in use in Indonesia, which suggests that they may have been secreted away as family or clan heirlooms and displayed only on ritual and ceremonial occasions. Certainly the generally fine condition of the examples known suggests that they have not been subjected to any sustained wear, given their age, which has been established by radiocarbon dating to the fifteenth–sixteenth centuries.

The *dodot*

One of the most distinctive items of Javanese noble dress which employed Indian cloth was the *dodot*, the over-sized outer wrap worn in combination with a *patola* or batik sarong or trousers, as described by Raffles (1817): 'The higher orders [of men] wear a *jarit*, of about seven or eight cubits long and about three cubits wide. The *sabuk* or waistband is generally of silk of the *chindi* or *patole* pattern....[On formal occasions] instead of the *jarik* or ordinary cloth, he must

127 'A Javan in Court dress', aquatint by William Daniell, *c.* 1816-17, published in T. S. Raffles' *History of Java* (1830 edition). The princely figure wears trousers made from what appears to be *patola*, together with a voluminous overcloth (*dodot*) of Javanese manufacture, most probably decorated with glued gold leaf (*prada mas* ; cf. 75), and secured with a gold belt.

wear the *dodot*, a cloth which is nearly double the dimensions.'[42] These spectacular cloths were the products of the workshops not of western India but of the Coromandel Coast. They were expressly designed to meet the clothing needs of the *priyayi* or nobility in Java, as their premier ceremonial garment. Typically, they measure 3.5 x 2 metres, and are characterized by either a repeat pattern or a composition consisting of a diamond-shaped centrefield, usually decorated with a floral motif reserved on a white ground, surrounded by borders with a related pattern on a coloured ground, usually red or blue [127, 136, 138].

The *dodot* appears to be of considerable antiquity: the name is used to refer to ceremonial male dress in Javanese texts of the late ninth century, and wearers are depicted in fourteenth-century reliefs showing courtly costume of the Majapahit period. Its most extravagant development, however, appears to belong to the period of rivalry between the courts of Yogyakarta and Surakarta following the collapse of the Mataram kingdom in eighteenth-century Java. That it came to be copied in locally produced batik is indicated by an aquatint based on an oil sketch by William Daniell which shows the manner in which it was worn in Central Java [127]. The voluminous garment displays the blue and cream characteristic of the batiks of Yogyakarta; it is gathered around the waist, secured by a gold belt, and hangs loosely to ankle length, revealing *patola* trousers beneath.

Outside Java, these cloths are today generally reserved for use as wall hangings and canopies on occasions important to the community [139]. Among the

128, 129 LEFT AND ABOVE LEFT Section of a long cloth, collected in the Toraja area of central Sulawesi, with a VOC stamp. Gujarat, for the Indonesian market; radiocarbon-dated 1720 ± 40 years. Cotton, block-printed mordant-dyed and painted; weft 90 cm. Victoria and Albert Museum, London.
◆ Piece goods were woven in long lengths, and cut at the point of sale. Those with floral designs were among the most popular Indian trade cloths in the seventeenth century; this one appears in a Japanese Namban screen painting of *c.* 1600, indicating its wide circulation. 'B' on the stamp refers to Batavia.

130 LEFT, BELOW Long cloth with flowering vine design (detail). Gujarat, for the Indonesian market; eighteenth century. Cotton, block-printed mordant-dyed, and painted. National Gallery of Victoria, Melbourne; gift of Michael and Mary Abbott, 1985.

131, 132 TOP RIGHT AND OPPOSITE, ABOVE *Kain sembagi,* skirt- or shoulder-cloth, with an ink stamp. Coromandel Coast, for the Indonesian market; late eighteenth century. Cotton, block-printed mordant-dyed; weft 89.5 cm. Victoria and Albert Museum, London. ◆ A typical coarse-weave cloth intended for mass circulation. The 'B' may signify Batavia.

133 OPPOSITE, BELOW LEFT Section of a long cloth (detail). Coromandel Coast, for the Indonesian market, found in Sulawesi; *c.* 1700–1730. Cotton, block-printed mordant-dyed. Collection Jeevak and Banoo Parpia, Ithaca, N.Y. ◆ The asymmetrical pattern, reminiscent of the French 'bizarre' silks fashionable in Europe between 1700 and 1715, is highly unusual for a Southeast Asian-provenanced trade cloth.

134 OPPOSITE, BELOW RIGHT Section of a long cloth (detail). Coromandel Coast, for the Indonesian market; second quarter of the eighteenth century. Cotton, drawn outline, painted mordant-dyed; weft 102 cm. Victoria and Albert Museum, London. ◆ This flamboyant symmetrical floral repeat echoes European chinoiserie of the 1720s [42].

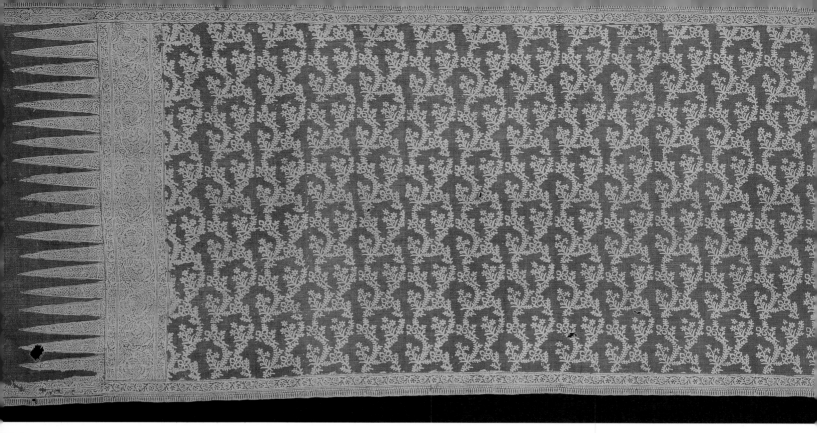

135 Folio from an illustrated manuscript of the *Ramayana Kakawin*, depicting the pleasures of residing in a heavenly abode. The women are wearing *kain kembangan*, 'flowered cloths'; those in circulation were both Indian imports and local cloths. The textiles depicted as pavilion awnings and curtaining have flower-in-lattice-grid designs, closely resembling Indian imports [cf. 139]. Ink on European paper watermarked 'J. Whatman 1811'. Bali, early nineteenth century. National Gallery of Australia, Canberra.

Tana Toraja people of central Sulawesi *dodot* could still be seen in the 1970s serving as banners and protective coverings, hung from tall bamboo poles over-looking the rice fields and from the projecting awnings of the clan houses [105]. Others protected the sacred drums during the celebration of the Merok festival.

The patchwork design

A remarkable *dodot*-style Indian cloth collected in western Indonesia graphically displays through its patterning the power and authority of trade textiles. In the centrefield is a dramatic truncated diamond or elongated hexagon filled with a patchwork design of aligned triangles forming a grid [90]. Some twenty patterns are depicted, representing a large proportion of the Indian trade textile repertoire found in Indonesia and presumably providing a barometer of the most desirable types. They include floral motifs on red, blue and white grounds, the Islamic-inspired endless knot, and stepped squares imitating *patola*. The borders are filled with mythical creatures including the Chinese-inspired fantastic lion (*kylin*) and Indian *gajasimha* (elephant-lion) [91]. The stylization of these mythical creatures is in the Javanese tradition, establishing that this cloth was intended for a Javanese cultural context. A related example is preserved in the museum in the Yogyakarta *kraton* (palace),[43] and examples even found their way into Japanese historical collections.

Magical properties ascribed to imported cloths are nowhere more vividly illustrated than in a very special and culturally specific textile, the Javanese *antakusuma*. This is a talismanic patchwork jacket imbued with supernatural protective powers. A number of these are recorded in nineteenth-century Java, where they were worn by such rulers as Sultan Hamengku Buwono V of Yogyakarta (r. 1822–55) and his successors [136], members of the Sultan's royal guard, and *kraton* priests.[44] The jacket's efficacy is seen to be embodied in the fragments of old, auspicious and potent textiles from which it is made. Most of these fragments are of Indian origin; they include both *patola* and painted cottons. The concept of the protective garment probably has its origins in

136 Sultan Hamengku Buwono VII of Yogyakarta (1877–1921), photographed by A. W. Nieuwenhuis in the early twentieth century. He poses in his robes of office: *patola* trousers, a batik *dodot* with a bold *parang rusak* pattern (a design reserved for the sultan's personal use since 1769), and the heirloom patchwork jacket known as *kyahi antakusuma* ('the venerable many-flowered'), considered by the Javanese to ward off evil and sickness. Koninklijk Instituut voor Taal-, Land- en Volkenkunde, Leiden.

Islamic culture, where supernatural properties were ascribed to clothing associated with revered religious teachers.

The patchwork design also found expression in the batik known as *tambal*. In all likelihood that is a late development, based on the Indian imports, though we cannot rule out that the idea of making cloth decorated to look like patchwork was itself originally inspired by the Javanese practice of producing talismanic *antakusuma* jackets. The complexity of this chain of development underscores the difficulties of establishing the generic origins of Indian trade textile designs.

137 ABOVE *Maa'* ceremonial banner [see also 44]. Gujarat, for the Indonesian market, found in the Toraja area of central Sulawesi; radiocarbon-dated 1340 ± 40 years. Cotton, block-printed mordant-dyed, block-printed and painted resist-dyed, 498 x 94 cm. Victoria and Albert Museum, London.
◆ The forested landscape, on blue ground for half the length and red for the other half, extends to the upper salvage, indicating that the design continued over a second width [cf. 217]. This spectacular display cloth must have been highly prized indeed, and preserved with the utmost care, to have survived six hundred years. It is one of several datable pieces [see also 146, 147] which testify to the trade in prestigious Indian cloths in the period before European contact.

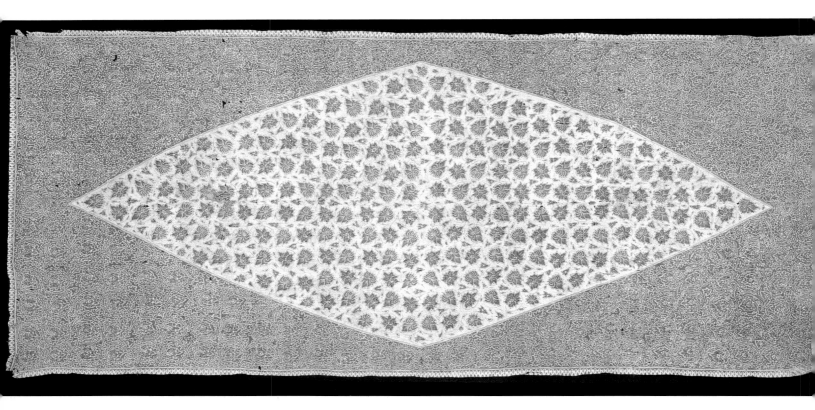

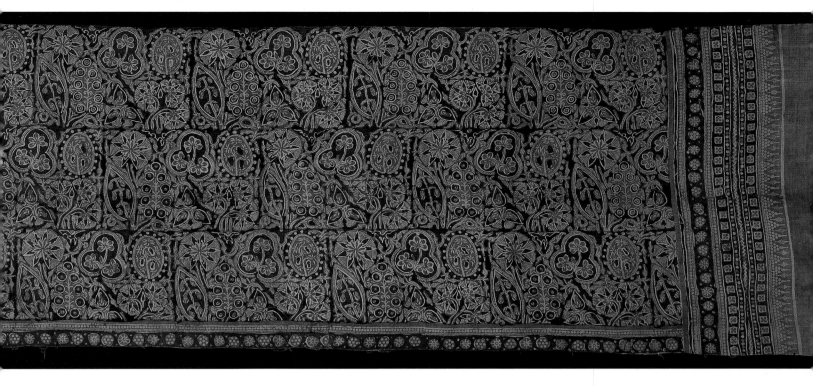

138 OPPOSITE, BELOW *Dodot*, ceremonial skirt-cloth. Coromandel Coast, for the Indonesian market, found in Sumatra; late eighteenth century. Cotton, painted mordant-dyed and resist-dyed, 270 x 119 cm. Courtesy of Spink & Son, London.

139 BELOW *Dodot*, ceremonial skirt-cloth (detail). Coromandel Coast, for the Indonesian market, found in Sumatra; nineteenth century. Cotton, painted mordant-dyed and resist-dyed. Victoria and Albert Museum, London. ◆ The complete cloth has a lozenge-shaped centrefield [cf. **138**], of which the grid- or patchwork-like pattern contrasts with the more flowing character of the surround [cf. **90, 91, 105**].

Large cloths known as dodot *were part of Javanese court dress, their use being restricted to members of the elite [127, 136]. Beyond Java they acquired other functions, as ceremonial banners and hangings, most notably in south Sumatra (where they are referred to locally as* kain lahore) *and in Sulawesi [105, 139].*

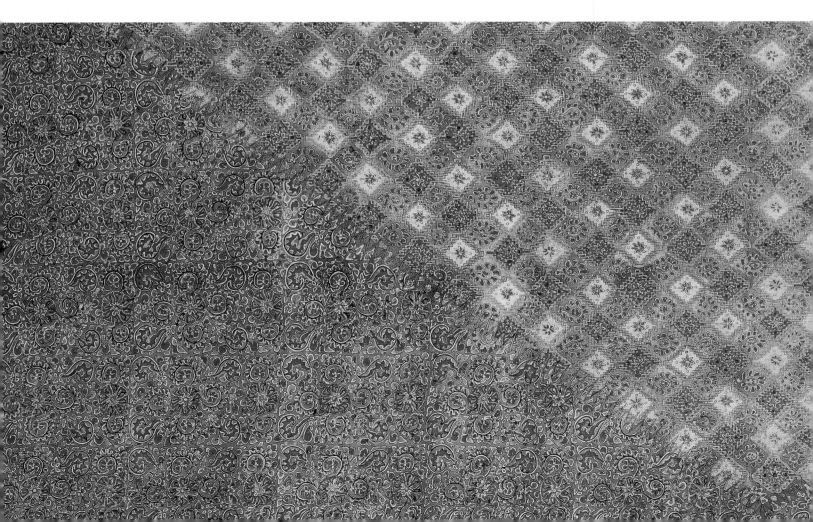

Palampores

A relatively late arrival on the Southeast Asian textile market was the Indian *palampore* (from *palang-posh*, 'bedcover'), a large cotton chintz cloth with a distinctive design usually featuring, in John Irwin's inimitable description, 'a tree with serpentine trunk and branches growing on a mound or rockery; often with partly exposed roots, and bearing a profusion of fruits, flowers and foliage of mixed and multifarious botanical associations' [143].[45] The *palampore*'s origins may be traced to Indo-Persian antecedents of the fifteenth and sixteenth centuries, and elements of the design through Iran to earlier Chinese sources. We are concerned here however only with its much later appearance in the Southeast Asian textile trade. This was in the later seventeenth century, when European design elements also began to be absorbed. Such cloths display the exuberant Indo-Persian flowering tree and rocky Sino-Persian landscape

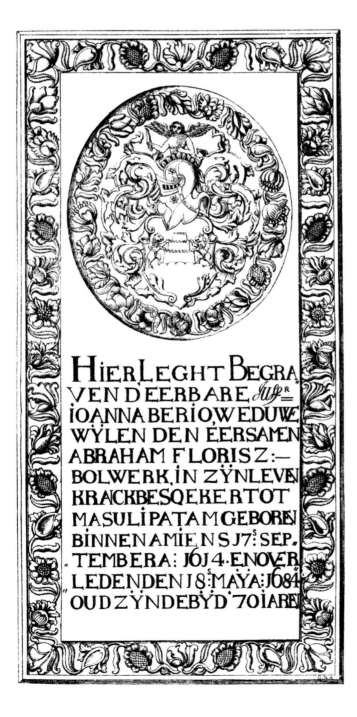

140 A tombstone in the VOC cemetery at Pulicat, southern Coromandel Coast, dated 1684. The stylized meandering floral motifs in the border provide direct, and dated, parallels with those in painted cloths from this region, especially *palampores* [cf. 143]. The Dutch inscription tells us that 'Here lies buried the Honourable Lady Joanna Berio, widow of the Honourable Abraham Floriszoon Bolwerk...' of Masulipatam.

supplemented with flower-pots and bouquets of a distinctly European flavour, or simply have stylized flowers and fruits with a floral border [141]. These types continued to be dominant in Southeast Asia until the nineteenth century, when smaller versions intended as prayer mats became increasingly popular.

The major production centres were on the Coromandel Coast; chief among them were Masulipatam, Golconda's principal port, and Pulicat, both renowned for the quality of their chintz painting. In the eighteenth century Nagapattinam became an important export centre, following first the relocation of the Dutch headquarters there in 1690, and then the consolidation of English control over Coromandel Coast trade. Both these developments were part of an overall shift of coastal trade from north to south.

Palampores were initially produced in a Chinoiserie style for the European market. In Asia they first found a market among the European employees of the foreign trading companies; used as coverlets and hangings, they represented a way for those so far from home to echo the fashion of the day. Considerable quantities were acquired for this purpose, to judge from frequent references to the demand for *palampores* in VOC and East India Company correspondence and accounts.

Over time, however, *palampores* made their way throughout the Indonesian archipelago, absorbed into the hierarchy of exotic cloths along with *patola* and painted cottons. Like them, they acquired added value through the social, ceremonial and ritual uses to which they were put. However, unlike other Indian trade cloth patterns, the flowering tree had only very limited impact on textile design in the region. One exception occurs among the Toraja people of central Sulawesi, where a number of locally made cloths adapted the motif as their principal feature. Significantly, perhaps, this is where a considerable proportion of the trade *palampores* known from Indonesia have been discovered.

The majority of the *palampores* found in the archipelago are of the flowering tree type. Far rarer are those with a design of stylized flowers, leaves and fruit. One such example is executed in red, blue and aubergine on a red ground, colours typical of the Dutch market *palampore* [42].[46] The coarse cotton suggests that it was made on the Coromandel Coast expressly for export to Indonesia, rather than to Holland where a finer cotton would have been expected. Pulicat, the Dutch textile centre and safe harbour north of Madras, is the most likely source. A remarkable group of carved tombstones preserved at the VOC cemetery there provide benchmarks for establishing when particular floral stylizations were in vogue. Designs of the type represented on this painted cloth appear in the decoration of the tombstone of one Lady Joanna Berio, dated 1684 [140]. Clearly related to that too is the floral border on a flowering tree *palampore* found in Indonesia, which thus may be dated to the last quarter of the seventeenth century [143]. A number of *palampore*-related textiles have survived from Indonesia, characterized by the use of the flower bud rather than the tree as their principal motif [142].

Figurative cloths

The figurative painted cotton cloths found in Indonesia represent a rare and intriguing class of trade textile. They can be classified into four broad types according to subject-matter: female figures, hunting scenes, entertainers, and a narrative scene from the Hindu epic, the *Ramayana*. The first three exhibit stylistic traits associated with western India, whilst the fourth was produced in the workshops of the Coromandel Coast.

141 BELOW *Palampore*, bedcover or hanging (detail). Coromandel Coast, for the Indonesian market, found in Sumatra; late eighteenth century. Cotton, painted mordant-dyed and painted. Victoria and Albert Museum, London.

142 RIGHT *Palampore* (detail). Coromandel Coast, for the Indonesian market, found in Sumatra; eighteenth century. Cotton, block-printed and painted outline, drawn and painted mordant- and resist-dyed. Victoria and Albert Museum, London.

143 OPPOSITE *Palampore* with flowering tree. Coromandel Coast, for the Indonesian market, found in south Sumatra; late seventeenth century. Cotton, painted mordant-dyed and painted; 173 x 89 cm. Collection Thomas Murray, California.
◆ The vibrant flowers point to an early date [cf. **220**]. Damaged corners suggests its use as a canopy.

Female figures

Designs of this subject take various forms, but essentially they show either a woman holding a parrot, flanked by attendants, or a group of musicians and/or dancers [26, 144]. In all instances the women are represented as sources of pleasure and entertainment, exhibiting the social skills of the courtesan as described in ancient Indian literature. They are depicted in a manner that is clearly rooted in the western Indian painting tradition associated with the Jain and Hindu schools of Gujarat and Rajasthan [145], which is characterized by distinctive stylizations of human form and costume details: witness the frontal posture of the figures combined with three-quarter-profile faces that have sharply pointed noses and wide, tear-shaped eyes, the swelling chest and narrow waist, and the flare of the *dhoti* and sari. Most diagnostic of all is the curious protruding eye, which extends in an unnatural and disturbing manner beyond the outline of the face. In painting this convention emerged around the twelfth century. The earliest reliably dated context for the style in textiles is provided by resist-dyed cotton fragments from Egypt. It persisted, in an increasingly extreme form, into the sixteenth century, maintained by an ongoing market demand from Indonesia. The exaggeration of the device in the painted cloths is a further corruption.

A number of variant designs with female figures are known but for purposes of analysis they can be classified into three groups, each representing a different stage of development in stylization.

The most lively and potentially the earliest in date are those cloths with a double register of figures [146]. The repeat design, applied by block-printing, is mordant- and resist-dyed in red and blue. The registration marks are clearly visible and indicate that large blocks were employed. Each block contains the complete motif. In the centre is a charmingly poised young woman (in a flexed pose reminiscent of the *salabhanjika* of early Indian sculpture) dressed in floral blouse and sari. In her raised hand she holds a parrot, which in an Indian context has amorous associations. The parrot has the stem of a fruit in its beak – perhaps a mango, which also has erotic connotations. The lady is attended by two women, presumably servants, one of whom holds a cloth parasol decorated with loops of fabric. Two *hamsa* appear in the landscape. The two registers are repeated along the length of the textile. It is coloured with a mordanted red and a resist-dyed blue ground which rather carelessly follows the silhouettes of the figures. This cloth has been radiocarbon dated to 1370 ± 40 years, remarkably early for extant textiles in tropical Southeast Asia.

The second group of female-figure cloths is decorated with a frieze of dancers. The transition from the single figure with two attendants to a continuous tableau is represented by a cloth collected in Indonesia. The basic element here is a mirror-image pair of dancers, printed from a single block [144]. This representation of paired dancers belongs to a medieval pan-Indian painting and sculptural tradition, as seen for example in the murals at the Alchi monastery, Ladakh, *c.* 1200.[47] A related textile version, of dancers with musical sticks, survives from Fustat.[48] In 1623 the Italian traveller Pietro della Valle saw a troupe of temple dancers (*devadasi*) perform at the city temple of Ikkeri, in the southern Deccan, with painted wooden sticks 'which they struck together after a musical measure'.[49] His description may be the closest we will get to an identification of the enigmatic women depicted on these cloths.

In the fully developed version of this second type [148, 149], a subtle and perhaps significant shift has also occurred in the subject-matter: the women are

144 Ceremonial cloth with female dancers (detail). Gujarat, for the Indonesian market, found in Sulawesi; sixteenth–seventeenth century. Cotton, block-printed mordant-dyed. Collection Mary Kahlenberg, Santa Fe, N.M. ◆ The design, of two dancers with parrots, flowers and geese, is contained in one printing block, the registration marks of which are visible bordering the head and feet of each pair of dancers. Comparison with the Jain manuscript [145] vividly illustrates the close relationship between that region's painting tradition and its decorated cloths.

145 OPPOSITE A female dancer, from a Jain manuscript, the *Uttaradhyana Sutra*; mid-fifteenth century. Gouache on paper. Victoria and Albert Museum, London. ◆ The indebtedness of Gujarati figurative painted textiles to manuscripts is especially apparent in the stylization of facial features, posture and gesture [cf. also 146–149].

all given equal importance, as providers of service and entertainment – parasol and fly-whisk (*chauri*) bearers, musicians and dancers. Their occupations provide a clue to the textiles' intended use, as a ceremonial backdrop for rulers, clan leaders and other dignitaries. The figures have now abandoned their relaxed posture; they are shown in rigid three-quarter profile, dressed in a bodice and long flared skirt, with feet in full profile. Each figure holds a stringed instrument and has a parrot poised on her raised hand; she wears a small crown and her earrings have acquired a *hamsa* design in the centre and a pearl border. Her arms and hands are decorated with painted henna, still a favoured body decoration in western India. In the background of one of the cloths [149], above each figure is an undeciphered inscription in Devanagari script. Here peacocks appear, together with parrots, amidst flowering vines adapted from Persian painting via the western Indian tradition. The end-panels resemble those of other Gujarati export types. The design is drawn in mordanted red with highlights in blue.

The third phase of development is marked by a more formal and schematic treatment of the figures, the effect being to render them rather doll-like. What began as a spirited style has become an exercise in decorative patterning. This is the type of Gujarati figurative cloth most commonly found in Indonesia. A unique variant belonging to this group was collected in the highlands of central Sulawesi [147]. It depicts a frieze of twelve women in Gujarati style, grouped in pairs, variously holding an umbrella, a parrot, a stringed instrument (probably a *vina*) or a fly-whisk. Conventions such as the rock outcrops along the lower border are familiar elements not from Gujarati painting but from Coromandel chintzes of the seventeenth century. The figure depicted on the extreme right holds a boat-shaped water flask of a type known from Mughal paintings of the same period. On the right end border appear two stamps, both in Devanagari script: the round stamp contains the numerals '1556' but the preceding letters, presumably indicating the dating system, are illegible. Other sections of the inscription have been reads as: '*Sri*. [This is the] signature of Muhamu(d) Shah in the year of 1556'. According to the Vikram *samvat* dating system prevalent in western India, 1556 would correspond to AD 1500. Gujarat was being ruled at this time by one Mahmud Shah I (r. 1459–1511), so the stamp can be taken to refer to the fact that the cloth was made in the year specified, in Mahmud Shah's reign.[50] If that reading is correct, this is the earliest inscribed dated Indian trade textile recorded in a Southeast Asian context, and a critical document for dating this group of figurative cloths.[51]

These imposing cloths featuring female figures are unrecorded in an Indian context and were presumably prepared expressly for export. All extant examples have come to light in Indonesia, and their precise provenance, where known, is central Sulawesi where they belong to the most potent class of ritual textiles used by the Toraja, the *maa'* (see pp. 86–87).

Hunting scenes

A textile type obviously intended for ceremonial use is the Gujarati-style hunting scene [152, 153]. The subject recalls a description by the thirteenth-century Chinese commentator on international trade, Zhao Rukua: the ruler of Gujarat, he noted, possessed 'over four hundred war-elephants and about one thousand cavalry horses'; 'when the king goes about he rides an elephant; on his head he wears a cap. His followers ride on horseback and carry swords.'[52] Some of the cloths depict the ruler riding on an elephant surrounded by his guard,

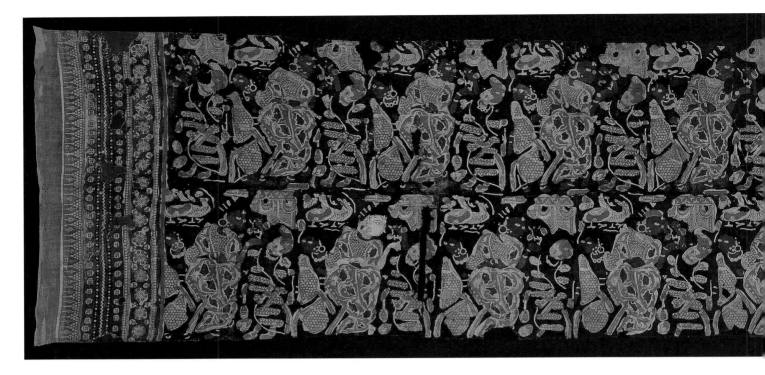

146 ABOVE Ceremonial cloth with repeat scenes of a woman with a parrot (half-length detail). Gujarat, for the Indonesian market, found in the Toraja area of central Sulawesi; radiocarbon-dated 1370 ± 40 years. Cotton, block-printed mordant-dyed and painted resist-dyed; weft 99 cm. Victoria and Albert Museum, London. ◆ The design, repeated over two registers, is printed from a large block in mordants [see 26]. The subject of a court lady or courtesan, borrowed from fourteenth-century Indian painting,

persisted in Gujarati painted textiles for some centuries, as seen in the other examples illustrated.

147 BELOW *Maa'* ceremonial cloth. Gujarat, for the Indonesian market; found in the Toraja area of central Sulawesi; dated by inscription to AD 1500. Cotton, painted mordant-dyed and drawn resist-dyed; 534 x 102 cm. National Gallery of Australia, Canberra; gift of Michael and Mary Abbott, 1989. ◆ This is the most complex and

pictorially sophisticated of the Gujarati figurative textiles found in Indonesia. It displays the distinctive stylized female figures, together with a tree motif which bears comparison with a landscape cloth also from Indonesia [137] and closely related Gujarati textiles retrieved from Egypt [45, 47]. The reading of the year makes this the earliest inscribed dated textile in Southeast Asia.

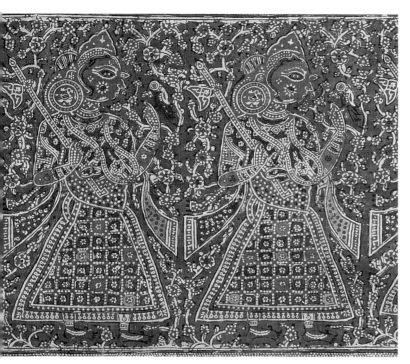

148 ABOVE, LEFT Ceremonial cloth with a procession of female musicians (detail). Gujarat, for the Indonesian market, found in Sulawesi; seventeenth century. Cotton, block-printed mordant-dyed and resist-dyed. Collection A.E.D.T.A., Paris.

149 ABOVE Ceremonial cloth with a procession of female musicians, and Devanagari inscriptions (detail). Gujarat, for the Indonesian market; seventeenth century. Cotton, block-printed mordant-dyed and resist-dyed. Collection Jyuraku, City Museum, Kobe.

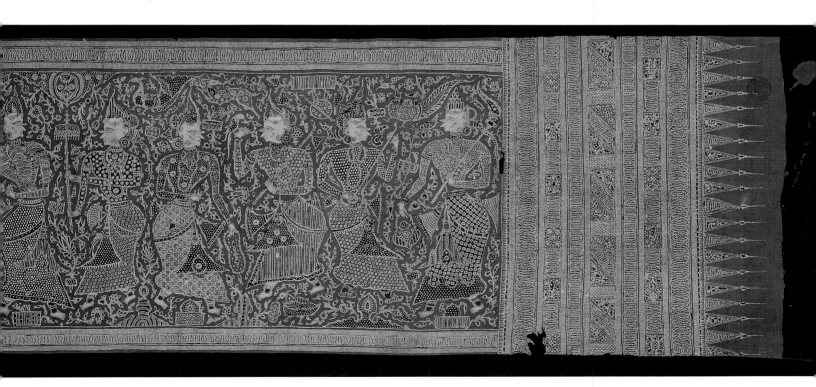

engaged in a deer hunt; others show him in his *howdah*, holding a bow, while his *mahout*, armed with a lance, slays a tiger. The example illustrated [152], wonderfully evocative of medieval Gujarat, was collected in eastern Indonesia. A further version of the subject, depicting a horseman hunting boar, appears in fragments of Gujarati cottons found in Egypt.[53]

The hunting-scene cloths are typically of a coarse-weave cotton, dyed by means of block-printing using both mordant and resist, with added colour. The earliest examples are crudely executed yet retain much of the vigour and charm of western Indian manuscript painting of the fifteenth and sixteenth centuries. The motif of elephant, horsemen and footmen is repeated in two registers over the length of the textile. Such a cloth could only have been intended for display. Although the design is block-printed, it is done with such skill that it retains much of the fluidity of painting, the casual application of the blue ground and highlights serving to disguise the repetitive process involved.

A later version, by contrast, makes no attempt at this painterly quality [153] The costume detailing and stately deportment of the procession are reminiscent of Mughal-inspired Rajasthani miniatures of the late seventeenth century, but the geometricized stylization of the subject and the treatment of the borders and ends evokes designs executed in the *patola* technique, such as the elephant pattern [110]. Clearly, a dialogue existed between the painted cottons and silk *patolas* intended for the Southeast Asian market.

Indonesia had always displayed a strong liking for cloths with elephant motifs, as witnessed by the demand for elephant *patola*. The rarity of the cotton cloths with royal hunting scenes and the regal nature of their decoration suggest that they were, like *patola*, restricted in their distribution. Repeated sightings from central Sulawesi affirm that it was an important market for the genre.

Entertainers

The problem of meaning and context is highlighted by a remarkable series of cloths which came to light in the early 1990s in the former Portuguese colony of East Timor. They represent a previously unrecorded aspect of the western Indian textile trade to Indonesia. They are of fine cotton rather than the

150 Ceremonial hanging with figures of entertainers. Gujarat, for the Indonesian market, found in East Timor; radiocarbon-dated 1750 ± 45 years. Cotton, block-printed and painted mordant-dyed and painted resist-dyed; weft 77.5 cm. Collection J. Luth, Hanover. ◆ Radiocarbon dating becomes increasingly problematic for objects this young, but the date given is broadly compatible with the stylistic characteristics of the rich floral and geometrical framework in which the unusual figurative subject is depicted.

coarse weave more commonly intended for the eastern islands. One has, set in decorative borders characteristic of western Indian workshops, a pictorial field peopled by a variety of figures: cowherd farmers, courtiers, nobles, foot and equestrian soldiers, and palanquin bearers [154]. Hindu deities mingle with mortals: the flute-playing figure of Krishna and an anthropomorphic representation of Garuda (Vishnu's vehicle) support religious associations. Masked theatrical characters occupy a stage in the upper register, reminiscent of the troubadours of Gujarat and Madhya Pradesh. A second cloth of this type has a more conventional tableau [150]: it depicts a highly animated female dancer, accompanied by musicians, performing before a nobleman seated on a cushioned platform. Soldiers, or perhaps members of the same theatrical troupe, engage in a sword fight for the nobleman's entertainment. The stylized portrayal of the dancer can be closely linked to Gujarati paintings. As in the case of the other figurative cloths discussed, they are unlike anything found in India.

Battle scene from the 'Ramayana'

Another figurative textile type with Hindu associations is that depicting a subject from the epic of the *Ramayana* [151].[54] The cloths all show the same climactic scene when Rama, with the aid of the monkey army, does battle with the evil multi-headed demon Ravana and the forces of Lanka. Both Rama and Ravana, dressed only in *dhoti*, are poised with their long bows drawn, about to discharge their magic arrows. The contesting armies are engaged in deadly combat and the landscape is littered with dismembered bodies. Members of Rama's monkey army carry rocks to build the land bridge from India to Lanka.

In village India such narrative textiles are widely used as backdrops for dramatic performances of scenes from the religious epics. Javanese didactic cloth painting (such as *wayang beber*) and Balinese Klungkung court painting had a long autonomous history, and the narrative intent of the imported cloths would not have gone unappreciated. In eastern Indonesia, on the other hand, the subject would have needed to be explained within the local belief system.

These narrative cloth paintings can be related to the medieval southern Coromandel Coast *kalamkari* tradition, especially the pictorial temple cloths which illustrate sequential scenes from the Hindu epics. Whilst sharing aspects of both function and technique, the *Ramayana* textiles have no close parallels in south India. Rather, they too appear to have been made expressly for Indonesia.

It remains an open question how early the *Ramayana* cloths began being produced. It is perhaps significant that they are not recognizable in lists of textiles ordered by European companies for their Indonesia trade, although at least one piece, in the Tropen Museum, Amsterdam, bears a VOC stamp. The earliest provenanced example entered the collection of the Musée de l'Impression sur Etoffes at Mulhouse in 1829, three decades after the demise of the VOC.[55]

Competition to Indian cloths

Forgeries

A threat to VOC control of trade came with the appearance of low-quality imitation chintz textiles from India. These cloths were made not by the true *kalamkari* technique, which involves complex mordant- and resist-dyeing, but by simply applying colour directly onto the untreated cotton. They could be produced at greatly reduced cost but were not colourfast, a key requirement of consumers. As early as 1648 the Company passed an edict prohibiting the

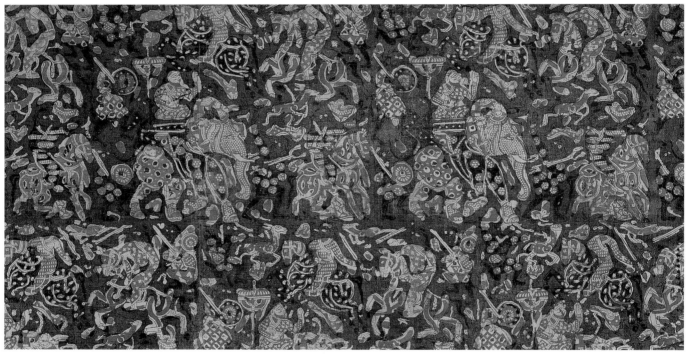
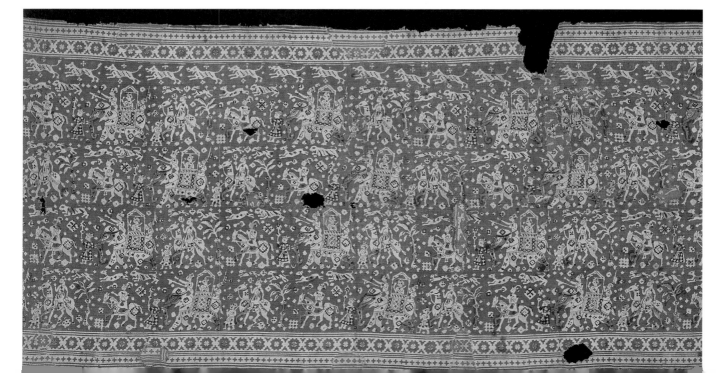

151 ABOVE Ceremonial hanging with a scene from the *Ramayana*. Coromandel Coast, for the Indonesian market, found in eastern Indonesia; eighteenth century. Cotton, painted mordant-dyed and painted, 450 x 95 cm. Victoria and Albert Museum, London. ◆ Rama, aided by the monkey army at left, overcomes the demon Ravana and the forces of Lanka. Although related in technique and style to south Indian temple cloths, *Ramayana* cloths are unique to Indonesia, where they have been mostly recorded in Sulawesi and Bali; some bear the stamp of the VOC, establishing a pre-1800 date for their manufacture.

152 OPPOSITE, CENTRE Ceremonial hanging with a hunting scene (detail). Gujarat, for the Indonesian market; late fourteenth–fifteenth century. Cotton, block-printed mordant-dyed and resist-dyed. National Gallery of Australia, Canberra, gift of Michael and Mary Abbott, 1988. ◆ The scene evokes the description of a king in Gujarat given by a thirteenth-century Chinese traveller (see p. 111). Strong parallels with radiocarbon-tested cloths [137, 146] suggest the early date.

153 OPPOSITE, BELOW Ceremonial hanging with a hunting scene (detail). Gujarat, for the Indonesian market; late seventeenth–eighteenth century. Cotton, block-printed mordant-dyed and painted dyes; weft 95.5 cm. Victoria and Albert Museum, London. ◆ The style of the figures and their costume details recall Rajasthani paintings of this period whilst the geometric treatment echoes *patola*.

154 BELOW Ceremonial cloth with figures of entertainers (detail). Gujarat, for the Indonesian market, found in Timor; eighteenth century. Cotton, mordant- and resist-dyed. Museum of International Folk Art, Neutrogena Collection, Santa Fe, N.M.

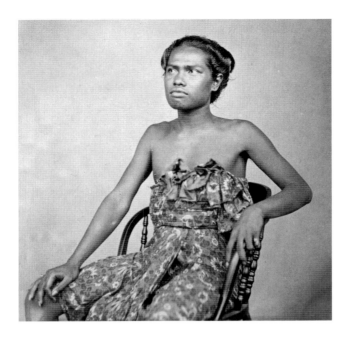

155 A Balinese prince, photographed
c. 1910. The young man is wearing a length
of floral patterned cloth, most probably
machine-printed cotton, gathered up around
his chest. Collection Yu-chee Chong Fine
Art, London.

importation and sale of these counterfeit *kalamkaris* and imposed severe
penalties for violations.[56] The Dutch were familiar with the problems of forgery
from their experience of the textile trade within Europe.[57] There, quality came
to be defined in terms of tightness and evenness of weave, thread count, uniformity of twist, alignment of warp and weft, degree of finishing applied, and the
use of a lead seal to designate that a cloth had passed inspection.[58] These criteria
were essentially those which the VOC's officers used to ensure consistency in the
supplies from their Indian agents. The maintenance of standards was a source of
tension between buyer and supplier and required constant vigilance.

A further category of counterfeit cloths appeared in the eighteenth and
nineteenth centuries, from Southeast Asian weavers and dyers. These convincing replicas were able to damage the sale of the more expensive genuine article;
they were, however, again not colourfast and were readily spoiled by moisture.
Raffles comments on such painted cloths in the Indian style that were being
made in Java in the early nineteenth century:

156 Page from a sample book of the Dutch
textile printing firm De Heijder & Co. of
Leiden, showing machine-printed cotton
imitations of Indian cloth for the Indonesian
market; late nineteenth century. Collection
Vlisco BV, Helmond.

> coloured cotton, in imitation of the Indian chintz, is also prepared; but it is not
> held in much estimation, on account of the superiority of the foreign chintzes
> imported, and the uncertainty of the colours, which the natives allege will not stand
> in the same manner as those which have undergone the process of the batek [i.e.
> wax-resist], frequently fading in the second washing. In these cloths, the patterns
> being carved on small wooden blocks are stamped as in India. They serve as cover-
> lids [bedcovers], and are employed as a substitute for the Indian *palampore*, when
> the latter is not procurable. The price is about four rupees.[59]

Similar complaints of unfast colours spoiled the reputation of English printed
cottons, a late arrival on the Javanese textile market, which though not strictly
forgeries were nonetheless designed to steal the market from the Indian
products. Raffles noted that some cloths, 'of peculiar patterns adapted to the
taste of the natives and Chinese', were popular, but that another consignment
suffered a different fate:

> a very extensive and valuable assortment of these cottons, imitated after the
> Javan and Malayan patterns, was recently imported into Java by the East India
> Company…[but] the natives discovered that the colours would not stand, and
> the remainder were no longer in any demand.[60]

Raffles lamented the technical inferiority of British cloth and urged British

157 Line drawings of batik designs, from a sample book or *batikmuster* prepared in Gresik, north coast Java, in 1822 by A. D. Cornets de Groot, the Dutch Resident (published by Rouffaer and Juynboll, 1914). The designs show a close relationship to those appearing on Indian imports of the period [cf. 6, 8, 84, 87].

manufacturers to learn from Asia the sources of their dye-stuffs and methods of fixing the colours. In time machine-printed British and Dutch cloths entered the Southeast Asian market, with a range of convincing imitations of Indian cloths which found a degree of local favour [156].

Substitution of local cloths

An even greater problem for the Dutch than forgeries was the substitution of locally produced cloths for imported ones; indeed, it has recently been argued that the terminal decline of the VOC textile trade in Indonesia in the course of the eighteenth century was economically and functionally related to the rise in local manufacture and trade.[61] Indonesia had long been involved in such trade, regional and long-distance, as witnessed by the presence of cheap Javanese cloths noted by Pires at Melaka in 1512. With the growing monopoly of the Dutch on the supply of Indian textiles and the inflated prices that resulted, consumers increasingly resorted to products from the region, distributed by a trading system in which Javanese and Makassarese played a key role. The Dutch did not originally attempt to control locally woven textiles because of their low value and small profit margins. Over time, however, VOC sales of Indian goods were affected, and in 1697 a proclamation was passed forbidding the trade in local cloth without a company licence.[62] Taxes on sales were imposed at those markets controlled by the VOC, but evasion was endemic.

The Company was powerless to prevent the local cultivation of cotton and production of cloth. Indeed, rulers actively encouraged their subjects to be self-sufficient, and the women of the court set an example with their batik making. The adoption of local fashion in the Sumatran courts of Palembang and Jambi, for example,[63] reflected a backlash against Dutch attempts to impose a monopoly on supply of Indian imports. The Dutch had reason for concern: in Ambon, the proportion of local (Makassarese and Javanese) cloth to foreign imports grew in the late eighteenth century from 55 to 80 per cent.[64]

That some of these cloths made in Indonesia deliberately imitated the prestigious imports from the subcontinent is evident from a study of the line drawings of contemporary batik designs prepared in Gresik in 1822 by A. D. Cornets de Groot:[65] most can be related to known Indian trade textile designs [157]. They suggest that the growth of the batik industry in the nineteenth century was largely prompted by a need to relieve shortages of Indian cloth and to circumvent the high prices asked for it. An alternative explanation may lie in the monetarization of the local economies: as silver and copper coins became more available, they may have partially displaced cloth as 'hoard money', as a store of wealth.

In Java, batik (also referred to as 'painted cloth') produced within the courts became important alongside Indian cloths, especially *patola*, and formed part of royal regalia. Each court established its character and authority through the invention and control of the use of particular designs. It is surely significant that some of the batik patterns of central Java which were restricted to members of the royal family can be recognized as being borrowed or adapted from Indian textiles: for example, those called *kawang piccus*, *jajakusama* and *cakar melik* are all *patola*-inspired while *sembagen huk* is based on resist-dyed Indian imports, known in western Indonesia as *sembagi*.[66] Indian imports inspired a fine tradition in batik versions [cf. 84, 85, 88], and European imitations are known to have been produced from the mid-nineteenth century.

VII

'CLOTHS IN THE FASHION OF SIAM'

They say that the chief merchandise they take from Malacca [Melaka] to Siam [is]…wide and narrow muslins, Kling cloths in the fashion of Siam [and] brocades from Cambay.

Tomé Pires, 1512–15[1]

158 OPPOSITE *Pha kiao*, floor cover or hanging (detail). Coromandel Coast, for the Thai market; late eighteenth century. Cotton, painted and block-printed mordant-dyed and painted resist-dyed. Victoria and Albert Museum, London. ◆ Indian painted textiles for the Thai market are characterized by trellis or lattice-pattern centrefields typically decorated with Buddhist celestial beings.

159 'Siamese man and woman', *c.* 1887. Both wear *pha nung* (skirt-cloths). His is drawn up between his legs as *pha nung chong kraben*; he has a waist sash which may be an Indian *patka* and a short scarf. The woman's breasts are covered with a long cloth, the *sabai*. Watercolour from *Burmese Drawings*. Victoria and Albert Museum, London.

The Indian textile trade with Thailand was centred at Ayutthaya, the capital of the kingdom of Siam from the fifteenth century until 1767, when it was sacked by the Burmese and the capital relocated south to Bangkok. Siam as a political entity corresponds with the modern provinces of central Thailand. The city, which emerged as the result of the integration of two local powers, Lopburi and Suphanburi, was strategically situated at the confluence of three rivers, enabling it to control the flow of commerce between the Gulf of Thailand and the hinterland which produced the valuable farming, forest and animal products so much in demand by the international markets [160]. Foreign trade was promoted by the court, to enhance prestige and generate revenue: by the eighteenth century over 25 per cent of royal earnings came from such commerce.[2]

Trade and its control

Evidence of trade goods in Thailand in the fifteenth century is provided from a number of sources. Large quantities of glazed ceramics, including Chinese and Vietnamese, have been retrieved from the riverbed at Ayutthaya, pointing to the role of that city as a major regional and international transshipment centre for ceramics.[3] There is also growing evidence to suggest that Ayutthaya's overseas trade was dominated by foreign entrepreneurs. An indication of the wealth and influence of such communities can be gauged from a discovery at the temple of Wat Ratchaburana, built under the direction of King Borommaracha II in the 1420s: when the relic chamber beneath the main tower was opened in 1957 it was found to contain a lengthy foundation inscription written principally in Thai but with additional passages in Arabic, Chinese and Khmer which provided the names of foreign donor-families who contributed to the endowment of the temple,[4] thus joining the king in a public act of religious patronage. Whilst the Chinese dominated Thai trade eastward, Arabic-speaking merchants played a major role in the Indian Ocean trade. Ma Huan, the Muslim interpreter who accompanied the Chinese admiral Zheng He on the great expeditions into the western oceans, provides in his account of 1433 some valuable observations on Thai commerce. He lists the natural products assembled at Ayutthaya but attaches no particular importance to the city, which suggests that it was not yet established as one of Southeast Asia's premier entrepots. He lays stress on a market town situated some 43 kilometres to the north, which must be the former capital of Lopburi, stating that 'in this place there are five or six hundred families of foreigners' and that 'all kinds of foreign goods are for sale'.[5]

Information on Ayutthaya's role in the fifteenth century is preserved in the *Rekidai Hoan*, a history of the royal household of the Ryukyu Islands south of Japan, which records that kingdom's relations with countries in East and Southeast Asia (see pp. 159–60). The documents suggest that commercial contacts with Thailand commenced as early as the 1380s. Indian textiles are first

121

mentioned around 1430: in that year the ruler of the Ryukyus received a cargo from Thailand which included, together with sappanwood (the source of a red dye much in demand in Japan), two 'variegated velvet carpets', most probably Persian or Indian, one length of 'soft western silk', and 'twenty bolts of red oiled cotton cloth'.[6] This latter item must refer to the highly glazed painted cottons dyed red with *chay* that are most closely associated with the Coromandel Coast port of Masulipatam. Contact appears to have been strongest in the late fifteenth century, when the *Rekidai Hoan* records Thai missions whose cargoes consisted principally of sappanwood and red cloth,[7] which may be from the Coromandel Coast, or may be the 'red Western cloth' identified by Ma Huan as coming from Cambay, Gujarat's principal port, each piece measuring 1.35 metres in width and 7.6 metres in length, and worth eight or ten gold pieces.[8]

It is evident from the writings of the Portuguese Tomé Pires, who was based at Melaka on the Malay Peninsula from 1512 to 1515, that Ayutthaya was a major regional trading centre by his time. What Pires was probably slower to realize was that direct trade between Ayutthaya and India had also grown in response to the Portuguese seizure of Melaka in 1511. Although he complained (in what is a foretaste of many seventeenth-century European commentators' laments) that the city attracted less commerce than it might because of its restrictive policies, it was nonetheless too important a source of highly profitable natural products for merchants to ignore. Pires notes that among the merchandise taken from Melaka to Thailand were 'Kling cloths in the fashion of Siam', 'Kling' being the term current for the Tamil-speaking Coromandel Coast traders, particularly those associated with Masulipatam and Pulicat. This is the first evidence of Indian cloths being designed expressly for the Thai market.

Pires also mentions textiles from elsewhere in India among Thailand's imports from Melaka: 'wide and narrow muslins' not only from the Coromandel Coast but from Bengal, and carpets and brocades from Cambay.[9] Duarte Barbosa, a contemporary countryman of Pires, states that the ports of Thailand and the kingdom of Pegu in lower Burma received great quantities of Indian textiles from both the Coromandel Coast (Pulicat) and Cambay, and that the cloths were highly prized. As we have seen, a great range of qualities were produced by Indian manufacturers for export, including coarse grades to satisfy demand at the poorer levels of society. In the latter market regional competition was a factor: Pires informs us that Thailand, already a discriminating importer of fine-quality Indian cottons, was also a major exporter of 'cheap coarse Siamese cloth for the poor people'.[10] he witnessed this traffic in Melaka, whence the goods were re-exported throughout the Indonesian archipelago in competition with Indian imports and locally woven textiles.

Thailand had control of a number of ports on the west coast of the peninsula to service its Indian trade.[11] The most important was 'Tanacary' or 'Tannasary', the modern port of Tenasserim. This was described by Barbosa as 'a great city, a sea-haven…here are many merchants both Moors and Heathens [Hindus] who deal in goods of every kind, and also possess many ships which sail to Bengala, Malaca and many other places'; their cargoes included 'cloth dyed in grain [indigo?], silk, coloured Meca velvets…Cambay cloths; the whole whereof they prize greatly in this Kingdom of Anseam [Siam]'.[12] Goods traded at Tenasserim and Mergui, a nearby port, were then moved by a complex river and land route to the Gulf of Thailand and hence to the capital and beyond. To facilitate this trade the Thai court maintained good relations with the provincial rulers of Tenasserim. As early as 1613 an agent of the East India Company,

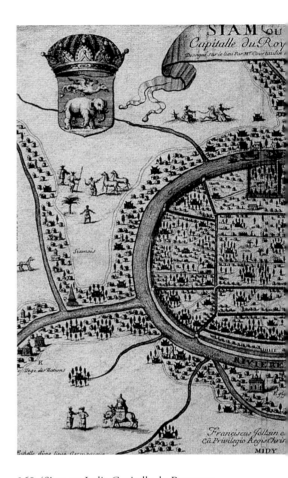

160 'Siam ou Iudia Capitalle du Royaume de Siam' (detail), drawn by Courtaulin and engraved by François Jollain, 1686. Ayutthaya, the capital of the kingdom of Siam, is shown here at the height of its power, built largely on the wealth of international trade. The map indicates the location of the Indian, Chinese, Malay, Burmese, Portuguese, Dutch and French trading communities, situated outside the moated and walled royal city. Collection of the Siam Society, Bangkok.

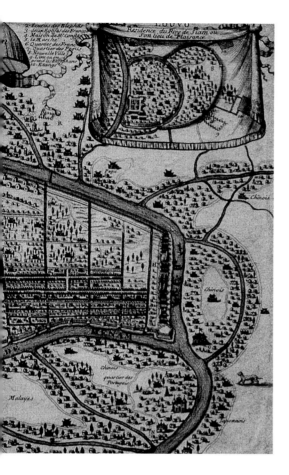

Thomas Samuel, reached the northern Thai capital of Chiang Mai with a consignment of Coromandel cloths which had travelled this route, intending to trade them for gold, rubies, benzoin, wax and deer skins.[13]

The royal monopolies

A major feature of Thai foreign trade relations from the mid-fifteenth century was the gradual imposition of royal monopolies. A degree of state control was reputedly instigated as part of administrative reforms undertaken by King Trailok (1448–88), but there is evidence that the process had begun even earlier: the *Rekidai Hoan* states that in 1419 Ryukyuan merchants complained of interference from Thai court officials.[14] The trend strengthened under Songt'am (1610–28) and during the reign of Prasat T'ong (1630–56) controls on trade were formalized into royal monopolies on particular export goods, a system which continued until the mid-nineteenth century. The distribution of imported textiles was closely controlled, but it was never declared a state monopoly.

At the centre of the administrative structure was the office of the *phra khlang*, or minister of finance, who was given specific responsibility to supervise commercial relations with foreigners. Beneath him, two further posts were created, the *chularatchamontri* and the *chodukratchasetthi*, harbour-masters of Indian and Chinese origin respectively, who were in charge of dealings with merchants from their country of origin. Those offices subsequently became known as the departments of the *Krom Tha Khwa*, or Port of the Right (the western side of Siam, facing the Indian Ocean) and *Krom Tha Sai*, or Port of the Left (the eastern region, facing the South China Sea).[15] The model appears to have been the *shahbandar*, the harbour-master with responsibility for foreign merchants who operated in ports throughout the Asian and Islamic world. The Law of Civil Hierarchy, under which these various posts were created, gave titles to all members of a ship's crew, and assigned a mark (*sakdina*) which defined where each foreign trader was ranked in the Thai social order.

The Dutch established a foothold at the capital in 1604, and were further encouraged by the Thai diplomatic mission to the Netherlands in 1607–10, the first such mission to Europe. Despite the initial encouragement, their fortunes at Ayutthaya were precarious. Joost Schouten, sent as chief of the VOC factory in 1633 to renegotiate trading terms, gives a detailed account of the regulation of commerce, so profitable to the Thai court:

> Revenue of the Crown is great…arising out of in-land Commodities, as Rice, Sappang, Tin, Lead, Salt-peter; as also the profits of the Sand and Mountain Gold, which are only sold by the Kings Factors to foreign Merchants: He hath also his Customs for out-landish [i.e. foreign] Wares; his Tributes and Presents from Subject-Princes, and Governors of Cities and Provinces, who know how much they must contribute, as also the profits of his Traffick with *Choromandel* and *China*: Add to these the inland trade, carried on by his Factors in the City of *Indica* [=Judica=Ayutthaya] or elsewhere, and his Majesty of Siam will be found to be one of the richest Princes.[16]

Writing specifically of Ayutthaya – which he called 'this royal admirable City, populous to a wonder' – Schouten remarks:

> in the chief City the trading is very good…the principal commodities are Choromandes [Coromandel] and Sura [Surat] vestments.…This City, by virtue of its great traffick, is frequented by several Nations, as the *Indians*, the more Western *Asiaticks*, European Moors, and Christian Merchants. The King himself is also a Merchant, and hath his own Ships and Factors trading to *Choromandel* and *China*.[17]

Although only limited statistical information survives from European trading records, and virtually none from Thai and Indian merchant sources, an impression can be gleaned of a substantial trade in both Coromandel Coast and western Indian (Surat) textiles. Schouten estimated that of the merchandise which could be profitably imported to Siam, 50 per cent was Indian cloth, and that the annual limit that could be sold there was about 15,000 pieces of various types.[18] Expansion later in the century probably reflects the growth in the re-export trade, particularly to Japan. The bulk of the Indian textiles for Thailand came via the VOC factory in Batavia. Smaller quantities were purchased by VOC officials in Ayutthaya from Indian merchants, particularly of those designs which it was judged could be most profitably resold elewhere.

A proclamation in 1630 making overseas trade a royal prerogative represented an attempt to break from the crown's earlier dependency on the wealth and influence of the foreign merchant communities, whose very success represented a threat to the monarch's authority. That foreigners might pose a military threat to the Thai state was dramatically illustrated by the revolt in 1612 of the Japanese mercenaries employed as bodyguards to the monarch;[19] in 1633 members of the Japanese community resident at Ayutthaya were massacred following the poisoning of their merchant-warrior leader Yamada Nagamasa.[20] As the numbers of foreign merchants rapidly expanded in the seventeenth century, the royal authorities established cantonments for them beyond the city limits, with only the Chinese and Muslim traders being permitted to live within Ayutthaya itself. Nonetheless, the Thai monarch remained heavily dependent on the commercial acumen of foreign merchants. The presence of Indian Muslims at court is well attested: one is depicted in a manuscript painting of 1776 [162]. Dr Engelbert Kaempfer, a Prussian who served as physician to the VOC on their mission to Siam and Japan in 1690, recorded that on the day of his royal audience his escort from the Company factory to the court included the king's *shahbandar*,

161, 163 ABOVE AND OPPOSITE, BELOW Ceremonial cloth (details). Coromandel Coast, for the Thai market; eighteenth century. Cotton, painted mordant-dyed, resist-dyed, and painted; weft 137 cm. Private collection, London. ◆ The finest Indian cloths were confined to court circles. This fragment has a lattice-patterned centrefield with a royal emblem which must have been expressly commissioned for court use – the Hindu deity Indra riding his seven-headed elephant Erawan. The lattice incorporates *thepanom* [cf. **68, 69**] and an image of Brahma in a cartouche at the intersections. The border design has close links with Khmer decoration, which was highly fashionable at the time in Ayutthaya [see **70, 71**].

162 A Buddhist Heaven; detail from a Thai cosmological manuscript, *Traiphum*, probably from Ayutthaya; dated 1776. Museum für Indische Kunst, Berlin.
◆ Few examples of Ayutthaya-period painting survive; this manuscript is an exceptional example, exhibiting the Thai decorative style at its finest. Many of the elements, including the flame-like treatment of architectural finials, and the use of strong primary colours, are also found in Thai-market painted Indian cottons. Indra is seated on a throne draped with a textile decorated in Thai style.
Note also the presence of a man in Indian Muslim dress at lower left; such people often served as advisers at the Thai court.

who was an Indian Muslim 'clad after the fashion of his Country, in a gown embroider'd with gold, with a turbant upon his head'.[21]

European merchants complained bitterly of the degree of state regulation of their activities which, together with the heavy bribes demanded by court officials, made commercial survival precarious. The system of inducements at Ayutthaya was described as being in excess of anything encountered elsewhere in Asian trade. The king also went beyond what was perceived as customary practice and proceeded to act, in effect, as the country's principal merchant. The experiences of Peter Floris, a Dutch agent in the employ of the *Globe* (the first English East India Company ship to engage in direct trade with Thailand) graphically illustrate the situation encountered. Upon arrival at Ayutthaya on 17 September 1612 he was given a royal audience and granted permission to engage in free trade. He was, however, frustrated in concluding any transactions, and so finally departed to Pattani, one of the Thai Peninsula states. An officer instructed to remain in Thailand to sell the English vessel's stock of Indian textiles reported that he had been unable to conclude a sale with 'the King' (in reality the king's representative) and that:'other shopkeepers dare not bee so bolde as to buye one piece of cloth till the King bee furnished and his price agreed....The King, not liking the prices of the taken goods, hath given it all back, having kept it above two months in his house. A pittiful case when Kings become merchants, but this is [so]...throughout the Indies.'[22] The 'house' must be the royal warehouse (*phra khlang sinkha*), where local products destined for export were stored and incoming goods of high value, such as textiles, weapons and porcelain, were held. The system gave the crown first option on all imports, and on its own terms. Failure to conclude a deal probably reflected unwillingness on the part of the merchant to pay the necessary gratuities.

All negotiations were conducted through the office of the *phra khlang*, and payments or gifts were to remain part of the procedure. It was made clear to representatives of the VOC, such as Antonius Caen who was sent from Batavia to negotiate a monopoly on the export of skins and sappanwood in 1632, that impediments to concluding trading deals would disappear if gifts were made to the *phra khlang.* According to Dutch sources other members of the nobility also expected a share. A list of expenses incurred by Dutch officials at Ayutthaya in 1693 survives, from which it is clear that the practice extended from the king's *phra khlang*, the Muslim and Chinese *shahbandars* and the city governor to lesser scribes and even the tollkeepers who regulated shipping downstream of the capital.[23] VOC expenditure in that year included a gift of Indian textiles valued at 300 guilders to the priests officiating at the funeral of the *phra khlang*'s son.[24] In 1727 the English country trader Alexander Hamilton was advised that 'some pieces of *Surat* goods' would encourage official cooperation.[25]

The king controlled the import trade and was able to profit through price maintenance in the domestic market. While some cloths were distributed only under the court patronage system (see below), unrestricted types were sold commercially at considerable profit for the crown. Simon de La Loubère, French envoy resident at Ayutthaya in 1687–88, complained that the king's agents even had shops in the markets.[26] The monarch had drawn a growing number of commodities under his control by instituting state monopolies on export items: sappanwood, tin, lead, benzoin, gumlac, deer hides, eaglewood, ivory and areca had to be sold to the king, who then regulated and profited from their resale to foreign merchants at what, in an open market, would have been uncompetitive prices.[27] He acted as banker to foreign traders, capitalizing their ventures as well as maintaining his own ships. Dutch attempts to monopolize the Thai trade (as they had done with partial success in Indonesia through their control of Batavia) encountered solid resistance from the king and his *phra khlang*. They abandoned their post at Ayutthaya several times in the course of the seventeenth century, it proving unprofitable largely because of the degree of royal competition. Jeremias van Vliet, who was in charge of the VOC factory at Ayutthaya from 1629 to 1634, observed that Coromandel and Surat textiles 'made and painted after the fashion of Siam...[were] in great quantities imported by the Moors, the Gentiles, the Siamese and other nations at Tannasary...but] the trade in these goods did not bring much profit to the Company.'[28]

Imported Indian textiles proved an attractive commodity for resale by the court to foreign merchants, as demand remained strong from Europeans eager to trade them elsewhere. Nicolas Gervaise, French resident at Ayutthaya from 1683 until 1687, noted that the king never paid for the gold, silver and jewels that were sold to him by foreigners, except in ivory, saltpetre, tin and painted cloth from the Coromandel Coast.[29] Thai royal trading ships sailed there regularly from Mergui and Tenasserim, and the king employed Muslim agents for the purchase of textiles at Masulipatam and elsewhere in the region.[30] The dominant group of foreign traders at Mergui and Tenasserim were Muslims from Golconda, the Indian state controlling the northern Coromandel ports. Sound diplomatic relations with Golconda ensured that the Thai king was able to secure regular supplies of Indian textiles, and on terms similar to those granted to the European companies.[31] In the 1680s, under the reign of King Narai (r. 1656–88), a group of defectors from the English East India Company were in the employ of the court, one serving as *shahbandar* at Tenasserim, another acting as the king's commercial agent at Masulipatam and Madras. In this period a number of Englishmen captained ships belonging to the Thai ruler on the Bay of Bengal trade.[32]

164 Procession during the reign of Phra Narai, showing noblemen in formal dress, after a mural dated 1681 in the ordination hall at Wat Yom, Ayutthaya. In this rare image of court dress in the Ayutthaya period the noblemen wear a skirt-cloth drawn up between their legs (*pha nung chong kraben*), a tight-fitting jacket tied to the right, a waist sash, and the hat of office [cf. 185, 191]. The monarch regularly distributed fine Indian painted cotton skirts in the Thai fashion to members of his nobility to be worn at court as insignia of rank. Copy on *khoi* paper, 1897. National Library, Bangkok.

The resale of Indian cloths within Thailand was so closely regulated by the king's agents that European merchants found it difficult to compete. Although the European presence grew in importance in the course of the seventeenth century, the balance of Asian trade remained in Asian hands until the latter part of the eighteenth century.[33] Nicolas Gervaise acknowledged that although the Dutch were the most successful of the Europeans, it was the Indian Muslim and Hindu merchants who carried on the bulk of the Indian Ocean trade: 'Every year their ships bring rich merchandise from the Indies.'[34]

Court protocol and patronage

The demand for the distinctive Thai-market Indian cloths can be related to the exercise of royal authority and protocol in Ayutthaya. The monarch insisted that the finest imported Indian textiles were reserved for the court, both for wear by courtiers and for use as royal gifts. This consolidation of royal authority brought with it the creation of an elaborate system for the granting of favours in recognition of service to the crown.

Court protocol was based on a strict system of social stratification. Van Vliet records that bearers of high office (the 'mandarins') were drawn from both noble and commoner families but that before anyone could hold mandarin office he was elevated to a noble rank, of which there were six grades.[35] The Jesuit Guy Tachard, who accompanied the French embassy of 1685 from Louis XIV to Phra Narai, confirms Van Vliet's description and adds that three types of princes were recognized: those of the royal family, princes of tributary states, and 'those whom the King has raised to the Degree of Princes'.[36]

Central to this system was the use of imported textiles as royal gifts, distributed according to rank. Sumptuary rules restricting specified types of cloths to particular classes of courtiers, court officials and visiting dignitaries were in force, as La Loubère noted during his stay in 1687–88: '*pagnes* [skirt-cloths] of distinct beauty, such as those of silk stuff with embroidery or without embroidery, or such as the very fine ones of painted cloth, are permitted only to those to whom the Prince presents them'.[37] Garments with gold-work on silk were more highly rated than painted cottons [200]. A long-sleeved jacket of brocaded satin was highly restricted in its circulation, it being 'unlawful for any Siamese to wear this sort of veste, unless the King gives it him, and he makes this present only to the most considerable of his officers' [191].[38]

Little information survives of restrictions on the wearing of specific designs, as observed by Zhou Daguan at Angkor in 1296 or as seen later in the palaces of central Java. A cloth depicting the Hindu god Indra on the multi-headed white elephant Erawan was presumably restricted in its use, given the royal nature of its design [161, 163]. White-ground cloths were generally reserved for members of the aristocracy, though it is unclear if this was ever prescribed [168, 180, 181].

Indian textiles also formed part of state gifts to visiting ambassadors and envoys. Listed among the items presented to the Persian Ibrahim Beg, a member of Shah Sulaiman's embassy to the court of Phra Narai in 1685–88, are twenty-nine rolls of Indian cloth. Lesser officials in the delegation received smaller gifts, all of which included cloth.[39] Father Tachard gives an account of the gift-giving to the Chevalier de Chaumont and his attendants that throws light on the role of textiles in court protocol:

> It is a custom established at the Court of Siam to give a Vest [i.e. jacket] to all who have the honour of being introduced into the King's presence, and it is always

  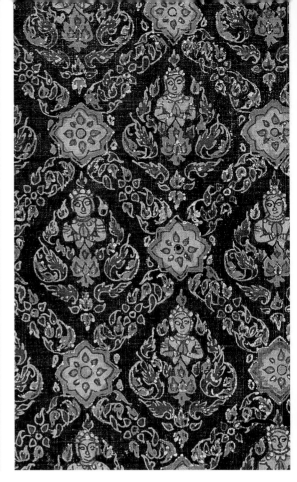

165 *Pha nung*, skirt-cloth (detail).
Coromandel Coast, for the Thai market;
eighteenth century. Cotton, mordant-dyed
and drawn resist-dyed, with painted gold.
Collection A.E.D.T.A., Paris.

166 *Pha nung*, skirt-cloth (detail).
Coromandel Coast, for the Thai market;
nineteenth century. Cotton, mordant-dyed
and drawn resist-dyed, with painted gold.
Victoria and Albert Museum, London.

167 *Pha nung*, skirt-cloth (detail).
Coromandel Coast, for the Thai market;
nineteenth century. Cotton, mordant-dyed
and drawn resist-dyed, with painted gold.
Victoria and Albert Museum, London.

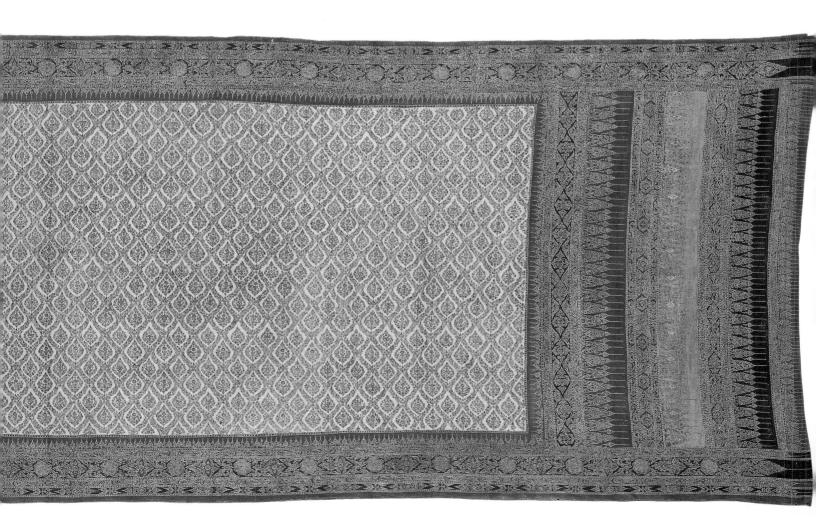

169 ABOVE LEFT *Pha nung*, skirt-cloth (detail: cf. 174). Coromandel Coast, for the Thai market; eighteenth century. Cotton, painted mordant-dyed and drawn resist-dyed, and painted. Victoria and Albert Museum, London.

170 ABOVE CENTRE *Pha nung*, skirt-cloth (detail). Coromandel Coast, for the Thai market; eighteenth century. Cotton, painted mordant-dyed and drawn resist-dyed, and painted. Victoria and Albert Museum, London.

171 ABOVE RIGHT *Pha nung*, skirt-cloth (detail; see also 175). Coromandel Coast, for the Thai market; early nineteenth century. Cotton, painted mordant-dyed, resist-dyed, and painted. Victoria and Albert Museum, London.

168 OPPOSITE *Pha nung*, skirt-cloth (half-length detail). Coromandel Coast, for the Thai market; nineteenth century. Cotton, painted mordant-dyed and resist-dyed, with painted gold; weft 113 cm. Victoria and Albert Museum, London. ◆ This is a high-quality cloth, with a three-register end-panel and a gold-on-white lattice centrefield. The application of the gold is not as refined as on the finest Coromandel Coast painted cottons [28] and was probably done locally, as was the practice in the Malay and Javanese realms [75].

brought to the Ambassadors at the end of the Audience when they present them the *Betle* [i.e. betel set, a traditional expression of hospitality in Southeast Asia]. The King being informed that the French made no use of *Betle*, and that perhaps a Suit of Cloaths made at Siam would not fit them, he would not have it given them at that time, but some days after he sent his Excellence twenty pieces of a very rich Stuff with flowers of Gold, and as much silk stuff for linings. He made a like Present to the Gentlemen of his Retinue, that they might make lighter Cloaths…and to suffer with less inconvenience the great heat of a Climate to which they were not accustomed.[40]

Tachard provides no clues as to the origin of these fine textiles, but in all probability they were Indian cottons made for the Thai market, many of which survive today with their customary Chinese silk linings. According to Jan Huyghen van Linschoten, who was based in Portuguese Goa at the end of the sixteenth century, the very finest painted Coromandel Coast cottons were more highly valued than silk.[41] To allow these textiles to form the core of state gifts reflected not only the esteem with which Indian painted cottons were held at the Thai court but their high international standing.

References to flowered cloths recur in diplomatic accounts. Phra Narai gave a jacket with golden flowers to the Chevalier de Chaumont, and a 'flowered cloth…from Hindustan' appears in the list of gifts he sent to Louis XIV with the returning embassy. That and similar textiles brought back by members of the mission no doubt helped create the vogue in France for '*les siamoises*', which contributed to the taste for this form of chinoiserie in late seventeenth-century Europe.[42]

Commissioning

The use of textiles to service a hieratic system of court patronage required commissioning to very precise specifications. Evidence for this practice is scant, but two seventeenth-century sources indicate that textile painters worked direct from designs supplied by their Thai clients.

As early as 1608 the Dutch East India Company ship *Eendracht* sailed from the port of Banten (Bantam) in west Java for the Coromandel Coast with instructions specifying the types of cloths required, together with samples showing the preferences of the various markets.[43] The reference to actual samples rather than pattern books indicates that the desired genres of cloths were already established in their respective markets.

The second reference to commissioning is contained in a letter from an officer of the English East India Company stationed in Ayutthaya to his superiors at Surat, dated 2 December 1662. The officer – Coates – lists the textiles marketable in the capital, notably red-ground chintz, 'long cloth and most sorts of cloth from the Coast [i.e. Coromandel] or Bengal', and 'sad [i.e. dark/sombre] coloured chints for lungees [skirt-cloths]'. He concludes by stating that 'The King of Siam expects those puttelaes to be made according to those patterns Mr Bladwell carried to Surat; if not to be procured, those patterns to be returned.'[44] 'Puttelaes' is probably a corruption of *percallaes*, a textile term referring to a South Indian high-grade plain cotton cloth best suited for chintz.[45] The reference to Surat does not necessarily indicate that the painting was to be ordered there: Surat was the English East India Company's Indian headquarters at the time. Rather, the type of cloth specified suggests that it was to be commissioned on the Coromandel Coast, renowned for the finest cotton painting.

Coates's letter indicates that the Thai court supplied agents with patterns for painted cloths. It also suggests that the grade of cotton was specified. The designs were probably not dissimilar from those which survive in later pattern books associated with the Indian–Thai textile trade, some of which are preserved at Pethapur in Gujarat, with families who produced the printing blocks for *saudagiri* fabrics [207, 208].

Interesting evidence of the Dutch East India Company's involvement in commissioning textiles for Thailand in another region comes from VOC records for 1713 from Bandar Abbas on the Persian Gulf. 'Gold and silver wrought stuffs' were to be made for the king of Siam; they were to be of a specified size, and they would need a separate loom to be erected for each design.[46] It is not recorded if these cloths were to be 'in the fashion of Siam' or were to follow Persian designs.

Correspondence dated 1785 between a Thai official and the British country trader Francis Light (later the founder of Penang) instructing him to acquire cloth of a special pattern for the king provides an insight into the methods of procurement.[47] It also indicates that a general understanding prevailed within the textile trade of what constituted a royal design, and suggests that such cloths could be obtained by agents other than those in the direct employ of the crown.

European descriptions of the use of cloths in court protocol make no mention of the role of another group of potential patrons, the leading families who dominated the upper echelons of Thai society and politics throughout the Ayutthaya and Bangkok periods. Members of these families were either nobles (*khunnang*) or wealthy commoners who held key posts as ministers, officials and provincial governors. Many were foreigners, especially Chinese, who had secured high social standing through their commercial successes. The four most powerful families in the late eighteenth century who held ministerial rank (*chaophraya*) were all involved with the post of foreign trade and were all of non-Thai origin, namely Persian, Indian, Mon and Chinese.[48] They would have been eager to emulate court fashion, and no doubt actively commissioned fine-quality painted textiles for their own use and for trade, presumably avoiding designs restricted under any court sumptuary rules. It is interesting to observe that it is precisely these families, many of whom acquired some degree of royal connection through intermarriage, who have heirloom collections of such cloths in Thailand today.

A royal commission of a very specific kind involved the shaped printed cloths intended for the tailored jackets worn by the royal guard (see pp. 141–43). These could only have been achieved through the supplying of accurate samplers and pattern templates, which points to a sophisticated system of ordering and supervision carried out by the king's commercial agents [188, 190].

'In the fashion of Siam'

Despite Tomé Pires' tantalizing observation at the beginning of the sixteenth century that the cloths of the northern Coromandel Coast were decorated 'in the fashion of Siam' we know little about the specific appearance of those textiles. Did they still have the simple floral repeat patterns seen in Thai paintings and reliefs of earlier periods, or were they already the elaborate resist- and mordant-painted cottons which were in wide circulation in the late sixteenth century, as described by van Linschoten? He wrote of a great traffic in Indian textiles with finely drawn floral and figurative designs, shipped from the ports along the length of the Coromandel Coast to Thailand:

> there is excellent faire linnen of Cotton made in Negapatan, Saint Thomas, and Musilepatan, of all colours, and woven with divers sorts of loome work [Dutch *loofwerck* = leafwork or foliage] and figures, verie fine and cunningly wrought... the best sort are named clothes of Sarasso [i.e. *sarasa*, fine painted cotton], some being mingled with gold and silver and such like stuffe of a thousand sortes, very beautiful to behold.[49]

Some surviving Thai market cloths fit van Linschoten's description: they display remarkably delicate drawing (pen-work, executed with the *qalam*), and designs dominated by floral patterns and figures, usually mythical [161, 180].

European commentators active in the region in the early decades of the seventeenth century confirm that particular cloths were destined for the Thai market. Henry Middleton, who captained the English East India Company voyage to Maluku (the Moluccas) in 1604–6, reported that his agent in Banten was holding '480 fardells of callicoes...including 59 fardells of girdles for Sysan [Siam]'.[50] Another Englishman, William Methwold, writing of his experiences of trade in Golconda (1626), recorded that to Tenasserim 'they carry red cotton yarne, red and white beethyles [muslin], paintings [Portuguese *pintados*, i.e. patterned cloths] of severall sorts befitting that countries [i.e. Siam's] weare.'[51] From such comments, from surviving examples, and from comparison with contemporary Indian textiles for other markets, it is clear that the painted and printed cottons produced for the Thai market form a readily identifiable group of Indian export textiles. Seventeenth-century examples tend to display larger, more freely drawn motifs [187], whereas in the course of the eighteenth century the designs become increasingly fine, displaying a dazzling command of the complex techniques of *kalamkari* drawing and dyeing. A Thai document lists eight types of textiles ordered by a noblewoman from the trader Francis Light in 1787. The patron required these cloths for presentation during a royal audience in Bangkok, and so the list can be taken as a clear, though not exhaustive,

172 The flame motif, a recurrent element of Ayutthaya and Bangkok period decorative arts. It is particularly a feature of resist-drawn painted cottons, where the painter could achieve considerable elegance of line using the metal *qalam* to apply fine trails of wax which served to protect the cloth from dye [cf. 173, 175, 176].

173 OPPOSITE End-panel of a *pha nung*, skirt-cloth (detail; cf. 176). Coromandel Coast, for the Thai market; eighteenth century. Cotton, painted mordant- and resist-dyed, and painted. Victoria and Albert Museum, London. ◆ This close-up illustrates the consummate skill of the cloth painters of the Coromandel Coast. The highly refined control of line, combined with a heightened sense of colour, achieves a vitality rarely seen, whether for the European or Asian market.

174 ABOVE *Pha nung*, skirt-cloth (half-length detail). Coromandel Coast, for the Thai market; eighteenth century. Cotton, painted mordant- and resist-dyed, and painted. Victoria and Albert Museum, London.

175 RIGHT, CENTRE End-panel of a *pha nung*, skirt-cloth (detail). Coromandel Coast, for the Thai market; early nineteenth century. Cotton, painted mordant-dyed, resist-dyed, and painted. Victoria and Albert Museum, London. ◆ A *kirttimukha* (mythical protector) face in the centre is flanked by *thepanom* adoring the mythical bird Garuda.

176 RIGHT, BELOW End-panel of a *pha nung*, skirt-cloth (detail). Coromandel Coast, for the Thai market; eighteenth century. Cotton, painted mordant- and resist-dyed, and painted. Victoria and Albert Museum, London.

statement of the types of designs acceptable to the Siamese monarch in the late eighteenth century. The cloths are named as follows:

pha khao kan nyaeng lai khru = 'white cloth with overall pattern of flower buds arranged in clusters of four'
pha khao umao nu'a di = 'fine quality white cloth'
pha khao kasa na thong na chua = 'patterned white muslin'
pha lai dok tang kan = 'flowered chintz'
pha lai thu' di = 'flowered chintz'
pha khem khapmot tat = 'striped cloth decorated with gold or silver thread'
pha dam nu'a di = 'fine quality black cloth'
phrae da rai si tang kan = 'multi-coloured silk cloth'[52]

Light was active in the private trade between Thailand and the Coromandel Coast and all of these cloth varieties most probably came from there.

The more spectacular cloths are those with designs based on vegetal and figurative elements, of which there are a great variety. Not all the features are Thai in origin: they include Persian floral border scrolls, Indian stepped squares, and winged cherubs of European inspiration.

The four-petalled rosette of the sandal flower (*lai pracham yam dok chan*) [181, 183], a motif popular in Thai art since Dvaravati times (*c.* eighth century), is the most common motif on Indian textiles for the Thai market, both painted cottons and silk brocades. It can appear within a trellis pattern (*ba khai*) or in the central field, where it is often combined with the stepped square (*lai yamum mai sipsong*, 'twelve-cornered design').

The arrangement of motifs is distinctly Thai in character. The typical skirt-cloth has a dominant centrefield, narrow longitudinal borders and elaborate end borders. The latter feature a flaming leaf related to the Malay–Indonesian *tumpal*, displayed in several registers; convention dictates two for female use and three for males, a distinction the origins of which are not known. Typical colours for these registers are black, green, red and yellow, in various combinations. The centrefield has a vegetal or figurative pattern, sometimes both, which is either freely arranged or structured in a trellis grid, and which can usually be read from a number of vantage points. Typical figurative motifs include deities or angels represented with hands held together in a gesture of respect (*thepanom*) [167], celestial nymphs (*apsaras*) [171], the mythical bird Garuda in mortal combat with serpent divinities (*nagas*) [175], and the Hindu deity Brahma, who assumed a special place in Thai Buddhist cosmology [177]. The designs on the finest cloths are executed with a finesse and delicacy of drawing only seen elsewhere in the best chintzes for the European market. An example decorated with golden *devas* against a white ground with flame-like leaf motifs in red, blue and green articulated as a trellis displays remarkable skill and sophistication [180]. The metamorphosis of spiralling leaves into a *kirttimukha* or *kala* (mythical protector) mask is an especially witty and fanciful detail. The rendering of the golden figures and the restrained use of red and green on the foliage echo the chromatic order seen in a mural at Wat Yai Suwannaram [182].

The textile painters clearly took great pleasure in the manipulation of organic and figurative elements. Plant forms are often represented metamorphizing into human or animal shapes. Celestial deities emerge organically from lotus flowers and foliage, as if caught in some act of magical transformation. In one cloth, the Indra-on-Erawan design referred to earlier is remarkably framed in a border composed of hybrid warrior creatures which combine elements of bird, monkey and crocodile [70]. Another cloth, probably also eighteenth-

177 Corner of a *pha kiao*, floor cover or hanging. Coromandel Coast, for the Thai market; late eighteenth century. Cotton, painted mordant-dyed and resist-dyed. Victoria and Albert Museum, London.
◆ The Hindu deity Brahma appears in a cartouche in each corner of the continuous border; at the sides his vehicle, Garuda, battles with snakes (*nagas*). On the reverse of this cloth is an ink stamp with the letters 'UEIC' in an intercepted square [179], indicating that it was traded by the English United East India Company.

century, has a centrefield of interlocking stepped squares alternately filled with *devas* and mythical lions (*simhas*) and a border of highly animated figures in grass skirts [183], related no doubt to the tribal hunters depicted in a great figurative chintz from the southern Coromandel Coast in the Brooklyn Museum.[53]

Murals, manuscripts and textile design

The designs seen on Indian cloths for the Thai market appear in other media as well, and comparison sheds light on their character and sometimes on their dating. The image of the lotus-born deity has a long history: in its Thai form it occurs, for instance, in architectural ceramics of the fifteenth and early sixteenth centuries [69].[54]

An invaluable source for identifying the repertoire of textile designs is the murals of later Ayutthaya and Bangkok period temples which span a period from the later seventeenth to nineteenth centuries. Temple murals depict a variety of textiles being worn by celestial deities, many dressed in costumes resembling princely attire.

Few temples at Ayutthaya escaped the 1767 sacking by Burmese armies; Wat Yai Suwannaram, at Petchaburi, preserves rare examples of mural painting. The ordination hall is attributed to the years 1603–57,[55] but the murals that interest us are more likely to date from a renovation known to have been carried out in the early eighteenth century. The paintings depict celestial worshippers (*thep chumnum*) wearing crowns and jewelry of regal magnificence, and a lower garment to which is added an elaborate waist sash [182]. These costumes provide a remarkable register of textile designs, many readily identifiable as known types of Indian trade cloths. They include various forms of floral and leaf trellis, geometric mandalas, and an assortment of star and circle medallions. This series of painted figures also shows the manner in which the garments were worn.

The surviving decoration of temple interiors provides another source of information for textile studies. Gilded decoration, typically in patterns that are also seen on textiles, was widely applied to the black or red lacquer ground on the woodwork of ceilings, pillars, doors and window embrasures. The *vihara* or image house of Wat Panan Choeng demonstrates this on a grand scale. This monastery is the oldest in Ayutthaya, but the decoration of the *vihara* is in the Bangkok style and dates from a renovation during the reign of King Rama IV (1851–68). The four massive pillars which support the roof are richly decorated with gold and green on a red ground, in a pattern known as *gruai choeng*. These colours, together with the use of a trellis field and flame border, closely resemble the classic Indian cloths for the Thai market of the eighteenth and nineteenth centuries [181]. The ornamented pillars in Wat Yai Suwannaram, which probably date from the renovations carried out during the reign of King Rama V (1868–1910), illustrate another series of textile patterns [198]. Some display *devas* set in a trellis with bands of leaves and flowers leading to a dramatic *tumpal*-type border at the base, while others are ornamented with alternating flower medallions and stepped squares, which again have direct parallels in textiles [183, 194]. Such decoration may be accepted as a memory of an earlier age when actual fabrics were used more extensively for interior decoration [193, 195]; indeed, the Thai term for large decorative hangings, *pha kiao*, literally means 'pillar cloth'.

Finally, a number of Thai manuscripts have decoration that is clearly related to known textile designs. In some instances they are datable, as by a royal emblem, and thus provide a date range for the patterns. A lacquer-and-gilt

178, 179 Two ink stamps on textiles for the Thai market. The intercepted square, which appears on the reverse of two *pha kiao* cloths illustrated [177, 183], has the initials 'UEIC', for the United East India Company, confirming that the English traded successfully with Ayutthaya, despite the dominance of Asians and the monopolistic aspirations of the Dutch. The stamp is of a design in use by the Company in the second half of the eighteenth century. The heart-shaped stamp (on 183) is unidentified, but may be presumed to indicate some aspect of quality or stock control by the UEIC.

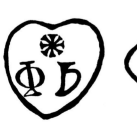

180 LEFT *Pha nung*, skirt-cloth (detail). Coromandel Coast, for the Thai market; late eighteenth century. Cotton, painted mordant-dyed, drawn resist-dyed, and painted. Victoria and Albert Museum, London. ◆ 'Golden' celestial worshippers, painted yellow on a white ground, are set in a flaming lattice composition to create a sumptuous and refined cloth [see 12], worthy of presentation at court.

181 BELOW LEFT *Pha nung*, skirt-cloth (detail). Coromandel Coast, for the Thai market; eighteenth century. Cotton, painted mordant-dyed, resist-dyed, and painted. Royal Museum of Scotland, Edinburgh.

182 BELOW A worshipping *yaksha* (a demon converted to the service of Buddhism) venerating the Buddha, from a mural in the ordination hall of Wat Yai Suwannaram, Petchaburi; probably early eighteenth century. The kneeling figure wears a *pha nung chong kraben* decorated with a pattern of stepped squares and diamonds, and a waist sash with a flaming leaf pattern, both relating to surviving examples of Indian painted cottons in the Thai style [cf. 183, 176].

183 OPPOSITE *Pha kiao*, floor cover or hanging (detail). Coromandel Coast, for the Thai market; second half of the eighteenth century. Cotton, painted mordant-dyed, resist-dyed, and painted. Victoria and Albert Museum, London. ◆ The dominant stepped-square pattern, and the border evenly surrounding the field, are characteristic of cloths intended for furnishing rather than costume [see 194]. This piece bears the intercepted-square stamp of the English United East India Company, together with another stamp, on the reverse [178. 179]

184 Cover and opening folio of the *Sarasangha*, a Buddhist text. Palm-leaf, with lacquer and gilt; early nineteenth century. Chester Beatty Library, Dublin. ◆ The treatment of the Garuda with *devas* in flaming foliage on the cover is echoed in a number of Indian painted cottons. The medallion on the opener bears the device of Rama II (r. 1809–24), which suggests a likely date for cloths in this style [cf. 171].

decorated palm-leaf manuscript, for instance, bears the device of Rama II, which places it between 1809 and 1824 [184]. The Garuda-with-*naga* crest is framed by celestial nymphs in leaf roundels, a design seen on Thai-market Indian cloths [158, 171].

The cloths and their uses

The importance of Indian textiles for the Thai monarchy cannot be exaggerated. The variety of uses assigned to the finest painted cottons link them to activities at the heart of court life and etiquette. They not only formed part of the monarch's domestic patronage system but also provided valuable commodities for commercial and diplomatic dealings with foreigners. As such, they assumed an economic importance which complemented their political and social role as demarcators of rank. Outside the court, they also assumed an honorific role in monasteries; and they occupied a place that was both prestigious and practical in the realms of dress and interior decoration.

Dress

As in India, the principal item of dress was an untailored length of cloth, which was worn in a number of ways. At its simplest, it was used by both men and women as a skirt-cloth (*pha nung*), or drawn up between the legs in the *dhoti*-like style known as *pha nung chong kraben*. Women could also wear it as a pleated skirt (*pha naa nang*). A separate length might be used as a shoulder- or breast-cloth (*phaa sabai krong thong*) [159].

The French envoys Gervaise and La Loubère, both writing of their observations around 1688, provide detailed descriptions of the manner of wearing Thai costume at the time. Here is Gervaise:

> Men's dress consists of only two pieces of silk or cotton: with one of these, which is 2 ells[56] long and ¾ an ell wide [approx. 240 x 90 cm], they cover their shoulders like a scarf, while the other, which is of the same width and length, they gird round their loins and, by tucking both ends in neatly behind, make a kind of breeches, reaching below the knee. This garment is called *pa-nonc* [Thai *pha nung*; Portuguese *panno*, French *pagne*]. The *pagne* worn by the mandarins is much fuller and richer than any others, being usually silver or cloth of gold or of the beautiful painted Indian cloth

that is commonly called *chitte* [chintz] from Masulipatam…when the north wind blows they wear a kind of jerkin of Chinese brocade or of some fine European cloth…and over this jerkin they put, in the same manner that a sash is worn by our military men, a length of gold or silver brocade, or of painted cloth as beautiful as they can find in the kingdom. The dress of women is not very different from that of men. Their *pagne*…[is] a little larger, and they let it hang…so that it just brushes the ground like a petticoat. It is usually black, which they consider the most beautiful and elegant colour, and it is often brocaded with gold and silver. A small piece of muslin is used to cover the breasts.[57]

La Loubère provides similar information, although his measurements differ slightly (he gives 2½ ells for the length, or *c.* 3 m); he notes that 'sometimes instead of a painted [cotton] cloth the *Pagne* is a silken Stuff, either plain or embroidered with a border of gold or silver'.[58] Engravings published in France by La Loubère [185, 186] illustrate the manner in which these garments were worn, with the woman's skirt-cloth simply secured at the waist and an undecorated shoulder- or breast-cloth casually displayed. The nobleman's skirt-cloth is drawn up in a *pha nung chong kraben*, and worn in combination with a tailored jacket and a hat of office. An eighteenth-century Thai illustrated manuscript provides more accurately observed depictions of noblemen's attire, with the *pha nung chong kraben* being worn with a tightly fitting cross-over jacket and a waist sash tied at the front [164]. The large flowering meander motif that is sketchily shown in La Loubère's engravings finds its closest parallel among surviving textiles in a piece of painted cotton which dates, judging from the large-scale floral motifs, from the late seventeenth century or early eighteenth century [187].

Tailored jackets were a favoured item in court circles. There is no evidence that they were a feature of Thai costume before the seventeenth century and they are believed to have been inspired by the example of Persian costume worn at the Ayutthaya court by diplomatic emissaries. Both La Loubère and

185, 186 Two engravings from Simon de La Loubère, *A New Historical Relation of the Kingdom of Siam*, 1691. The nobleman, wearing the tall conical hat of rank, is dressed in a skirt-cloth which is drawn up between his legs and secured at the waist in the style known as *pha nung chong kraben*; the woman's skirt is a simple wrapper (*pha nung*), combined with a shawl.

187 LEFT *Pha nung*, skirt-cloth (detail). Coromandel Coast, for the Thai market; late seventeenth–early eighteenth century. Cotton, drawn outline, painted mordant-dyed, resist-dyed, and painted. Victoria and Albert Museum, London. ◆ Large meandering flowering vines provide the structure of this design, with only a narrow end-panel. The skirt-cloths worn in La Loubère's engravings [185, 186] appear to be of this type. Most surviving cloths, by contrast, are later, and show a development after the mid-eighteenth century of highly elaborated end-panels which rival in importance a much reduced centrefield [168].

The distinctive soldier's shirt illustrates how precise the process of commissioning textiles for Thailand in India could be: its design, with kala *or demon faces on the chest and sleeves, would have necessitated the use of detailed pattern books and meticulous laying-out (see p. 142).*

188 OPPOSITE, ABOVE *Su'a senakut*, soldier's shirt or tunic. Coromandel Coast, for the Thai market; late eighteenth century. Cotton, painted mordant-dyed and resist-dyed; extended width 155 cm. Royal Ontario Museum, Toronto.

189 OPPOSITE, BELOW LEFT A celestial temple guardian, represented wearing a *su'a senakut*. Lacquer and gilt painting on a wooden door of the chapel of Wat Suthat, Bangkok; late nineteenth century).

190 OPPOSITE, BELOW RIGHT Procession during the reign of Phra Narai showing palace guards wearing *su'a senakut* shirts, after a mural dated 1681 in the ordination hall of Wat Yom, Ayutthaya. Copy on *khoi* paper, 1897. National Library, Bangkok.

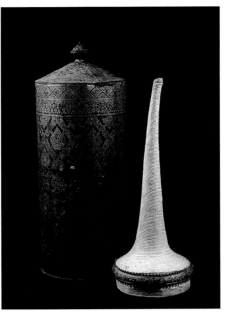

Tachard commented on this prestigious item of court attire, and it is depicted in contemporary engravings.

Gervaise's reference to the 'jerkin' and sash worn by male members of the nobility is the first detailed description of this item of court dress. Depictions of the Siamese ambassador Kosa Pan received at Versailles in 1686 provide us with European impressions of such a garment [191]. The ambassador also wears the distinctive conical hat of office which identifies him as a member of the nobility. In his account of the journey written for his king, Kosa Pan refers to it as a headdress of muslin 'in the new Persian style favoured of Your Majesty', with a gold band to denote his ambassadorial status.[59] The eight other nobles who formed the diplomatic mission wore the same style of headdress. An example of this flamboyant hat of office is preserved, together with its storage box, in the National Museum in Bangkok [192] and confirms the accuracy of the engraving. The gilded decoration of the cylindrical storage box provides an illustration of the distinctive flaming flower and leaf design much favoured in seventeenth-century Thai art, including painted cotton textiles commissioned from India.

A tailored garment for which Indian textiles were expressly commissioned is the soldier's shirt (*su'a senakut*) [188]. The design was carefully painted on the uncut cloth, the intended seams edged with blue. The colour-scheme is dominated by red and purple. The red is a mordanted madder, the purple achieved by combining alum and iron mordants. The jackets are decorated with the fearsome *kala* mask as their central motif. There is both literary and pictorial evidence to indicate that they were worn by members of the royal guard in the seventeenth century. A description of Thai soldiers in red-dyed muslin jackets is provided by the Portuguese missionary Sebastian Manrique in his *Itinerario*. It is, he says,

> a general Custom at Siam that the Prince, and all his Retinue in the War or Hunting, be cloath'd in Red. Upon this account the Shirts which are given to the Soldrs, are of Muslin dy'd Red; and on the days of Ceremony, as was that of the entry of the King's Ambassadors, these Red Shirts were given to the Siamese which they put under their Arms [weapons].[60]

A nineteenth-century manuscript copy of now badly deteriorated murals in the chapel (*ubosoth*) of Wat Yom, Ayutthaya, dated 1681, depicts the royal guards [190]. The garments must have been issued in considerable quantities, though few survive. Such *kala* shirts, complete with demon sleeves and cloud collars, are worn by celestial guardians depicted at the nineteenth-century Wat Suthat, Bangkok [189]. In addition to the remarkable jacket illustrated, two other examples are preserved in the National Museum, Bangkok.

Textiles as decor

The second major use of Indian textiles in Thailand was as items of decor. Mural paintings and illustrated manuscripts of the late Ayutthaya and Bangkok periods depict textiles in use as wall hangings, curtains and room partitions, throne and platform covers, floor covers and carpets [5, 193, 195]. As we have seen (p. 135), textile patterns provided the principal decoration of the Buddhist temple interior, reflecting a time when actual cloths were a regular feature of monastery decor. Traditionally, the main *vihara* was open-sided and hangings served to define inner and outer spaces and to demarcate the sacred from the mundane worlds. Descriptions comment on the use of rich hangings in the royal audience hall and throne room, and refer to the opulent use of sumptuous textiles whenever the king and his entourage moved beyond the palace, be it by

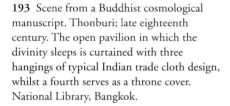

193 Scene from a Buddhist cosmological manuscript. Thonburi; late eighteenth century. The open pavilion in which the divinity sleeps is curtained with three hangings of typical Indian trade cloth design, whilst a fourth serves as a throne cover. National Library, Bangkok.

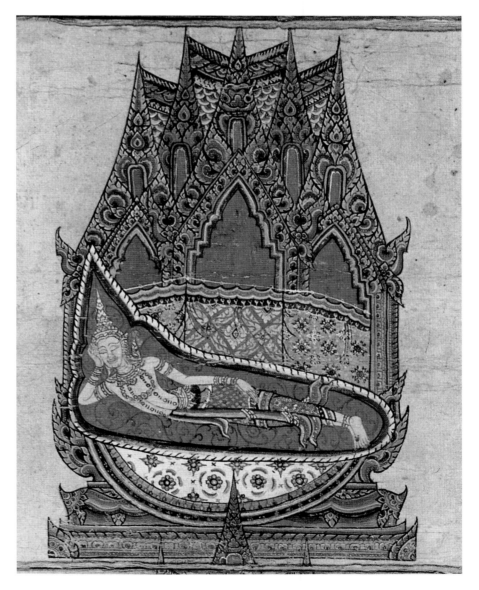

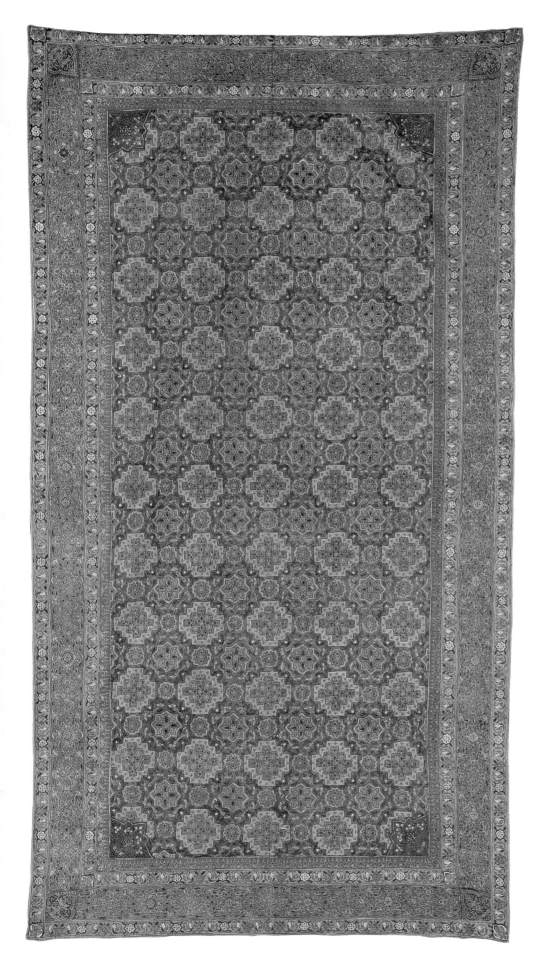

Prestigious imported textiles were a regular feature of palace decor in Southeast Asia, as witnessed by historical depictions in murals and manuscripts. A range of Indian painted cottons, characterized by the use of four even-width borders, were ordered for use among the Thai nobility as screening, curtaining, and covers for seating platforms on formal occasions. Their name, pha kiao, means 'pillar cloth', and their patterns are often echoed in the painted decoration of Thai temple interiors [cf. 198].

194 LEFT *Pha kiao*, floor cover or hanging. Coromandel Coast, for the Thai market; nineteenth century. Cotton, painted mordant-dyed, resist-dyed, and painted. Victoria and Albert Museum, London.

195 BELOW A celestial palace with textile curtaining, from a mural of the *Ramayana* story on the enclosure wall of Wat Preah Keo Morokat in the Royal Palace compound, Phnom Penh, Cambodia; nineteenth century.

Monks were, on occasion, presented with Indian painted cottons of first-grade quality. Forbidden to wear extravagant robes, they frequently cut them up and made them into wrapping cloths for manuscripts stored in the monastery library; another use, as seen here, was as a shoulder bag.

196 ABOVE Cloth used for wrapping a Buddhist manuscript. Coromandel Coast, for the Thai market. Cotton, painted mordant-dyed and resist-dyed; late eighteenth century. Chester Beatty Library, Dublin.

197 RIGHT *Yaam* or *thung*, monk's shoulder bag. Coromandel Coast, for the Thai market; eighteenth century. Cotton, painted mordant-dyed and resist-dyed, and painted; width 33 cm. Victoria and Albert Museum, London.

palanquin, elephant or royal barge. The houses provided for the French envoys in Ayutthaya during La Loubère's visit had their walls 'hung with painted cloth, with ceilings of white muslin',[61] as was the rest-house (*sala*) provided for the Persian diplomat ibn Muhammad Ibrahim in 1685: 'inside walls and posts were covered with various kinds of cloth, such as chit and red shila' – that is, painted chintz and red-dyed cottons.[62] The effect of the finest Indian painted cloths, when hung in elegant interiors, would have evoked an atmosphere of wealth and elegance. In a palace context they served as 'moving walls', to screen or partition interiors or to designate inner and outer spaces on religious or courtly occasions. Textiles intended for this purpose are larger and squarer than those for attire; the field is typically decorated with regular motifs repeated and the border is of equal width on all four sides. In addition to the general term for such cloths, *pha kiao* ('pillar cloth') [cf. 198], other terms exist for cloths with specific functions, for example *pha sujane* for floor coverings [194].

Cloths in a monastic context

A postscript must be added to this account of the traditional functions of imported Indian textiles in Thailand, in which we look at their use by the *sangha* or community of monks and nuns. Textiles with specific functions in a religious context include the *pha puu kraap*, a floor cloth used when venerating an image and as the cover for the throne on which a statue of the Buddha is placed. The latter use is recorded both in painting and in sculpture: stucco images at Wat Chai Wattanram, Ayutthaya, for instance, show the enthroned Buddha seated on a textile with a raised pattern, probably a brocade.

Thai monks and nuns only ever wore the prescribed saffron or white robes which were presented by pious members of the laity, but there is evidence that Indian painted cloths of the highest quality were also received by the community as gifts from high-ranking members of the nobility and wealthy lay worshippers. Although never worn, they were used in other ways. Some were tailored to make containers in which the monks could store their robes. One piece of superb quality was turned into a monk's shoulder bag (*yaam* or *thung*) [197]. Presumably it was presented by its owner or bequeathed upon his or her death to the family monastery, where it was adapted to the needs of the *sangha*.

The majority of such gifts were used as wrappers for the protection of the palm-leaf Buddhist texts, themselves descended from Indian originals. This prestigious role reflects the status and value assigned to the cloths, of which remains are still to be seen today in the libraries (*ho trai*) of monasteries in rural Thailand. Many of the finest cotton fabrics are lined with coarser Indian cottons or Chinese silk. The designs are typical of the eighteenth and nineteenth centuries. A well-preserved example is in the Chester Beatty Library, Dublin [196].

Fashion by decree

Thai demand for painted Indian cottons and silk brocades [200] continued throughout the nineteenth century, though significant changes were to alter irreversibly the character of the trade. Fashion played a part in these changes. A growing taste for Chinese silks meant that they played an increasingly dominant role as part of royal gifts. A further factor in the reduced demand for Indian textiles of high quality was the vogue among women of the nobility to weave their own cloths, a trend observed by Sir John Bowring in his visit to Bangkok in 1855: 'Some of the most costly garments worn by the people of high rank

198 Lacquered and gilded wooden pillar in the Sala Kanparien or preaching hall of Wat Yai Suwannaram, Petchaburi. This seventeenth-century royal monastery was extensively renovated in the late nineteenth century during the reign of King Rama V. The pillars are richly decorated with a variety of patterns which echo known textile designs, including the stepped square seen here [cf. 183, 194].

were, as we learnt, manufactured in their homes; and they prided themselves on their being able to produce textiles more valuable than any they imported from foreign countries.'[63] The favoured medium was silk with supplementary weft silk and gilt thread decoration [201]. The design structures follow the established conventions: a large centrefield with a repeat pattern, narrow longitudinal borders, and a series of registers at the ends with the flame-leaf *tumpal* motif. Bowring tells us that sumptuary laws were in force limiting the use of certain garments to those of high rank, but regrettably he is not specific about the types of cloth which were thus restricted. There was clearly a shift in favour of locally woven cloth for use in court circles and as royal gifts.

199 A senior member of the Thai court dressed in the manner prescribed by Rama V, which combined the traditional skirt-cloth (worn drawn up between the legs, as *pha nung chong kraben*) with a European-style jacket, most probably tailored in Indian silk brocade. This photograph of *c.* 1904–8 comes from the collection of F. Badman, the king's English tailor. Victoria and Albert Museum, London.

200 OPPOSITE, ABOVE *Pha yok*, ceremonial cloth (detail). North India, probably Varanasi, for the Thai market; late nineteenth century. Silk with gold brocade. Victoria and Albert Museum, London.

201 OPPOSITE, BELOW *Pha yok*, ceremonial cloth (detail). Thailand, possibly from Chonnabot. Silk, with woven warp and supplementary weft decoration gold brocade. Victoria and Albert Museum, London.
◆ Thai silk-weaving was actively encouraged by the monarch in the later nineteenth century, when this large cloth was probably made.

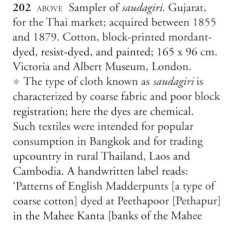

202 ABOVE Sampler of *saudagiri*. Gujarat, for the Thai market; acquired between 1855 and 1879. Cotton, block-printed mordant-dyed, resist-dyed, and painted; 165 x 96 cm. Victoria and Albert Museum, London.
◆ The type of cloth known as *saudagiri* is characterized by coarse fabric and poor block registration; here the dyes are chemical. Such textiles were intended for popular consumption in Bangkok and for trading upcountry in rural Thailand, Laos and Cambodia. A handwritten label reads: 'Patterns of English Madderpunts [a type of coarse cotton] dyed at Peethapoor [Pethapur] in the Mahee Kanta [banks of the Mahee

river] expressly for the use of the Siamese. The Dyers are supplied with cloth by Bombay merchants and the charge for dyeing any of the enclosed patterns is at the rate of one penny per yard.'

203 ABOVE RIGHT Samples of *saudagiri*. Gujarat, for the Thai market; acquired between 1855 and 1879. Victoria and Albert Museum, London. ◆ A handwritten label reads: 'Guzarat. Eleven patterns of Madderpunt prints stamped at Wasna [district] zilla Bawesee [town name] in the Mahee Kanta expressly for exportation to Siam where the demand for such goods

appears to be largely increasing, judging from the large additions to the number of persons successfully occupied as Dyers, both at Peethapoor and Wasna during the last few years.'

204–206 BELOW, LEFT TO RIGHT *Pha nung*, skirt-cloths (details). Gujarat, for the Thai market; late nineteenth century. Cotton, block-printed mordant- and resist-dyed, and block-printed. Victoria and Albert Museum, London. ◆ These cloths typify the finer quality *saudagiri* intended for popular consumption in Thailand in the later nineteenth century.

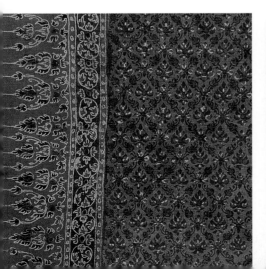

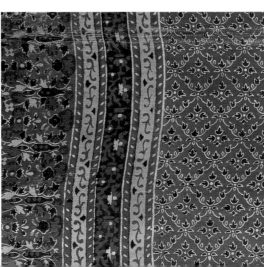

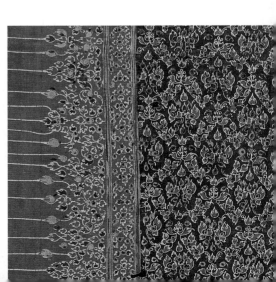

A third blow to the Indian textile trade was instigated by Rama IV (1851–68), who introduced elements of European attire to court. This major break with tradition marked the beginning of the fashion for mixed Thai and European dress. Following a state visit to Singapore and Batavia in 1869 by his successor Rama V, a decree was issued requiring that European-style tailored garments be worn at court, together with 'modern', i.e. Western, hairstyles. That royal decree, part of a strategy towards modernization, resulted in a rapid decline in orders from the upper echelons of society for Indian painted cottons. For men, the new fashion meant tailored jackets worn either with trousers or with *pha nung chong kraben*. Rama V adapted the Western-style jacket into a long-sleeved shirt more appropriate to the tropics, known as *rajapataen* ('royal shirt'). For women, court-approved dress consisted of a *pha naa nang* or *pha nung chong kraben* skirt with a European blouse and a *sabai* shoulder wrap. Although European cloth was widely used and Rama V employed his own English tailor, F. Badman, Indian silk and gold brocade were still appreciated, as seen in a turn-of-the-century photograph of a high-ranking nobleman [199].

The final phase

The court continued to use the finest Indian cloths for the most significant ceremonies, including coronations, a reflection of the symbolic authority they retained. At annual religious events such as the Swinging Festival (*Sao Ching Cha*) and the First Ploughing (*Roek Na*), a nobleman deputizing for the king is required to select a patterned Indian cloth from a number that are reserved for the occasion; even today his choice is deemed auspicious.[64]

Such textiles also retained a place in high-level diplomatic exchanges. It is surely significant that among the royal gifts presented by Rama IV's ambassador to Queen Victoria in 1857 was 'a piece of Indian cloth stamped with gold tissue devices worn on state occasions' and a 'red silk cloth figured worn daily'.[65] Whilst the royal status of these textiles has been preserved into this century, they had however ceased to be part of the royal patronage system at court and so lapsed from wider circulation within the ranks of the nobility.

The import of Indian painted cottons continued, but largely for the use of commoners. In mid-nineteenth-century Bangkok, Sir John Bowring noted: 'As to the ordinary dresses of the people, they are almost wholly made from cotton stuffs of foreign origin.'[66] The effect is illustrated in the engravings which accompany Henri Mouhot's *Travels in Siam, Cambodia and Laos 1858–1860*. This shift in status, from restricted high-quality textiles to mass-market wear, represented a major restructuring of the Indian textile trade to Thailand.

It also reflected a change which had already occurred in the Indian production centres themselves, away from the Coromandel Coast where the finest hand-drawn cloths had traditionally been made to the printing workshops of western India. The decline in quality was dramatic. The changeover from small-volume high-quality to a mass-consumption coarse product is exemplified by the textile known as *saudagiri*. The term is derived from the Persian *sauda* ('trade goods') and came to be applied in western India, probably in the nineteenth century, to cloths printed expressly for the Thai market. Pattern books survive, none of which is thought to be older than the mid-nineteenth century; they consist of ink drawings on paper, annotated with the name of the design in Gujarati [207, 208]. The samples of *saudagiri*

207, 208 Folios from a block-printed pattern book used in the production of *saudagiri* textiles for Thailand. Gujarat, Pethapur; early twentieth century (collected in Pethapur in 1984). National Crafts Museum, New Delhi. ◆ The designs – for characteristic centrefield and end-panel motifs – are annotated in Gujarati with their names. These pages illustrate the manner in which information about preferred patterns was transmitted between client and producer, and was preserved in the workshop. No doubt such books were, in the past, carried by merchants to Thailand when securing orders.

collected from Gujarat before 1880 by the Victoria and Albert Museum typify the low standard of production which characterized these mud-resist block-printed fabrics [203, 205].

The trade struggled on into the twentieth century, as witnessed by extant pattern books of that date which catalogue the designs in demand and name the merchants involved. According to the records of Maneklal Gajjar in Pethapur, Gujarat, ink-drawn designs continued to be sent from Bangkok by the Maalbari Trading Company to their agents in Surat who commissioned the textiles in Gujarat, usually at Ahmedabad. The cloths were known in Thailand as *pha surat* or, increasingly, by the name of the Indian agent, hence *pha Maalbari, Maskati, Vasi*, or *Baghwall*. According to an interview conducted by John Irwin in 1957 with A. E. Maskati of Ahmedabad, that family had been active sending printed textiles to Thailand since 1852.[67]

With the opening of the Second World War, the historic trade was fatally disrupted. A legacy persisted after the war in the form of locally produced block-printed cloths in the *saudagiri* style, known as *phaa phim*. They too have now succumbed to the pressures of mechanization, with machine-printed textiles alone preserving the memory of a five-hundred year long commercial and cultural dialogue between Thailand and India.

KANTON

CHINA

On the river [of Canton] there were merchantmen belonging to the Po-lo-men [Indians], the Po-sseu [Persians], the K'ouen-loeun [Malays], and others besides of which it is difficult to determine the number....There were also three monasteries of the Po-lo-men where Brahmans were residing.

Kanshin, *c.* 750[1]

For much of her early history, China had only very limited indigenous sources of cotton.[2] As a consequence, it was imported from a variety of places, including Central Asia, India and Southeast Asia. Indian goods were traded via Southeast Asia, local ports serving as entrepots: for commerce with the south of the country, Vietnam was a critical staging post. In this chapter, we shall examine what scant evidence there is relating to this aspect of the Indian textile trade, together with the role of Vietnam as an important intermediary in the process.

China and the introduction of cotton

There are indications that China represented one of the earliest eastern markets for Indian textiles. The oldest Chinese source is the *Hanshu* ('History of the [Former] Han Dynasty'), where the author Ban Gu (AD 32–92) lists cloth among the goods from India presented to the Emperor Wudi. Indian inscriptions indicate that merchant communities from the subcontinent were settled in insular Southeast Asia from the early centuries AD, principally to facilitate the gathering of the sea and forest products of the region known to be marketable in China; in the fourth century the Chinese pilgrim Faxian observed Indian merchants who were conducting trade with his country.[3] An Indian tribute mission to the Emperor Wu in 503 presented cotton among its gifts, a rare and highly desirable fabric.[4] Around this time a new word for cotton, *gu bei* or *ji bei*, appears in Chinese sources.[5] It is derived from the Malay word *kapas* (Sanskrit *karpasa*), suggesting that cotton in China and the Malay world shared a common source, India, transmitted via Southeast Asia. A term for cotton cloth also appears, *thu lu pu*, a transliteration of the Sanskrit *tula*, meaning woven cloth. Indian cotton was also reaching China overland from Bengal via Assam and Yunnan and via the Central Asian overland route.

Secular inscriptions by Tamil-speaking merchants from South India appear in Southeast Asia as early as the third or fourth century, contemporary with the earliest religious Sanskrit inscriptions found in the region, and then again in the ninth century, by which time the merchants were a regular feature of commercial life at the South China ports of Guangzhou (Canton) and Quanzhou in coastal Fujian. By then they were obliged to share this lucrative commerce with Persian and Arab merchants (*Po-ssi* and *Ta-shih* in the Chinese sources). Mosques and temples were built in the ports for the use of the expatriate merchant communities [209]. The cosmopolitan character of these trading communities can be judged from an account of the massacre of foreigners in Guangzhou in 878 in which, according to the Arab writer Abu Zaid, Muslims, Jews, Christians and Parsees perished.[6] Despite such setbacks, commerce gradually resumed and the Arab historian and geographer Mas'udi (d. 956) wrote in his *Muruj al-Dhahab* that 'ships from Basra, Siraf, Oman, India, the islands of Zabaj [Southeast Asia] and Sanf [Champa, central Vietnam], come to the mouth of the river of Khanfu [Guangzhou] in China with their merchandise'.[7] Such was the volume of trade that a customs shipping office was

209 View of Canton (Guangzhou) from the Pearl River (Zhujiang), with European and Chinese ships at anchor. Detail of an engraving first published in Philippus Baldaeus, *Naauwkeurige Beschryvinge van Malabar en Choromandel,* Amsterdam, 1672. Within the city walls two historical landmarks are visible: the minaret of the Huai-shengsi, the oldest mosque in south China, dating from around the ninth century, and a pagoda, possibly that of the Yanxiang temple, dated 1009.

established in Guangzhou in 971 to regulate the flow of imports and to collect taxes. In the twelfth century foreign commerce was actively promoted by the Song administration and merchant vessels were encouraged to visit the southern ports. A system of first- and second-category value goods was created: trading in first-category goods – luxury commodities such as aromatics, animal horn, precious stones and pearls – was state-regulated; second-category goods, which included foreign textiles, could be traded on the open market after payment of import duty, varying in this period between 10 and 15 per cent. Official concern was repeatedly expressed in the Chinese dynastic histories, the *Songshi* and the *Yuanshi*, about the outflow of metal, both precious (gold and silver) and base (copper), used to pay for the growing tide of imports.

The categorization of Indian textiles as unrestricted goods in the Song dynasty is the clearest indication that they were now intended for a broader market. No longer was Indian cotton such a rare commodity: it was available in growing quantities, allowing its wider use in society. The strength of demand is further indicated by the government's need in the thirteenth century to impose cash limits on its trade with South India, which was the major source of textiles.[8] Nonetheless, cotton goods remained relatively expensive: Ibn Battuta, an Arab traveller, was able to observe in 1344 that a piece of cotton could command a price equivalent to many pieces of silk, in which China was rich.[9]

The Chola dynasty of South India, whose territories included the textile-producing centres of the Coromandel Coast, sent a series of missions to China to encourage trade, beginning in 1015 and continuing until the close of the thirteenth century. The obstacle to assessing the scale of textiles in this trade is that their relatively low unit value meant they rarely featured in tribute lists, unlike high-value items like pearls and aromatics. The eleventh-century entries under 'Coromandel' in the *Song huiyao* (*c.* 1279) make clear that attention was focused on the luxury goods, praising the 'pearls as big as peas' which, together with Borneo camphor, were scattered in front of the imperial throne.[10]

Zhao Rukua, the harbour-master of Quanzhou in the early thirteenth century, notes in his *Zhufan zhi* ('Description of Barbarous Peoples') of 1225 that 'foreign cloth' (*fan bu*) was readily available, and names Gujarat, Malwa, Malabar and the Coromandel Coast as regions from which Indian cotton goods were supplied to the ports of South China.[11] Around 1300 the *Nan zhi* ('Gazetteer of the South') lists a variety of imported cloths, both white and patterned.[12] The presence of a strong Indian merchant community in Quanzhou is confirmed by a Tamil–Chinese bilingual inscription of April 1281 recording the dedication of a Hindu image installed there for worship.[13] The despatch from the city two months earlier of an official Yuan dynasty envoy to South India underscores the reciprocal nature of the trading relationship.[14]

At the time of Zhao Rukua, China got the bulk of her supplies of cotton, both raw and woven, from India and parts of Southeast Asia, notably Vietnam and Java. The plant was commercially grown on Hainan Island from around the twelfth century. Its cultivation quickly spread to the mainland but it was not produced on a large scale until the fifteenth century, when a rapid increase in urbanization led to an unprecedented demand. Locally produced cloth continued to be supplemented by both high-quality Indian cloth and lesser-quality goods from Southeast Asian sources.

More specific evidence directly relating to the Indian textile trade comes from a fourteenth-century Chinese commentator, Wang Dayuan. He records in his *Daoyi zhilue* ('Brief Account of the Barbarian Isles') of 1350 that 'patterned cloth' was imported from Nagapattinam, the Chola dynasty's principal port and a major centre for the export of cotton goods from the southern Coromandel Coast. He also refers to a Chinese merchant community resident there and notes that they built a temple for their use.[15] This reflects a new development in Sino-Indian trade, the active role of Chinese merchants in securing at source the textiles, spices and aromatics demanded at home.

Wang Dayuan also provides some of the earliest direct evidence of Indian cloth being employed in a complex system of secondary trading and exchange which linked Southeast Asia and South China. He mentions 'patterned cloth' entering China from a number of trading centres in insular Southeast Asia, including Srivijaya in eastern Sumatra, Palawan and Mindoro in the Philippines, and the Sulu and Maluku (Moluccas) regions of eastern Indonesia.[16] It is not clear from his account whether the cloths were local products or Indian goods acquired through trade.

However, there is reason to believe that the bulk of 'patterned cloth' in circulation was of Indian origin. It was customary for local rulers to present what was most highly valued within their culture. Given the status of Indian cloths in Southeast Asia, it is highly likely that they were preferred over home-produced examples for use in tribute and exchange. Such gifts had an additional benefit too: they acted as indicators of the tributary state's international connections and so served to enhance its standing in the eyes of China. Another Chinese official's account, Huang Xingzeng's *Xiyang chaogong dianlu* of 1520, catalogues twelve types of textile brought to China by Thai missions as tribute,[17] most of which, from our knowledge of Thai court protocol, were probably Indian.

In addition to the Coromandel Coast ports, Bengal features prominently in the Chinese sources. Ma Huan in 1433 refers to 'five or six varieties of fine stuffs' made in Bengal which were known to the Chinese.[18] Irregular tribute missions sent by the rulers of Bengal bearing a variety of cotton and woollen cloths feature in lists for the reigns of the Yongle (1402–24) and Zhengtong (1435–49).[19] Not everything that entered the country was of a quality judged appropriate for diplomatic exchange. Among the many Indian cottons imported to supplement domestic sources, the one in greatest demand was *bafta* (Chinese *bibu*), a finely woven white fabric which was already popular in fourteenth-century China. Other fine cottons included the coloured *manzheti*; a superior strong calico (*shanabafu*); a muslin favoured by wealthy Bengalis for use as turbans (*xinbailedali*); *chaotaer*, a soft cotton similar to Chinese *sansuo*; and a cotton velvet (*moheimoluo*).[20] China, the home of the silk industry, had no need of Indian silks.

In the fifteenth and sixteenth centuries the Ryukyu merchants played a pivotal role in the East Asia trade (see pp. 159–60). The situation is described with remarkable precision by the Portuguese Tomé Pires, who was based in Melaka (Malacca) between 1512 and 1515: 'The *Lequjos* [Ryukyu people] trade in China and Malacca. In China they trade in the port of *Foqum* [Fujian]....They sail from Malacca to China, and go to Japan. They take the same merchandise as the Chinese...in [up to] three junks every year, and they take a great deal of Bengal clothing.'[21]

Apart from the fragmentary evidence cited above, the Indian textile trade to China is difficult to chronicle in any degree of detail. Periodic bans imposed by the Ming government on Chinese participation in overseas trade prohibited their direct involvement. These restrictions may have acted as a further stimulus to the accelerated development of local cotton cultivation.

The role of Vietnam

Vital to the traditional trade to China were the ports of coastal Vietnam which were encountered en route. The Cham kingdom of central Vietnam and the Red River delta area to the north in the Bay of Tonkin had served the China trade since antiquity. In the sixteenth and seventeenth centuries the major ports were Hoi An and Pho Hien [210]. Hoi An (formerly Faifo), an ancient port on the estuary of the Thu Bon River near Danang, emerged in the mid-sixteenth century as a significant entrepot for the China and Ryukyu–Japan trade. It attracted foreign merchants in significant numbers, and Chinese and Japanese communities settled there. According to the Vietnamese annals, the governor Nguyen Hoang established a secure and peaceful port with a stable market at which 'the boats of merchants from all kingdoms gathered'.[22] A Japanese scroll painting of 1630 exists which depicts the arrival of a Red Seal ship belonging to the Chaya family of Kyoto (see p. 162–63). Large timbered houses to the north of the river denote the town, and south of the estuary thatched buildings labelled as the Chinese quarter probably represent their market. Today that area is rich in Chinese ceramic shards,[23] no doubt both trade wares for re-export and others for use by the expatriate community which was estimated in 1642 to number five thousand.[24] At Hoi An Chinese and Japanese merchants could have purchased Indian cotton cloths traded via Melaka, Ayutthaya and Batavia: the Dutch opened a factory here in 1633, followed by one in Tonkin in 1637, and were eager to exchange Indian cloth for the ceramics and silks which could be re-sold in Japan. The latter trade was disrupted by the Tokugawa prohibition of the 1630s and the role of Japanese merchants was assumed by the Dutch who, along with the Chinese, retained privileged access to the Japanese market.

The northern Vietnamese port of Pho Hien was situated on the Red River 50 kilometres south of the capital Thang-long (modern Hanoi), which was one of the largest cities of Southeast Asia in the sixteenth and seventeenth centuries, along with Ayutthaya and Melaka. It rose to prominence as Thang-long's international port in the early seventeenth century, and is first mentioned in that role in a stele dated 1625.[25] Trade was highly regulated, with designated streets for the sale of particular goods, which ensured control for purposes of royal taxation.[26] The English East India Company's Tonkin factory operated at Pho Hien from 1672 until 1679, when it was transferred to Thang-long, closing in 1697. Though the English never made their Tonkin operation a success, the letters sent by Company officials to their directors in London throw considerable light

210 View of Hanoi, showing a Vietnamese galley on the Red River and flags flying above the English and Dutch factories (right), the latter established in 1640. Detail of a drawing by Samuel Baron from *A Description of the Kingdom of Tonqueen*, 1685.

on the nature of the trade. The purchase of Vietnamese silk, yarn and woven cloth for export to Japan (and later to England where it proved very marketable) was the prime objective. Tonkin was also seen as a springboard for business in China. There is no evidence that the Company promoted Indian textiles in Vietnam, though others did, as the record of a vessel arriving at Pho Hien from Manila in 1674 shows, its cargo including twenty bales of Indian piece- goods.[27]

Vietnam continued to serve its historical role as a conduit for the Chinese ports, but increasingly the European ships that came to dominate the India–China trade by-passed Tonkin and sailed direct to Guangzhou.

The nineteenth century

It is difficult to gauge the volume of the Indian textile trade to China until the later eighteenth century, when the English East India Company embarked on a vigorous campaign based on cotton goods and opium, both targeted at a mass market. Calcutta emerged in the 1770s as the dominant port, although Madras maintained a steady trade. The Company began sending ships with cotton goods direct from Madras to China. Further supplies reached China via the ports of Southeast Asia, especially Melaka, Acheh, Penang and Kedah. Much of this trade was in private hands. Independent English country traders could, with the consolidation of their nation's authority in the region, procure Coromandel Coast cloths at privileged rates for re-sale in both Southeast Asia and China. Progressively, textile production centres fell under direct English control, as the Dutch and French lost ground, and local producers were obliged to operate on English terms. Indian merchants were increasingly squeezed out of this trade, especially as direct sailings on the large East Indiamen became the norm. The smaller Asian vessels continued to dominate coastal traffic and much of the south Coromandel trade to Southeast Asia. Some communities, such as the Chulias – Muslim Tamil merchants – continued their historic pattern of operation in Southeast Asia, settling in key ports and entrepots; Kedah became a favoured centre.

As English contacts with China grew, stimulated by the Commutation Act of 1784 which dramatically increased the importation of tea from China to England, so too did the imbalance of trade. In order to offset this, the Company actively fostered the dispatch to China of opium and cotton goods from the Bay of Bengal and Coromandel regions.

From the beginning of the nineteenth century, the textiles which dominated the Coromandel Coast trade were increasingly generated in the hinterlands south of Madras, especially in Thanjavur district. This shift reflected a cost restructuring, as the fine-quality goods associated with Masulipatam and Pulicat and their regions were largely abandoned in favour of poorer-grade cottons from the handloom weavers of Tamilnadu. Those cloths represented a new and ominous development, for they were intended to compete directly with the textiles produced and traded locally within Southeast Asia. Where China was concerned, they provided an expansion of supply to a mass market.

The trade to China was of growing importance for the East India Company. The strengthening of this commerce, seen for example through control of the Bay of Bengal, the securing of Penang Island in 1786 and the founding of Singapore in 1819, had the effect also of strengthening the textile trade to Southeast Asia. The English thus found themselves well positioned to exploit the commerce in cloth between India, Southeast Asia and China.

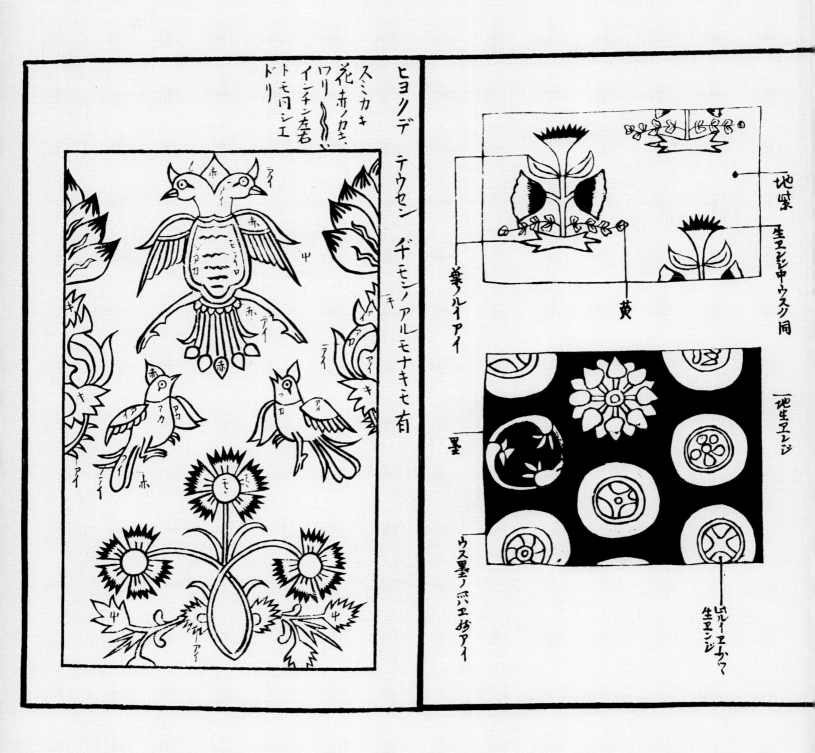

'STRANGE PAINTEINGES': THE JAPAN TRADE

You are to note that the people of this country doe not buy our sortes of Indian cloth soe much for necessity as for the new and strange fashions and painteinges, beinge a people desireinge change, for they have great stores of silke and linnen stuffes made here better and cheaper than we can afford our India cloth. So we must strive to p'cure [procure] strange sortes of cloth with strange painteinges every yeare…

Ralph Coppendale, 5 December 1615[1]

211 Pages from an edition of the woodblock-printed *Sarasa benran*, first published in Edo (Tokyo) in 1781, showing Indian painted and printed cotton designs popular in Japan, with annotations describing the colours to be employed when copying these patterns by stencilling techniques (see p. 177). Victoria and Albert Museum, London.

Indian textiles in Japan fulfilled a function unlike that in any other country in Asia. Their primary role was not to satisfy a popular demand for relatively inexpensive cotton garments, as in Indonesia, or to supply high-quality items which could be used in the internal and international market for gifts or trade, as in Thailand, but to satisfy a love of the exotic [p. 1; 216, 228]. While elsewhere in Asia accuracy of design was the key requirement, here the market was driven by a thirst for novelty: historical collections of Indian cloth in Japan display the greatest variety seen anywhere outside the subcontinent.

When members of the newly formed English East India Company ventured to Japan in 1613 and established a tenuous foothold at the remote port of Hirado on the western coast, they quickly came to learn of the vagaries of the local taste for Indian cloths. The explanation for this apparent fickleness lay in the nature of the market itself. Japan had traditionally been self-sufficient in textiles. The Dutch official François Caron, whose experience with the VOC trade here extended from 1619 to 1641, wrote that the country was abundantly wealthy and provided for all the needs of its inhabitants.[2] Significant quantities of silk were in fact imported from China and especially from Vietnam, but they came in the form of yarn and undyed cloth, to supplement domestic supplies, and were worked into Japanese fabrics. The demand for finished foreign cloth did not extend beyond what was desired by the wealthy as curiosities.

Patterns of trade

Japan's overseas trade before the seventeenth century was limited in volume. Religious and commercial contact with China occurred from at least the late Tang period, as witnessed by records of the arrival of Chinese Buddhist monks in the seventh century, and by the presence of Tang textiles and ceramics. There is little to suggest that the Japanese took an active role in this early trade, beyond providing a willing market for exotic luxury imports. Many of the surviving items are associated with Buddhist temples, to which they would have been presented by noble devotees or eminent monks.[3] Over time the temple authorities came to be the custodians of remarkable collections of rarities. This proved to be a blessing, as they were less vulnerable to the widespread destruction which characterized periods of Japanese history, when the households of innumerable feudal lords (*daimyo*) and their hereditary holdings were lost in clan warfare.

In the period leading up to unification in the late sixteenth century, Japan's international trade was largely conducted by merchants from China and especially from the Ryukyu, a group of islands including Okinawa situated off the southern coast of Japan [11]. A detailed account is preserved in the *Rekidai Hoan* ('Precious Documents of Successive Generations'), a history of the ruling household's diplomatic and commercial relations.[4] The Ryukyuan merchants served as intermediaries, supplying commodities between China, Korea and

Japan. In Southeast Asia, commercial relations were maintained with Vietnam, Thailand, Pattani, Melaka (Malacca), Sumatra and Java.

The *Rekidai Hoan* contains references to 'crimson cotton', the identity of which is unclear but which in all probability included Indian cloth; the records for 1430, as noted in Chapter VII, include a reference to 'twenty bolts of red oiled cotton cloth' arriving from Thailand,[5] which almost certainly originated on the Coromandel Coast. This source points to the presence of Indian textiles in East Asian waters in the first half of the fifteenth century and also affirms Thailand's role as an entrepot in international trade in this early period. At the beginning of the sixteenth century Tomé Pires was aware of the pivotal role of Ryukyuan merchants, linking Melaka, China and Japan in a commercial web.[6]

The Portuguese were the first Europeans to establish contact with Japan, in 1542–43. They made annual sailings in their famed 'black ships' (*nau*) from China, and after 1554 from their own base at Macao. The ships carried Chinese raw silk, gold and porcelain which were traded for Japanese copper, silver and dyes.[7] The vessels, their cargoes, and the attire of the merchants and crews who accompanied them are recorded in screen paintings of the period, known as *namban byobu* after the name the Japanese gave to the new arrivals, *namban-jin* ('barbarians from the South'). A screen attributed to the painter Kano Domi[8] depicts a Portuguese ship unloading at the port of Nagasaki. Each year the vessels were delayed for some months awaiting favourable monsoons, affording the Japanese artists ample opportunity to study the strange foreigners.

Whilst the Portuguese sources of the early seventeenth century indicate that the bulk of the textiles carried from Macao were Chinese silks, the screen paintings depict the merchants and most notably their crew wearing what appear to be Indian painted cotton garments. The characteristic ballooning trousers of the Portuguese are made of a dark fabric, typically with striped, medallion or floral decoration. The versions worn by their servants (mostly Asian slaves of Indian or Malay origin) are made of fabric decorated with a floral vine meander or Mughal flower motif [214]. Comparison may be made with samples of Indian painted or printed cottons preserved in Japan. The practice of making European trousers from the finest painted Coromandel Coast cottons is attested by the Dutch trader Jan Huyghen van Linschoten, writing from Goa at the end of the sixteenth century: the best of the painted cottons, are 'higher priced than silke, because of the finenes and cunning workmanship: they are called Rechatas and Cheyias, wherof the Christians and Portingals in India make breeches'.[9]

The Portuguese operated a highly profitable trade between Macao and Japan, supplying textiles and spices from their Indian and Southeast Asian bases, and silk and porcelain from China. Their dominance, shared only with a small number of Chinese and Japanese traders, came to an end at the beginning of the seventeenth century. A key factor was growing disquiet over Portuguese Jesuit missionary activities, sparked by the scale of Christian conversions in the south of the country. Protestant Dutch merchants, newly arrived, further kindled fear of Portuguese territorial ambitions in the minds of the local *daimyos*. In response, the government stimulated the growth of native shipping and this, together with pressure from rival European traders, most notably the Dutch, weakened and eventually eliminated the Portuguese from the Japan trade.

Private Japanese traders played a significant role in commerce with Southeast Asia in the late sixteenth century, though the absence of port or company records makes it difficult to assess. Several European observers record the presence of Japanese merchants in Southeast Asian waters in the period

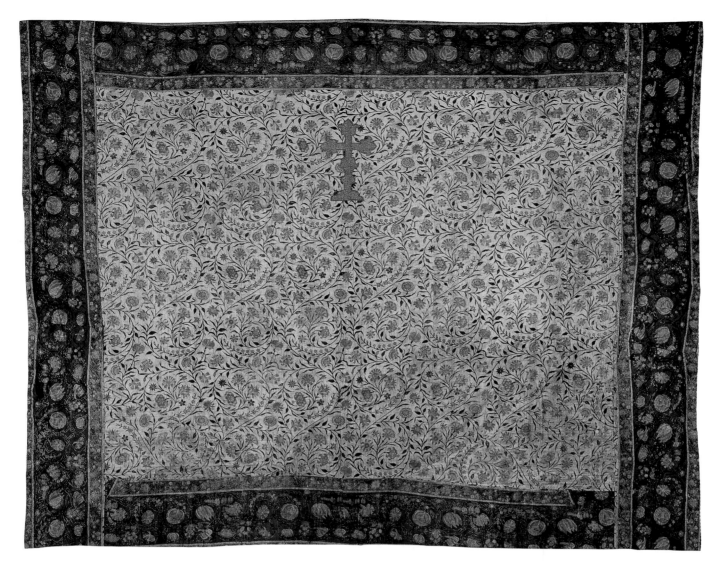

212 Liturgical cloth, possibly intended as an
altar hanging for one of the communities of
Japanese Christians converted by foreign
Jesuits and friars (see p. 167). Coromandel
Coast, for the Japanese market; early
eighteenth century. Cotton, painted
mordant-dyed and resist-dyed, and painted.
Kanebo Museum of Textiles, Osaka.

213 A cloth shop; detail from a Namban
screen painting. Kyushu, possibly Nagasaki;
late sixteenth century. Kobe City Museum.
◆ Bolts of cloth are displayed: judging from
the colours and patterns visible, they are most
probably Chinese silk brocades and Indian
painted cottons, as well as local fabrics.
The shopkeeper is watching with curiosity a
Jesuit and two Franciscans passing her shop.
The likely setting of this painting is Nagasaki,
on the harbour island of Deshima where
foreigners were quarantined.

following the loss of direct China trade in 1557, engaged in purchasing goods for their home market. Many came to Manila to buy raw silk from the Chinese ships that called there. They were also in search of the famous antique 'Luzon' jars much in demand for use as tea ceremony apparatus.

Political unification of Japan was achieved in the late sixteenth century. In 1600 Shogun Tokugawa Ieyasu secured power and instigated an era of calm and relative prosperity. The Tokugawa clan was to rule the country until 1868. Ieyasu was alert to the benefits which could accrue to the ruling household through the regulated growth of foreign trade, and embarked on a policy of fostering international commerce. In 1604 he imposed the *itowappu* system, which required the leading merchants in Kyoto, Sakai and Nagasaki – and later Edo (now Tokyo) and Osaka – to form associations to guarantee the purchase of the imported raw silk offered for sale.[10] The scheme resulted in the massive consolidation of wealth by the Tokugawa shogunate through taxation on this trade.

Social stability, together with the rapid expansion of the merchant classes, generated unprecedented levels of demand for previously restricted luxuries such as silk garments and sugar. The tea ceremony underwent a major boost in the mid-sixteenth century as an aesthetic pastime of the urban merchant elite. Imported ceramic and metal utensils were greatly in demand for use as tea caddies and tea bowls; Thai and Vietnamese ceramics were admired for their rustic qualities.[11] Indian painted cotton textiles were much sought after as covers and wrappers for these wares.[12]

François Caron provides a succinct description of Japan's trading partners in the first half of the seventeenth century:

> The Trade of this Country (which is but small in respect of the vastness of it...) is carried on by strangers, the principal whereof are the Chinese...the *Portugals* have been acquainted with this People above an hundred years; the *English* of late, who finding but little profit and great expenses, abandoned this Traffik again. The *Siamese* and *Camboiders* used also to arrive with a Ship or two, though not now so often as formerly. Lastly, the Netherlander...trade these forty years.[13]

The one participant that Caron failed to mention was the Japanese themselves, who between 1600 and 1639 were strongly encouraged to engage in foreign commerce. While direct evidence of their activities earlier had been lacking, the scale of their operations now becomes clear through records of the Shogun Ieyasu's Red Seal permit system (*shuinjo*). Established in the late sixteenth century, this required all Japanese vessels sailing abroad to operate under an official licence; all likely host ports in Southeast Asia were requested to deal only with those ships presenting the seal. The system proved effective and Japanese trade prospered: between 1604 and 1639 more than 350 vessels sailed under these conditions.[14] These ships were engaged principally in regional trade, such as the purchasing of raw silk from Chinese merchants in Vietnam and Formosa, and from the Portuguese at Macao. Raw silk was the single largest Japanese import and it has been estimated that more than 50 per cent was carried on Japanese ships. The bulk of this commerce was funded with newly mined Japanese silver, which flooded into Southeast Asia and was in great demand in India; gold and copper were also widely used, contributing significantly to the volume of coinable metals in circulation in the region, and greatly facilitating the emergence of a sustainable monetary system in Southeast Asia.

Japanese settled at foreign ports, the largest number at the Thai capital of Ayutthaya, where both merchants and mercenaries resided in an area known as *ban jipun*, 'the Japanese quarter' [160]. In the decade between 1604 and 1616 an

214 A Dutchman and his Javanese servant, depicted in a woodblock print from Nagasaki; eighteenth century. British Museum, London. ◆ The Dutchman is wearing a floral patterned jacket suggestive of Indian painted cotton, his servant a Malay-style jacket (*baju*) with Mughal-inspired stemmed flower motifs [cf. 35].

average of three Japanese ships a year arrived, typically with a cargo of silver and swords to be traded for assorted skins, dye-woods and Indian textiles.

Regular sailings to Ayutthaya and Melaka enabled Japanese merchants to acquire goods from beyond the region at internationally competitive prices. They also established themselves along the routes, in areas such as Taiwan and the islands of Nan-dom in the Gulf of Tonkin; a community existed too at the port of Hoi An (modern Faifo) in the Cham region of central Vietnam. Cotton fragments in Japanese collections labelled 'Champa' may date from this period of intense commercial activity.[15] These contacts were seriously disrupted by the Tokugawa seclusion policy, enacted as an attempt to reduce foreign influences, which banned Japanese overseas trade from 1639 to 1685.

The early seventeenth century was a boom period for commerce in Southeast Asia and Japan. The Dutch were aggressively policies aiming at a monopoly in Asia. In Japan, having learnt from the Portuguese experience, they were careful to avoid any actions which would suggest colonial ambitions. In this way they were able to establish themselves as the most successful European traders in the country. They arrived in Banten (Bantam), the great emporium in west Java, in 1596 and in April 1600 their first ship, *De Liefde*, reached Japan.[16] The first ship of the Dutch East India Company arrived from Batavia (modern Jakarta) in 1609, and quickly sought permission for a factory at Hirado. Initially, they experienced competition from Japanese vessels operating privately in Southeast Asian ports, but after 1639 that competition ceased. The Portuguese, too, were banned in 1639. In 1641 the Dutch factory was moved to Nagasaki, Japan's only international port, under direct orders from the shogun. That year was also marked by another major shift in the struggle for control: combined forces of the Dutch and the rulers of the north Sumatran kingdom of Atjeh captured Melaka and so broke the nexus which linked the Portuguese possessions of Goa, Melaka and Macao in a powerful commercial chain.

The promise that Japan held for foreign traders is well described in the official records of the English East India Company. In 1613 the *Clove*, under the command of John Saris, arrived at Hirado from Banten. Company correspondence is rich in references to the varieties of Indian cloths which proved saleable in this most difficult of markets. Richard Wickham wrote from Hirado in 1617 to John Jourdain in Banten requesting '100 fine serassas [*sarasa*, or chintz] of St Thome [Madras region]' and complaining that 'the last Tapy [Tapti River, Surat] serassas being somewhat coarse are not vendible, neither being the first chint Bramportes [first-quality Burhanpur chintz] nor rumall chints [Andhra chintz]' [cf. 226].[17] Cambay and Surat cloth, from Gujarat, including chintz from Ahmedabad, are the trade textiles most frequently mentioned in the English records of this period, although ports along the Coromandel Coast are also referred to. By 1623 the English had abandoned their Japanese activities, having been unable to compete with the Dutch and with Asian traders.

The status of the best Indian textiles which reached Japan can be gauged from a Dutch description of an official reception held on 25 October 1626 in Kyoto: Conrad Krammer, the VOC official at the court, listed among the gifts presented by Shogun Hidetada to his son Prince Iemitsu 'one hundred Indian gowns richly wrought', and among the gifts from the shogun's secretary to the prince, twenty 'Indian gowns'.[18] No indication is provided as to the precise identity of the fabrics.

An analysis of the imports recorded at the Dutch factory at Hirado for the year 1636 provides a revealing insight into the composition of the trade in this period. The cargo arrived on ten VOC ships – five from Taiwan, three from Batavia and two from Atjeh. Of the value of the imports, raw silk and woven silk made up 80.4 per cent, leathers (shark and deer skins) 5.6 per cent, and dye-stuffs (sappanwood), drugs and spices 2.8 per cent, whilst cotton fabrics represented only 1.4 per cent. Within the latter category, nine varieties are named: 'gauze, Parcallen, Guinea stuffs, Chelas, Sarassa, Red chintzes, Gangans, Baftas and Gingham'.[19] Some of these terms can be associated with extant varieties: guinea, a plain weave dyed in stripes or checks associated with Gujarat; *chelas*, a cotton cloth striped or chequered; *sarasa*, painted cotton, chintz; red chintzes, a variant chintz distinguished from *sarasa*; *baftas*, plain cotton, sometimes dyed red; gingham, cotton woven with dyed yarn, in stripes or checks.

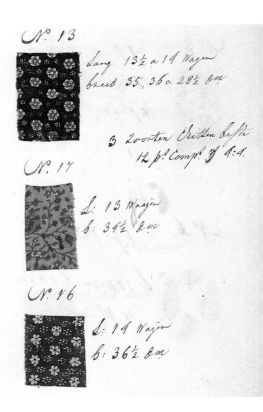

The Dutch had been particularly keen to exploit the Japan market, attracted by the profits to be had from the silver and copper they received in payment. François Bernier, a French observer of India in the years 1656–68, was aware that the gold and silver supplied by the Dutch were of Japanese origin, traded in exchange for Gujarati and Coromandel cloths and Bengal silks.[20] In 1645 they had introduced Bengal silk with considerable success, as an alternative to Chinese sources. They purchased up to a third of all Bengal's silk yarn production that year for export to Japan and Holland; they wanted more, but competing demand from local weavers and from the weaving centres of western India, notably Ahmedabad and Surat,[21] the home of *patola* production, was too great.

215 OPPOSITE Page from a Dutch order book (*Eisch Boek*), used to identify patterns marketable in Japan; early nineteenth century. Cotton samples, dyed with block-printed mordants and resist. Algemeen Rijksarchief, The Hague.

216 OPPOSITE, BELOW LEFT Nobleman's outer jacket (*jinbaori*), tailored in the late Edo period (early nineteenth century) for Maeda Yoshiyasu; height 107 cm. The tails are fashioned from Indian *sarasa* similar to that shown below. Coromandel Coast, for the Japanese market; eighteenth century. Cotton, painted mordant-dyed and drawn resist-dyed. Collection Maeda Ikutokukai Foundation, Tokyo.

217 BELOW Ceremonial banner (detail). Coromandel Coast, for the Indonesian market, found in Sulawesi, eighteenth century. Cotton, painted mordant- and resist-dyed; weft 71 cm. Victoria and Albert Museum, London.

218 RIGHT Coverlet (detail). Bengal, probably Satgaon, under Portuguese supervision; first half of the seventeenth century. Yellow tasar silk embroidery on cotton. Tokugawa Art Museum, Nagoya.
◆ This probably found its way into the Tokugawa clan collection as a gift from Portuguese merchants.

Indian textiles clearly continued to enter Japan throughout the seventeenth century at a volume far greater than VOC records alone suggest. Another source of supply was Thailand. The Coromandel merchants are known to have maintained very close commercial ties with the rulers of that country throughout the century, despite mounting pressure from the European Companies. The monarch sent his own ships and representatives to Japan. The first such vessel recorded in Japanese sources arrived at Nagasaki in 1612; in 1616 came a diplomatic mission seeking to trade forest products for swords.[22] Japanese records list 130 ships from Thailand in the second half of the century.[23] From our knowledge of the commercial activities of the Thai ruler, it is highly likely that Indian painted cotton textiles formed part of the trade, if only as diplomatic gifts. Indian cottons in Thai taste certainly feature in Japanese historical collections [267].

Although diplomatic activity was short-lived (the last recorded mission was in 1629), private Thai trade with Japan continued throughout the century. The vessels sailing on behalf of Thai interests were manned largely by Chinese crews and business was conducted by the Chinese, who were exempt from the trading restrictions. There is some evidence to suggest that Indian textiles were also traded direct with Japan by Indian merchants. The VOC *Daghregister* at Batavia records that in 1661 a group of Indian Muslims sailed from Ayutthaya for Japan in a Chinese junk.[24] The Dutch noted such incidents with growing annoyance as they underlined the ineffectiveness of their attempts to impose a commercial monopoly. The use of private Chinese vessels by other nationals was common practice and it must be assumed that a considerable quantity of Indian textiles reached Japan by this method. The last step in the Dutch strategy of centralizing trade through Batavia came with the closure of Banten as a free port in 1682. Indian and European merchants operating in Southeast and East Asia had traditionally used it as a major entrepot for the exchange of goods, particularly textiles, and its loss seriously impaired their operations.

In the course of the eighteenth century an active Japan trade was maintained, with Thai and Indian commodities being loaded in Ayutthaya for sale in Japan, and Japanese goods (especially weapons and refined metals) being acquired for re-sale both en-route in China (in exchange for porcelain and silk) and in Thailand. In the face of this Chinese-dominated trade, aided as it was by kinship loyalties, the Dutch were increasingly at a disadvantage. Whilst they retained their monopolistic posture at Batavia, in reality they were obliged to share the Japan trade increasingly with the Chinese.

Dutch order books (*Eisch Boeks*) provide a guide to the identity and prestige of the Indian textiles in eighteenth-century Japan [215]. In them were recorded the curious and rare goods (*rareteijten*) required for presentation by the VOC to the shogun and influential officials. The practice of making special orders may have begun as a means of cultivating favourable relations following the lifting of the prohibition on Japanese private trade in 1685. The earliest extant *Eisch Boek* is for 1725, and they continue throughout the Edo period into the nineteenth century.[25] Among the items ordered in 1810 were 'chitzen' (chintz) – Indian painted cottons. Japan continued to receive Indian textiles throughout the nineteenth century, the volume and designs reflecting prevailing local taste and fashion.

The textiles
Uses and adaptions

Indian cloth was employed in Japan in a number of ways which were unique to that country and which satisfied very specific cultural needs. Demand came in large measure from the Kansai region, which included the cities of Kyoto, Nara, Osaka and Kobe. This area had a unique concentration of wealthy temples, noble families and prosperous merchants, all potential consumers for imported textiles. Kyoto was the centre for commerce in seventeenth-century Japan and prided itself as also being the cultural heart.

One of the first markets for foreign textiles was the temple: from around the fourteenth century rare and expensive imports regularly served for the making of *kesa*, the ceremonial robes worn by Zen Buddhist priests. They were also used in this early period for costume robes for Noh, a form of theatre patronized by the elite. Most of the textiles were probably Chinese, though Indian luxury cloths may also have been employed.

The Portuguese were active in Japan in the second half of the sixteenth century and it is therefore not entirely surprising to discover in the Tokugawa family collection at Nagoya an Indo-Portuguese cotton coverlet of that date [218]. It is richly embroidered in yellow wild silk (*tasar*) with Indian hunting scenes around a central medallion depicting a couple beneath a flowering tree. Embroideries of this type were commissioned by the Portuguese in the sixteenth and early seventeenth centuries for export to Europe, chiefly to Lisbon; many bear the coats-of-arms of eminent Portuguese families. They are known as 'Bengalla quilts', and their production is likely to have been organized from Satgaon on the River Hooghly, the old mercantile centre of Bengal; the Portuguese had settled there, attracted to the region by the quality of its textiles and the famed skills of its workers. A non-Bengali provenance for the Tokugawa coverlet is also possible, however: according to Alfonso de Albuquerque, the second Governor of India (i.e. Cochin) from 1509 to 1515, artisans skilled in this type of textile work were also recruited to produce cloths in Melaka.[26] In all probability our

219 Fragment of Indian *sarasa* (detail), from the collection of the *daimyo* of Hikone province, Japan. Coromandel Coast; seventeenth century. Cotton, painted mordant-dyed. Collection Ii family, Tokyo National Museum. ◆ While a complete example of this design displaying the Sacred Heart has been recorded from south Sumatra, this fragment is unique in Japan. It is presumably a legacy of Jesuit missionary activity there; although that was outlawed in 1614, cloths with Christian imagery may have continued to enter the country clandestinely.

example formed part of a gift presented by the Portuguese to the shogun.[27]

A class of Indian textiles in Japan about which little is known is the cloths produced for the indigenous Christian community. Following the arrival of the Portuguese, and greatly stimulated by Francis Xavier's visit to Japan in 1549–50, Christian evangelizing achieved considerable success. The southern island of Kyushu quickly had significant conversions, numbering tens of thousands. The Japanese authorities reacted with prohibitions, the first in 1587, with brutal repressions in 1596 and 1612, and finally with the imposition of a total ban in 1614. There is evidence, however, especially in southern Japan where Christianity had taken root most firmly, that it was never fully exterminated during the long period of interdiction that lasted until 1873. Adherents met for worship in secret; they became known as *kakure krishitan*, 'hidden Christians', and survived by concealing themselves in the remote western islands off Kyushu, where they exist to this day. Meticulously preserved religious objects, such as portable oratories, devotional paintings, lecterns and sacrament boxes, have come to light in recent years, mostly in Japanese private collections.[28]

The vestments, altar cloths, hangings and furnishings needed by the clergy were supplied initially from Lisbon; in time, however, they came to be made in India and shipped from Goa via Macao. A textile with explicit Christian imagery survives as a fragment in the Hikone Castle collection of the Ii family [219]. It has the Jesuits' Sacred Heart motif mordanted on cotton, and is a rare reminder of the production of cloths in the service of the Society of Jesus for use in their evangelizing work in Asia.[29] A seventeenth-century date is possible: the alternating flower motif is a familiar feature of *namban* gilded lacquer (*maki-e*) and inlaid mother-of-pearl ecclesiastical objects. Many of the objects are in the *namban* style of the early seventeenth century.

Another cloth expressly made for Christian worship is a painted cotton with the quality and character of a classic Coromandel Coast piece of the early eighteenth century [212]. It has a red altar cross set against a red and green floral pattern on a white ground and is lined with an Indian striped coarse cotton fabric of the type known in Japan as *onisarasa* (devil's or demon's *sarasa*). It was probably intended as a portable altar cloth or backdrop in clandestine services.

The *samurai* or warrior class also made use of foreign textiles, particularly Indian *sarasa*, which served widely as linings and backing fabrics on suits of battle armour in the Tokugawa period. They were also favoured, along with foreign woollen cloth (notably English broadcloth), for the making of the *jinbaori*, the outer jacket worn by samurai and noblemen, especially when on horseback. The integration of the textiles into the design requirements of the garment is particularly inventive [216, 217], although there is no evidence of them having been commissioned in India specifically for the purpose, as was the case, for example, with some ecclesiastical textiles or with the soldier's jacket produced for the Thai market [188].

The main use of *sarasa* in tailored attire appears to have been as small-sleeved robes (*kosode*) rather than as outer garments (kimono) [220, 223]. Concealment of these brightly coloured robes ensured that the dress aesthetic prescribing 'quiet taste' (*sabi*) was observed. An early nineteenth-century hanging scroll depicts a lady raising the hem of her kimono as she walks, revealing the distinctive leafy floral pattern associated with Indian *sarasa* on the lining. *Sarasa* was also favoured for sleeping jackets and other garments not in the public gaze.[30] The social custom of not displaying one's wealth in an obvious manner still prevailed when Stewart Culin visited Japan early this century: he

220 ABOVE *Kosode*, underrobe. Tailored from an Indian *palampore* with flowering tree design [cf. 143]; early eighteenth century. Cotton, painted mordant-dyed and resist-dyed. Tokyo National Museum.

221 BELOW Cloth case for a scroll box, made from Indian *sarasa*. Coromandel Coast, for the Japanese market; eighteenth century. Cotton, painted mordant-dyed. Prefectural Museum of Art, Yamaguchi City.

222 RIGHT Tobacco pouch, made from Indian *sarasa*. Coromandel Coast, for the Japanese market, late eighteenth–nineteenth century. Cotton, block-printed mordant-dyed; 16 x 7.5 cm. Collection Tomoyuki Yamanobe, Toyama-Kinenkan Museum, Saitama-Ken.

223 RIGHT *Kosode*, underrobe. Tailored in the Taisho–Meiji period (1912–26) as a patchwork of eighteenth- and nineteenth-century Indian painted cottons, with nineteenth-century European printed cottons and Japanese stencilled cloths. Cotton, height 144 cm. Kobe City Museum.

224 RIGHT Japanese woman wearing an *obi*, waist sash, tailored from modern printed Indian cotton, photographed at Saitama-Ken near Tokyo in 1993.

observed that 'old *sarasa* is very expensive and a man may wear a *sarasa* undergarment that costs much more than his silk robe'.[31]

A splendid *sarasa kosode* demonstrates how extravagant these 'concealed' robes could be [220]: with its beautifully painted flowering tree design in resist-dyed reds of varying intensity and added green and yellow, it has the flamboyance of the finest Coromandel Coast painted cottons of the 1720s. Such patterns were primarily intended for the European market, where they echoed the vogue for French 'bizarre' designs of the early eighteenth century.[32]

A number of robes were made of a patchwork of painted Indian cottons. They appear to have been tailored in the late Edo and Meiji periods (late eighteenth–early twentieth centuries), but contain textiles which are considerably older [223]. A *kosode* belonging to the Mitsui family includes samples in a variety of styles: there are Mughal floral designs on a white ground, imitation double ikat,[33] and Thai market designs, as well as other cloths which are Indian in style but are Japanese stencil-resist (*wasarasa*).[34]

Indian *sarasa* was fashionable, at least from the late Edo period, for use as a woman's waist sash (*obi*), and the practice continues among older members of society [224]. Some of the *obi* today are made of new Indian printed cottons; others are older cloths, often from many sources assembled into a patchwork. The cost of older *sarasa* was high. Culin noted that 'very fine old *sarasa* is sold by the square inch and costs more than the finest brocade'.[35] Textile dealers in Kyoto continue the tradition of selling prized samples, usually in small swatches, mounted for study, or made up into tea bowl presentation cloths.

The most singular function that Indian textiles assumed in Japanese society was as wrappers (*furoshiki*) and containers for treasured objects, known in the literature of connoisseurship as *meibutsu* ('objects of fame'), and intimately associated with the tea ceremony. The term is frequently used in catalogues of famous tea utensils in the late sixteenth century.[36] The criteria for *meibutsu* are as much to do with the recorded provenance of the object as with its intrinsic aesthetic merits, and *kowatari sarasa* ('*sarasa* of foreign origin imported of old') itself assumed rarified status as *meibutsu-gire* ('famed fabrics'). Many such pieces remain in use today in important tea ceremony collections.

Indian *sarasa* was a favoured material for making cloth containers in which scroll boxes were stored [221]. In the Edo and Meiji periods (eighteenth and nineteenth centuries) it was used as a covering for small purses, tobacco pouches, seal containers and other personal items [222]; these appear to have been popular, judging by the number which survive. *Sarasa* was also utilized in nineteenth-century literati circles to cover books.

Fragments of many varieties of Indian textiles are preserved in the albums of *meibutsu-gire* which it became fashionable to assemble in the late Edo period [225]: highly prized samples, often the remains of or offcuts from the making of tea caddy pouches (*shifuku*) or wrapping cloths, were mounted on Japanese paper and identified by the name of the design, the country of origin, or a term identifying the cloth's original function. A great variety are represented, mostly cotton but also silks. An album in the Kanebo Museum of Textiles, Osaka, has a fragment of Gujarati silk *patola*, an Indian textile rarely recorded in Japan.

Two categories of Indian textiles are distinguished in the albums: *moru*, which has Mughal associations and is typically characterized by the use of floral patterns and gold or silver threads, and *sarasa*. Many of the *sarasa* can be identified with cloths found in insular Southeast Asia, especially those associated with the Malay–Sumatran region of western Indonesia [217, 227].

The prestige of antique exotic textiles of all kinds in Japan is nowhere better illustrated than in the practice of incorporating treasured fragments in hand-scrolls. A number of examples of Indian *sarasa* are preserved in this manner, typically in the composition of the mount. Very rarely do we witness their preservation as the central painting, but a vigorously drawn cloth depicting an Indian woman and two Portuguese men was so treated [p. 1]. The piece appears to be a fragment from a larger scene; the nearest stylistic parallels are with the famous Brooklyn Museum curtain panels dated to *c.* 1610–20,[37] and in all probability it once formed part of a panel of similar date. The confident and fresh painting style, employing a combination of resist- and mordant-dyeing, is distinctive and idiosyncratic. The costumes are also regionally specific: that of the woman belongs to southern India, and that of the men, with their full breeches, to Portugal. Cloth of this quality must have come from the southern Coromandel Coast, perhaps from Pulicat.

Sarasa was collected in its own right from the early years of the Tokugawa shogunate. The activities of the Maeda family, the feudal lords of Kaga Province, are particularly illuminating in this regard [216]. It is recorded that the third Lord Toshitsune, a renowned connoisseur of the tea ceremony, sent envoys in 1637 to Nagasaki to acquire examples of the finest foreign textiles.[38] The family collection, preserved today in the National Museum in Kyoto, is dominated by Chinese cloths but includes examples from India, Iran and Southeast Asia. One of the most remarkable is a painted cloth with gilded decoration depicting lions and fabulous creatures (*kylin*) in a snake-infested landscape [228]. It is a mordanted and resist-dyed finely woven cotton, produced on the Coromandel Coast in the second half of the seventeenth century. The design is heightened with glued gold leaf. A variant treatment of the lions-in-landscape subject, without gold, occurs on a cloth preserved in the Fries Museum, Leeuwarden, in northern Holland, where chintz was popular among the wealthy farming communities of the seventeenth and eighteenth centuries.[39]

The most extensive collection of *meibutsu-gire* was that of the Ii family, of Hikone Castle, which was assembled in its present form in the Edo period [219, 226, 227, 229, 230].[40] It provides an index of Indian textile designs imported into Japan at the time. As a group they are remarkable for their range, which falls into four broad categories – figurative, landscape, geometric, and floral – and a fifth combining several of these elements .

Many of the figurative designs occur on painted cottons of the South Indian *kalamkari* type [229]. They include winged angels, birds and animals. The land-scapes are remarkably varied; many have extravagant flower, leaf and animal motifs which suggest that they may have formed part of flowering tree cloths of the *palampore* type. The floral designs range from Mughal-style meanders to finely drawn flowers in elaborate vine-leaf meanders, and simple block-printed repeats. The geometric designs are equally varied, from simple repeat patterns to complex endless knot and cartouche schemes of Islamic inspiration [227]; some directly imitate the *patola* of Gujarat and the single ikats of Andhra Pradesh [226]. Some samples combine geometric and floral elements in curious hybrid arrangements unknown in any traditional Indian context.

It is rare that Indian trade cloths can be associated with a specific production region, but several of the Ii collection samples closely resemble cloths employed in the binding of manuscripts in the royal library of Maharaja Sarabhoji II (1798–1833) of Thanjavur, south India [34, 35, 37]. The latter were at first ascribed to the nearby weaving village of Karuppur, locally renowned for

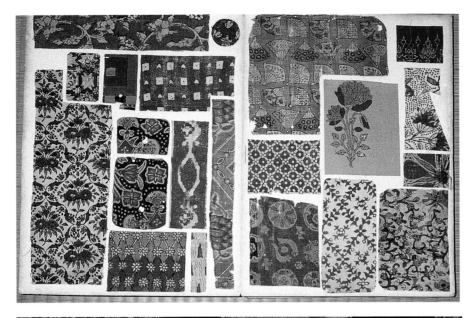

225 LEFT Samples of historical Indian textiles, preserved in a late Edo period album. Like the other fragments on this spread, they are *meibutsu gire* ('famed fabrics'). Private collection, Kyoto.

226 LEFT, CENTRE Fragment of Indian *sarasa* (detail), from the collection of the *daimyo* of Hikone province, Japan. Coromandel Coast, for the Japanese market, eighteenth century. Cotton, painted mordant-dyed, resist-dyed, and ikat. Collection Ii family, Tokyo National Museum. ◆ This is one of a number of fragments, recorded only in Japan, that incorporate elements of a regionally specific style of ikat dyeing associated with the *telia rumal* cloths of Chirala, coastal Andhra Pradesh. The presence of these samples suggests that actual *telia rumals* may have once formed a part – largely unrecorded – of the Coromandel Coast's eastern trade.

227 LEFT, BELOW Fragment of Indian *sarasa* (detail). Coromandel Coast, for the Japanese market; late eighteenth century. Cotton, painted mordant-dyed and resist-dyed. Collection Ii family, Tokyo National Museum.

228 OPPOSITE, ABOVE Fragment of Indian *sarasa* (detail). Coromandel Coast, for the Japanese market; seventeenth century. Cotton, painted mordant-dyed and resist-dyed, with glued gold leaf. Collection Maeda family, Kyoto National Museum. ◆ This was designed to cater for a fascination with the exotic which prevailed in Japan as well as in Europe (see p. 171).

229 OPPOSITE, BELOW LEFT Fragment of Indian *sarasa* (detail). Coromandel Coast, for the Japanese market; late seventeenth–eighteenth century. Cotton, painted mordant- and resist-dyed. Collection Ii family, Tokyo National Museum. ◆ The style most directly relates to Indian *kalamkari* painting as seen on temple cloths of southern India [cf. ill. p. 1].

230 OPPOSITE, BELOW RIGHT Fragment of Indian *sarasa* (detail). Coromandel Coast, for the Japanese market; eighteenth century. Cotton, painted mordant-dyed and resist-dyed. Collection Ii family, Tokyo National Museum. ◆ Painted cottons in Chinoiserie style produced for eighteenth-century Europe were also marketable in Japan [cf. **220**].

supplying cloths to the Thanjavur court.[41] That exclusive attribution can no longer be accepted; the varying coarseness of the weaves and the extraordinary variety of designs suggest that they were produced in a number of centres in Thanjavur District, but probably including Karuppur.

The fact that some of the Ii collection patterns are not found outside the country would suggest that they were produced to Japanese specifications, or at least with Japan as their intended market; the most common are a number of heraldic designs and a variety of interlocking hexagon and other geometric patterns. Other cloths are in Chinese style, such as an aquatic landscape with birds [230]; objects in Chinese taste had an established place in Japan.

The majority of Indian samples in the various *meibutsu-gire* books I have examined have designs intended for Southeast Asian markets rather than expressly for Japanese taste. This makes sense in terms of the historical trade sources, which repeatedly speak of Indian textiles purchased for supply to Japan in such ports as Banten, Batavia, Pattani or Ayutthaya. The variety represented also supports the observation of Ralph Coppendale in 1615 that the Japanese were a people liking change, always yearning after 'new and strange fashions', which would have encouraged a high degree of eclecticism.

The Gion Festival

The Japanese passion for foreign luxury goods is seen most dramatically today in the collections of cloths and carpets preserved by the Gion Matsuri

231 Processional floats, decorated with historical textiles from the merchant guilds' collections, being drawn through Kyoto during the Gion Festival. The earliest eye-witness description of the festival is provided by a Portuguese missionary in 1561, and it remains an annual event in the streets of the merchant quarter.

Tsuki-boko, the merchant guilds of the Gion district in Kyoto. Each July, in a display of prosperity expressed through a celebration of the exotic, these remarkable textiles are used to decorate all four sides of wooden floats which are paraded through the streets [231]. Similar floats occur at the neighbouring towns of Nagahama and Otsu. They are of two types – *hoko*, huge juggernauts which are pulled by thirty or forty men, and *yama*, palanquins which are carried by a similar number. The Gion guild collections include Indian cloths, Indian, Persian and Chinese carpets, and European tapestries. An early eighteenth-century Coromandel Coast *palampore* was until recently hung on the Minami-kannonyama guild's float [232]. It has an Oriental-style landscape with cranes and pine trees characteristic of cloths produced for export to Europe; designs of this type were particularly favoured in Holland, and in all probability Dutch merchants introduced this piece to Japan.[42] Of the carpets, many were inventoried in the eighteenth century, though at least three appear to be seventeenth-century Indian work;[43] Persian carpets are known to have been imported by the Dutch as early as 1636,[44] as are a group of Flemish tapestries.[45]

How did the guilds acquire these rare and wonderful textiles? The rise of the merchant class in Japan gained momentum in the seventeenth century, and represents a transfer of wealth from the nobility and *samurai* classes. It is recorded that foreign textiles were among gifts regularly presented to the shogun and his nobles by Europeans to ensure the renewal of their trading rights. With the gradual indebtedness of the nobility to merchant money-lenders, valued foreign textiles would appear to have changed hands to settle debts. The display of such luxury goods in the Gion and other festivals served to assert the economic ascendancy of the merchant classes in Japanese society and to underscore the value of imported Indian textiles.

Indian cloths and Japanese textile design

Whilst the volume of Indian textiles entering Japan was never great, they had a disproportionately large impact on Japanese textile design. They inspired a whole school of imitations, known as *wasarasa* ('Japanese *sarasa*'). Foreign *sarasa*, and especially Indian which was seen to be the most exotic, had been the preserve of the nobility, a privilege which had extended gradually to the wealthy merchant classes. With the growth of towns in the mid-Edo period (later seventeenth century), elite taste began to be imitated by the less wealthy sections of urban society. To satisfy this demand local workshops began producing relatively inexpensive cotton fabrics in Indian style.

Japanese imitations of Indian *sarasa* were made by a variety of techniques. As madder, the dye used in mordanting, was not available in Japan, a process was developed which replicated the effect. This was achieved by resist-dyeing with such sources as sappanwood, which was imported in great quantities from Thailand. Occasionally woodblock printing was used, for instance at Nabeshima.[46] A traditional paper-stencil method of applying the resist dye was also employed, in combination with a new spraying or blowing technique believed to have been introduced by the Dutch at Deshima, their residential quarter in Nagasaki; the resulting cloths were known as *fuki-e* or 'blown pictures'.

The area of Horikawa in Kyoto emerged in the eighteenth century as the centre for the manufacture of *wasarasa*. With increasing demand other centres appeared, such as Sakai, Nagasaki, and Nabeshima. Each quickly acquired a distinct character, though the bulk of the designs imitated Indian *sarasa*. With paper stencils it was possible to achieve results very similar to both traditional

232 Ceremonial hanging. Coromandel Coast, for the Japanese market; first half of the eighteenth century. Cotton, painted mordant-dyed and resist-dyed; 260 x 250 cm. Collection Minami-kannonyama Festival Preservation Society, Kyoto. ◆ This cloth was used until very recently to decorate the processional car of the Minami-kannonyama guild during the Gion Festival [cf. 231]; its original colours faded where it was exposed to light.

 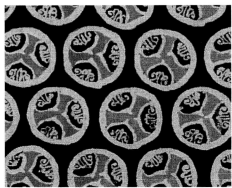 

These were among the most popular patterns for Indian sarasa *circulating in eighteenth-century Japan. With their circles, diamonds and intersecting octagons they are distinctly Japanese in taste, and can securely be said to have been made expressly for the local market.*

233–235 ABOVE Fragments of Indian *sarasa* (details). Coromandel Coast, for the Japanese market; eighteenth century. Cotton, painted mordant- and resist-dyed. Victoria and Albert Museum, London (233) and Collection Ii family, Tokyo National Museum (234, 235).

kalamkari and block-printing, but the Japanese cloths are usually very flat and even, lacking the depth of colour achieved by immersion-dyeing processes. Some *wasarasa*, however, consists of direct copies of such fidelity that distinguishing them from the Indian originals can often be difficult without samples of both being available for direct comparison. Other designs were done in the 'Indian manner' but with a distinctly Japanese flavour, revealed in the sombre blues, browns and greens of the colour schemes employed. This was a manifestation of the restrained taste known by the term *sabi*, which was recognized as early as the seventeenth century by East India Company officials who wrote of the market's preference for 'sad', i.e. dark or dull, colours.

The publication in Edo (Tokyo) in 1781 of *Sarasa benran*, a manual of Indian *sarasa* patterns available for replication by the technique of 'blown picture' stencilling, was a watershed, marking the rise in popularity of these Japanese imitations and serving to stimulate further their dissemination. The book features woodblock-printed illustrations of the more popular types, with notes of the appropriate colours [cf. 233–235 and 236–238]. The frequency with which new editions appeared[47] reflects growing demand among the urban population for textiles with richer patterns more in keeping with Indian designs. It was widely in use as a catalogue from which clients could select the *sarasa* patterns of their choice.

The Japanese market for Indian textiles was never of great commercial consequence, as it was in Indonesia at the height of the spice trade in the seventeenth century. Nonetheless, the presence of Indian painted cotton cloth, in a variety of designs, had a lasting impact on Japanese taste, and reflected an impassioned curiosity for the exotic.

236–238 Pages from an edition of the woodblock-printed *Sarasa benran*, first published in 1781 in Edo (Tokyo). Victoria and Albert Museum, London. ◆ The designs were copied from Indian *sarasa* available in eighteenth-century Japan (as seen in rare examples preserved by the *daimyo* Ii family of Hikone Province, opposite). They were then imitated locally by stencilling, in colours specified on the woodcuts. Such products were known as Kyo or Sakai *sarasa*.

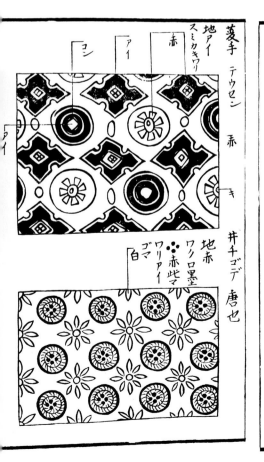

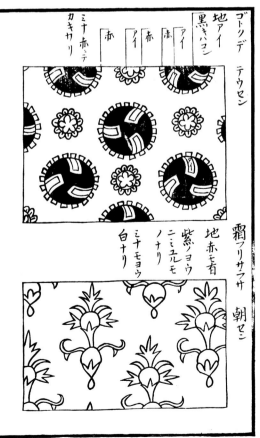

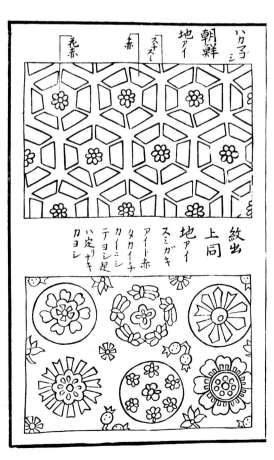

◆◆◆◆◆◆◆◆◆◆◆◆◆◆◆◆◆◆◆◆◆◆
NOTES
◆◆◆◆◆◆◆◆◆◆◆◆◆◆◆◆◆◆◆◆◆◆

I TEXTILES, CULTURE AND SPICES
(pp. 6–17)

1. Raychaudhuri, 1962; Chaudhuri, 1965, 1978; Das Gupta, 1979; Prakash, 1985; Arasaratnam, 1986; Hossain, 1988.
2. Laarhoven, 1993: 7.
3. Most notably the Tropen Museum, Amsterdam, the Rijksmuseum voor Volkenkunde, Leiden, and the Museum voor Volkenkunde, Rotterdam.
4. Irwin and Brett, 1970; Ramaswamy, 1985; Laarhoven, 1993.
5. Inventory of the Church of the Conceicão, Lisbon; Vassalo e Silva, 1993: 16–17.
6. Compare Geary, 1986.
7. Bayly, 1986: 288.
8. This interpretation is supported by the integration of the names of foreign cloths into those of the local versions.
9. Foster, 1904: 107.
10. Steensgard, 1973: 407.
11. For a summary history of the VOC, see Gastra in Meilink-Roelofsz, Raben and Spijkerman, 1992.
12. Excluding the unidentified threads recovered from Mohenjo Daro, contextually dated to *c.* 2000 BC. For radiocarbon datings, see below, p. 186, and Barnes, 1997b.

II TECHNIQUES AND PRODUCTION CENTRES
(pp. 18–33)

1. Schwartz, 1957: 24.
2. When European attention did finally turn to the study of Indian textile technology, it was as part of the spirit of technological enquiry which fuelled the Industrial Revolution. The ultimate effect of such studies was to make commercially redundant many of those very weaving and dyeing traditions, through mechanized looms and the development of synthetic dyes.
3. Tolat, 1982.
4. Katiresu, 1906. The name in Tamil is *shayaver*, a compound from *saya*, 'colour', and *ver*, 'root'. The botanical family of the plant is *Cinchonaceae*. The secret of the colour brilliance of the *chay* dye was its high calcium content, the result of shell deposits in the soil of delta regions.
5. Southeast Asia was the sole source of sappanwood (from the Malay *sapang*, 'red') until the discovery by the Portuguese of a similar dye-wood in South America. 'Brazil-wood' then gave its name to the country, Brazil.
6. Schoff, 1912.
7. A fourth-century AD treatise on state administration, based on earlier texts possibly originating in the Mauryan period, *c.* third century BC; Thapar, 1960.
8. For the etymology of 'chintz', see Irwin, 1959: 77.
9. For a fuller description of mordanting, see Irwin and Brett, 1970, and Gittinger, 1982: 19–21.
10. For a survey of *kalamkari*, see Varadarajan, 1982.
11. The Georges Rocques Manuscript, 1678; see Schwartz, 1969.
12. This information is based on personal observations and an interview with M. T. Gajjar of Pethapur in 1990.

13. See Bilgrami, 1990.
14. Where no penetration of the indigo occurs on the reverse of the cloth, it is very likely that the dye solution was applied by brush rather than by immersion in a dye bath.
15. De Bone, 1976: 54–55.
16. The *patola* technique was first described in detail by the Staffordshire silk manufacturer Thomas Wardle in 1886.
17. Barbosa, 1918–21: II, 198.
18. Cit. Buhler and Fischer, 1979: 321.
19. Francisco d'Andrade's account, in Nicholl, 1975: 22.
20. Lach, 1965: 642.
21. Guy, 1996.
22. Raychaudhuri and Habib, 1982: 271.
23. Das, 1992: 62–65.
24. Jayakar, 1955; Metha, 1961.
25. Schoff, 1912: 40–47.
26. Moreland, 1931: 35.
27. Mundy, 1914–19, II: 56; Arasaratnam and Ray, 1994.
28. Tavernier, 1977, I: 141.
29. For a masterful survey of the Coromandel Coast trade 1650–1740, see Arasaratnam, 1986.
30. See Murphy, 1991: 134.
31. Koloniaal Archief, no. 1262, 31 September 1682, cited in Brennig, 1975: 240.
32. Cited in Brennig, 1975: 137.
33. This unit, known as a *punjam* in Tamil, consisted of 120 threads in seventeenth-century sources, and by the nineteenth century rather less.

The Painting of Chintz
(pp. 34–37)

1. Ruurdje Laarhoven discovered this text in the course of archival research for her doctoral thesis (see Laarhoven, 1994).I am grateful to her for granting permission for her translation from the original Dutch to appear here in print for the first time.
2. Schwartz, 1966.
3. F. W. Stapel (ed.), *Pieter van Dam, Beschryvinge*, II, pt 2: 205–10. The observations were made one or two years earlier because it took that time for correspondence to reach the Netherlands. Van Rheede tot Drakesteyn was contracted as a naval cadet with the VOC in 1657, received the rank of approximate equivalence to second lieutenant in 1662 in Cochin, and soon became lieutenant, then captain. He was Commander of the Malabar Coast Office 1668–76, extraordinary Council Member in 1677, and repatriated in 1678. He returned as Commissioner-General in 1684 and inspected offices in Capetown, Sri Lanka, Bengal, Coromandel, and Surat. He died travelling near Bombay in 1691. Biography translated from Stapel, *General Missiven*, III (1666): 510, n. 2.
4. For *chay* see above, p. 19 and n. 4. While a red dye was made from it, in VOC documents 'chay' is often a general term for colour.
5. Mannar is a small island between Sri Lanka and Madura after which the Mannar Gulf is named.
6. *Ruynas* (in VOC sources) or *runas*, from the Persian for a type of madder, was a trade item of the Company.
7. *Patta* is the name of a tree, *saya* the colour of the dye.
8. *Mirabolanus citrini* is a plum-like fruit of the Mirabolans family.
9. *Kanji*, also written as *cansy* or *cangi*, is the Malay term for ricewater or starch.
10. Also used were the fibres of plants, such as pineapple and aloe; see G. P. Rouffaer, 'Vragen

over de Zuid-Dekhan'sche (Tamiel'sche) Wasteekenkunst en verfkunst', *BTLV* 716: 3.
11. Stapel (cit. at n. 3), noted that the Sanskrit *sura* is the general name for the fermented sap of the cocospalm and other palms.
12. Dark red and blue colours reminiscent of the neck of a dove.
13. The translator noted that this was an incorrect guess of van Rheede: the silk cloths and clothes were painted entirely by hand.

III INDIAN CLOTH AND INTERNATIONAL TRADE
(pp. 38–53)

1. Pires, 1944: 42, 46.
2. Dr Shokoohy, Indian Ocean Trade Seminar, University of London, November 1996. A number of mosques of considerably earlier date survive in southern India which are also legacies of international trade with the Arab world, such as one in Trichinopoly, Tamilnadu, which bears a foundation inscription dating the structure to the eighth century; personal communication from Dr Raja Mohamad, 1997.
3. The prevalent style of early Islamic architecture in India was Persian. Arabic mosque architecture of this period differs in having a projecting *mihrab*.
4. Goitein, 1966: 338, 349–50.
5. Mortel, 1994: 22–23.
6. This study was begun by Pfister, 1936, 1938.
7. Ahmad, 1989: 6–7.
8. Hirth and Rockhill, 1911: 92–93.
9. Latham, 1958: 293.
10. Digby, 1980: 130.
11. Goitein, 1967–83.
12. Huntington, 1980: 33,42.
13. Pliny, 1826: bk xii, chts. 48, 63.
14. Whitcomb and Johnson, 1979, 1982, and Vogelwood-Eastwood, 1990: no. 52.
15. Kubiak and Scanlon, 1989: frontispiece no. 2. The term 'Z-spun' refers to the direction of twist on a combined thread made of up of two or more spun yarns; see Emery, 1966: 11.
16. Ashmolean Museum, Oxford, Newberry Collection; Barnes, 1997a, 1997b.
17. Personal communication from George Scanlon.
18. Goitein, I, 1967: 107.
19. Goitein, 1967–83.
20. Goitein, I, 1967: 45.
21. An alternative explanation, however, may be that such records do not accurately reflect the situation, as cloths were generally classified by function and colour rather than fabric type.
22. Goitein, IV, 1983: 185.
23. Ibid.: 151.
24. Ibid.: 170.
25. Ibid.: 159.
26. Pearson, 1994.
27. This office appears to have evolved into that of *shah-bender* or *shahbandar*, the foreign merchants' representative, to be found in every major Southeast Asian port.
28. A Chinese glazed stoneware jar, probably of Guangdong manufacture, was excavated from the foundations of the Great Mosque at Siraf, dated by associated coins as anterior to 850. See Guy, 1987: fig. 7.
29. Shahriyar, 1981.
30. Stern, 1967.
31. Barbosa, 1918–21: II, 56.
32. Fryer, 1698: 223.
33. Tavernier, 1925: I, 46.
34. Ibid.: 47.
35. It is revealing that in the years 1914–31, Indonesian Muslims made up 50 per cent of all pilgrims to Mecca; Lombard, 1990: 62.
36. Goitein, IV, 1983: 173–75.

37. Dated 1555±55 years; Barnes, 1996: fig. 5.
38. Coomaraswamy, 1927.
39. Barnes, 1993: no. 37.

IV THE ASIAN TRADE BEFORE EUROPEAN
INTERVENTION
(pp. 54–63)

1. Karashima, 1995: 6–8.
2. Archaeological evidence indicates trade contacts
   even earlier; see Glover, 1989.
3. Guy, 1994.
4. Chou ta-kuan [Zhou Daguan], 1967: 22–23.
5. Ibid.: 27.
6. Ibid.: 37.
7. Ibid.: 23.
8. Reynolds, 1982: 176. According to Zhou
   Daguan, sericulture had recently been
   introduced into Cambodia by Thai settlers
   for commoners' use, but the palace used
   imported silks for weaving; Chou ta-kuan,
   1967: 37.
9. The *sima* inscriptions record the granting of
   land revenue and labour, usually for the benefit
   of a temple.
10. Wisseman Christie, 1993: 183.
11. Barrett Jones, 1984: 33, and Wisseman
    Christie, 1993.
12. For the implications of the term *tulis* for the
    evolution of batik, see Wisseman Christie,
    1993.
13. Scheurleer and Klooke, 1988: pls. 14–17.
14. Ma Huan, 1970: 87.
15. Robson, 1981: 108–9.
16. As described in the *kidung* literature; see
    Robson, 1981.

V THE MALAY WORLD
(pp. 64–75)

1. Pires, 1944: 45.
2. Ibid.
3. Ma Huan, 1970: 108–9, and n. 2.
4. Barbosa, 1918–21: 176.
5. Pires, 1944: 269.
6. Ibid.: 45.
7. Ibid.: 207.
8. Floris, 1934: 71.
9. Glamann, 1958: 141.
10. VOC records cited in Andaya, 1989: 37.
11. Pires, 1944: 161.
12. Crawford, 1820.
13. Marsden, 1966: 177.
14. Anderson, 1971.
15. Ma Huan, 1970: 110.
16. Ma Huan would not have described Chinese
    silk as 'foreign cloth'.
17. Marsden, 1966: 367, 377.
18. Ibid.: 323.
19. Anderson, 1971: 83.
20. Watson, 1989: 42.
21. Gallop, 1991: 56.
22. These were typically luxury novelty items, such
    as clocks, telescopes, mirrors and glass
    chandeliers, all of European manufacture.
23. Niessen, 1991: 8.
24. Watson, 1989: 33.
25. Sandbukt, 1988: 126.
26. Drakard, 1990.
27. As noted by Johan Splinter Stavorinus, a VOC
    officer and astute observer of Batavian society;
    trans. Moore, 1978: 21.
28. Hilgers-Hesse, 1985: 196. For a description of
    a Jambi wedding, with the ceremonial gift
    exchange of cloth, see Kerlogue, 1996: 12–13.
29. Kerlogue, 1996: 14–15.
30. Watson, 1989: 31.
31. Pires, 1944: 108 and 180.
32. Ibid.: 207.

VI INDONESIA
(pp. 76–119)

1. Pires, 1944: 180.
2. Raffles, 1830: I, 95.
3. For a Gujarati tombstone found in Java, see
   Lohuizen-de Leeuw, 1966, and for their
   distribution elsewhere in the Indian Ocean, see
   Porter, 1988.
4. Jones and Temple, 1928.
5. Meilink-Roelofsz 1962: 165.
6. Van der Chijs, 1885–1900: I, 238.
7. Lombard, 1990: I, 108.
8. Pelrus, 1995.
9. I am indebted to R. Laarhoven for this
   information. For these and other VOC
   regulations, see van der Chijs, 1885–1900.
10. Laarhoven, 1993: 7.
11. Nieuhof, 1988: 269.
12. Arsip Nasional Republic Indonesia, Jakarta.
    Archive: Bijlagen resoluties kasteel Batavia inv.
    nr 8, fols. 335–43, 29 July 1721. Personal
    communication from Remco Raben, 1994.
13. Algemeen Rijksarchief, The Hague. Archive:
    Schepenbank Batavia inv. nr 11983, criminal
    papers, fols. 102 ff.
14. Nagtegaal, 1996: 147–49.
15. Personal communication from Femme Gastra,
    December 1992.
16. The cloth dated 1763 is a large cotton with a
    floral meander design. It appeared on the art
    market in 1989; present location unknown. For
    the 1766 example, see Yoshimoto, 1996: 99.
17. I am grateful to Vesta Curtis and Venetia Porter
    of the British Museum for their readings of the
    Persian inscription.
18. Barnes, 1996: fig. 14.
19. Foster, 1926: 113.
20. Raffles, 1830: I, 95.
21. Ibid. : 94.
22. Nooy-Palm, 1979.
23. Nooy-Palm, 1980: 88.
24. Nooy-Palm, 1979: 257-76.
25. Nooy-Palm, 1979.
26. Prakash, 1984: 251.
27. Buhler and Fischer, 1979: 322.
28. Van der Chijs, 1885–1900: III, 37, 120.
29. Fox, 1977: 98.
30. Forth, 1981: 463.
31. Barnes, 1989a, and 1989b: 49.
32. Graham, 1994: 237.
33. Holmgren and Spertus, 1991: 83–84, col. pl.
    10.
34. A *patolu* with inscriptions published by Buhler
    and Fischer (1979: II, 32) is not strictly
    comparable, the inscription being across the
    end-border, not integral to the central field
    design. This cloth is of a type produced for the
    Indian domestic market.
35. Vogelsang-Eastwood, 1990: no. 52.
36. Barnes, 1997: nos 1017–19.
37. Hamilton, 1994: 32, 158.
38. Buhler and Ramsayer, 1975.
39. Barnes, 1989.
40. Holmgren and Spertus, 1989: no. 17.
41. See below, p. 186.
42. Raffles, 1830: 96–98.
43. Personal communication from Ebeltje
    Hartkamp-Jonxis, 1992.
44. Veldhuisen-Djajasoebrata, 1984: 77–78.
45. Irwin and Brett, 1970: 16.
46. Cf. Hartkamp-Jonxis, 1987: no. 107,
    frontispiece.
47. Guy, 1995, fig. 60.
48. Ill. Gittinger, 1982: 52.
49. Grey, 1892: II, 258–59.
50. Information based on a reading of the
    inscription by P. C. Parikh, to whom I am
    indebted.

51. When this cloth was first published the date
    was interpreted as a Saka era date, which
    corresponded to AD 1634; see Guy, 1989: 58.
52. Hirth and Rockhill, 1911: 92.
53. Gittinger, 1982: fig. 13.
54. The popularity of the *Ramayana* in post-
    classical Java is witnessed by the appearance of
    an early fifteenth-century Javanese version, the
    Ramayana Kakawin; see Santoso, 1980.
55. Depierre, 1909.
56. Van der Chijs, 1885–1900: II, 121.
57. The publication of Savary des Bruslon's
    Dictionnaire universel du commerce (1723) was
    a turning point in the regulation of quality
    control in France and Flanders.
58. Reddy, 1986: 265–67.
59. Raffles, 1830: I, 190–91.
60. Ibid.: 241.
61. Laarhoven, 1993: 15–16.
62. Van der Chijs, 1885–1900: III, 429.
63. Watson, 1989: 40.
64. Laarhoven, 1993: 15–16.
65. Rouffaer and Juynboll, 1914.
66. Veldhuisen-Djajasoebrata, 1980.

VII 'CLOTHS IN THE FASHION OF SIAM'
(pp. 120–51)

1. Pires, 1944: 108.
2. According to the *Khamhaikan Chao Krungkao*
   ('Testimony of the People of the Old Capital'),
   cited in Kasetsiri, 1992: 75.
3. Guy, 1986.
4. Charnvit, 1976: 81–82.
5. Ma Huan, 1970: 106.
6. Kobata and Matsuda, 1969: 64.
7. Ten bolts of red cloth are mentioned in each
   shipment; ibid., 87–92.
8. Ma Huan, cited in ibid.: 87.
9. Pires, 1944: 108.
10. Ibid.
11. The political control of these ports shifted
    between Thailand and Burma, and today both
    lie within Burmese territory.
12. Barbosa, 1918–21: II, 164.
13. Penth, 1994: 26–27.
14. In a document dated 1425; Kobata and
    Matsuda, 1969: 55.
15. Kasetsiri, 1992: 78.
16. Schouten, 1889: 125.
17. Ibid.: 130 and 148.
18. Smith, 1977: 92.
19. Floris, 1934: 56.
20. Nakamura, 1939.
21. Kaempfer, 1966: 24.
22. Floris, 1934: 73–74.
23. Smith, 1977: 96.
24. Pombejra, 1992: 51.
25. Hamilton, 1930: 101.
26. La Loubère, 1986. It is a measure of the interest
    in reports such as those of La Loubère (1691)
    and Tachard (see below) that they were
    translated into other European languages with
    remarkable speed, La Loubère appearing in
    Dutch simultaneously, and in English two years
    later.
27. Smith, 1977: 59.
28. Van Vliet, 1910: 89.
29. Gervaise, 1989: 217.
30. Ibid.: 238.
31. See Arasaratnam, 1986, for a study of this
    tradein the period 1650–1700.
32. Bassett, 1990: 12–13.
33. The disparity between European and Asian
    sources makes statistical comparisons
    problematic, as does the sub-contracting of
    Asian ships by European companies; see Das
    Gupta, 1986: 12–13.
34. Gervaise, 1989: 62.

35. Van Vliet, 1910: 63.
36. Tachard, 1981: 167. Tachard, published in French in 1686, appeared in English in 1688.
37. La Loubère, 1986: 26–27.
38. La Loubère, *Du royaume de Siam*, Paris, 1691: I, 98; translation by Emily Lane.
39. Ibrahim, 1972: 75–77.
40. Tachard, 1981; 156 and 175.
41. Van Linschoten, 1885: I, 91.
42. Smithies, 1986: 76. Some forty years later Savary des Bruslon's *Dictionnaire universel du commerce* (1723) refers to a problem posed by the unregulated (and untaxed) weaving of cotton–linen blend cloth in the *siamoise* mode in the French countryside; see Reddy, 1986: 268.
43. Terpatra, 1911, quoted in Floris, 1934: 71, n. 6.
44. India Office Records, *Records of the Relations*, 1915–21: II.
45. Irwin and Schwartz, 1966: 69.
46. Floor, 1987: 22.
47. Simmonds, 1963: 599.
48. Wyatt, 1986.
49. Van Linschoten, 1889: I, 91.
50. Middleton, 1943: 184.
51. Morehead, 1931: 39.
52. Simmonds, 1965: 220–22. The letter is from Lady Chan, widow of the governor of Thalang, peninsular Thailand, July 1787.
53. Repr. Gittinger, 1982: 92.
54. For this and other examples of recurring motifs in Thai design, see Guy and Richards, 1993.
55. Srinuan, 1984: 43.
56. A French ell (*aune*) varied between around 1.2 and 1.4 metres; in 1837 it was standardized at 1.2 metres.
57. Gervaise, 1989: 91–92.
58. La Loubère, 1986: 25.
59. Smithies, 1986: 44.
60. Manrique, 1927: 74. Manrique's account of his travels between 1629 and 1643 was first published in English translation as early as 1649, reflecting the keen interest across Europe in first-hand descriptions of Asia.
61. La Loubère, 1986: 30.
62. Ibrahim, 1972: 54.
63. Bowring, 1969: 238.
64. Quaritch Wales, 1931: 240, 247, and personal communication from Phaothong Thongchua, 1994.
65. Moffat, 1961: 205.
66. Bowring, 1969: 238.
67. John Irwin, 'Diary notes on a brief tour of block-printing centres in western India, February 1957', unpublished typescript, Victoria and Albert Museum; see also Archambault, 1989: 71.

VIII CHINA
(pp. 152–57)

1. Cited in Sastri, 1939: 118.
2. Some cultivation of cotton occurred in the western extremities of the kingdom, in Turfan and Khotan; see Kuhn, 1988: 58.
3. Legge, 1886.
4. Ray, 1995: 45–46.
5. Hirth and Rockhill, 1911: 218.
6. Lo Hsiang-lin, 1967: 177.
7. Tibbetts, 1979: 37.
8. Rockhill, 1914: 420–25.
9. Battuta, 1929: 284.
10. Wong, 1979: entry 15.
11. Hirth and Rockhill, 1911: 218.

12. The *Nan zhi* is an account of the commerce of Hainan Island by Chen Dazhen and Lu Guisun, published in the Dade period (1297–1307); translation provided by Craig Clunas.
13. Guy, 1993: 299.
14. Recorded in the *Yuan shi*, Rockhill, 1914: 431.
15. Guy, 1993.
16. Wang Dayuan, 1349; translation provided by Craig Clunas.
17. Lee, 1995: 178.
18. Ma Huan, 1970: 162–63.
19. Ray, 1993: 144.
20. I have followed Ray, 1993: ch. 4 in his identification of Chinese terms with Indian textile types.
21. Pires, 1944: 130.
22. Taylor, 1993: 49–50.
23. I observed this whilst surveying the area in 1990. Significant quantities of Chinese and northern Vietnamese ceramics were also retrieved from shipwrecks off Hoi An in the late 1980s and 1990s. These finds are largely undocumented, but for a comparable cargo found off the southern coast of Vietnam near Con Dao Island, see Christie's, *The Vung Tau Cargo*, sale catalogue, Amsterdam, 7 April 1992.
24. Reid, 1993: 312.
25. Phan Huy Le, 1993: 6.
26. François Baron (1685), cited in Reid, 1993: 91.
27. Farrington, 1993: 133.

IX THE JAPAN TRADE
(pp. 158–77)

1. East India Correspondence, Ralph Coppendale at Hirado, Japan, to Robert Larkin at Pattani, Thailand, 5 Dec. 1615; IOR: E/3/3, no. 317, in Farrington, 1991: 344.
2. Caron 1986: 85.
3. The oldest group of non-excavated textiles in Japan, imports from Central Asia and Tang China, known as *jodai-gire* ('ancient fabrics'), are preserved in the Shoso-in, the imperial storehouse in the grounds of the Todai-ji temple at Nara.
4. The *Rekidai Hoan*, discovered in Okinawa in 1932, chronicles the commercial dealings of the Ryukyu royal household between 1424 and 1827. Papers pertaining to relations with Korea and Southeast Asia between 1425 and 1638 were published by Kobata and Matsuda, 1969.
5. Kobata and Matsuda, 1969: 64.
6. Pires, 1944: 130–31.
7. Japan was famed for its high-grade silver, as witnessed by Luis de Camões (Camoens) in his *Lusiads*; Camoens, 1952.
8. Kano Domi was active in the late sixteenth and early seventeenth centuries. A Christian convert, he was renowned as a painter of *namban* pictures. In 1603 he departed Japan for Manila.
9. Van Linschoten, 1885: I, 91.
10. Iwao, 1976: 8.
11. Southeast Asian ceramics are known by a number of terms in tea ceremony connoisseurship, most notably *namban* ('southern barbarian' wares) and *shimamono* ('island goods').
12. Nishida, 1993.
13. Caron, 1986: 80.
14. Iwao, 1976: 10.
15. Samples of Cham textiles are preserved in albums in the Kanebo Museum of Textiles, Osaka, and the Ii collection, Tokyo National Museum.
16. *De Liefde* was in fact shipwrecked off the coast of Kyushu, but some of her crew survived and settled in Japan as independent merchants (*vrijburger*).
17. Farrington, 1991: 586.
18. Caron, 1986: 120.
19. Kato, 1976.
20. Bernier, 1891: 203.
21. Tavernier, 1977, vol. 2: 2–3.
22. Ishii, 1971: 162–63.
23. Ibid.: 164.
24. Arasaratnam, 1986: 145.
25. Omori, 1991: 200–201.
26. Mendonca, 1978: 15. As early as 1526 the Portuguese were using 'tapestries' and other pictorial cloths from Portugal as presents to local rulers in Southeast Asia; Nicholl, 1975: 22–23. It would appear therefore that Portuguese, Bengali and Melakan pictorial cloths, woven and embroidered, were distributed as gifts to heads of state.
27. No record of its provenance is preserved at the Tokugawa Museum, Nagoya.
28. Mendes Pinto, 1993: 182–88.
29. Ogasawara, 1993.
30. Kobe, 1984: nos. 180–82.
31. Culin, 1918: 133.
32. Hartkamp-Jonxis, 1987: no. 131.
33. Holgrem and Spertus, 1991, coined the termed '*geringsing* chintz' to describe Indian painted cotton imitations of Balinese double-ikat silk, known locally as *geringsing*.
34. Ill. Yoshioka and Yoshimoto, 1980: pl. 11.
35. Culin, 1918: 134.
36. The most eminent of these is the *Chaki Meibutsu Shu* (Catalogue of Famous Tea Utensils), written in the Momoyama period (1573–1615).
37. Published by N. Gwatkin in Gittinger, 1982: figs. 79–99.
38. Kirihata, 1978.
39. See e.g. Hartkamp-Jonxis, 1987: no. 148.
40. The Ii collection, consisting of 450 textile samples, is in the Tokyo National Museum, and has been extensively published; see Ogasawara, 1980, 1989, and Nishida, 1993.
41. The Thanjavur group was first noted by W. S. Hadaway in his *Cotton painting and printing in the Madras Presidency* (1917), and swatches were transferred to the Victoria and Albert Museum in 1920.
42. Hartkamp-Jonxis, 1987: no. 143. Other examples are now in the Cooper-Hewitt Museum, New York, and the Royal Ontario Museum, Toronto.
43. See Kajitani and Kojiro, 1992; Gion, 1994: 52–63; Walker, 1997: 136, fig. 59.
44. According to François Caron, who was in Japan between 1619 and 1641, Persian carpets were purchased by the VOC factory in Hormuz in the Persian Gulf and shipped via Batavia to Japan; Caron, 1986.
45. One such Flemish tapestry is recorded as being installed in the Tokugawa family temple of Zojo-ji, near Tokyo, shortly after the death of Tokugawa Ieyasu in 1616. It relates closely to other examples in Kyoto guild collections which were made in the workshops of Brussels in the 1590s and presumably shipped to Japan shortly thereafter; see Vlam, 1981: 480–85.
46. Yoshioka, 1993: 95.
47. With minor alterations, in 1781, 1784 and 1808.

◆◆◆◆◆◆◆◆◆◆◆◆◆◆◆◆◆◆◆◆◆

BIBLIOGRAPHY

◆◆◆◆◆◆◆◆◆◆◆◆◆◆◆◆◆◆◆◆◆

BEFEO   *Bulletin de l'Ecole Française d'Extrême-Orient*

BTLV   *Bijdragen tot de Taal-, Land- en Volkenkunde*

BMJ   *Brunei Museum Journal*

IESHR   *Indian Economic and Social History Review*

JESHO   *Journal of the Economic and Social History of the Orient*

JIA[I]   *Journal of Indian Art [and Industry]*

JITH   *Journal of Indian Textile History*

JMBRAS   *Journal of the Malaysian Branch of the Royal Asiatic Society*

JRAS   *Journal of the Royal Asiatic Society*

JSS   *Journal of the Siam Society*

Abraham, M., *Two Merchant Guilds of South India*, New Delhi, 1988.

Ahmad, A., *Indo-Portuguese Trade in the Seventeenth Century (1600–1663)*, New Delhi,1991.

Alam, S. M., 'Masulipatnam – A metropolitan port in the seventeenth century', *Islamic Culture*, vol. 33, no. 3, 1959: 169–87.

Albuquerque, B. de, *The Commentaries of the Great Alfonso Albuquerque* (1688), ed. W. de Gray Birch, London, 1880.

Algemeen Rijksarchief, The Hague, *Vereenigde Oostindische Compagnie, VOC : Uit Indie Overgekomen Brieven en Papieren and Bataviaas Inkomend Briefboek.*

Andaya, L. Y., *The Heritage of Arung Palakka: A History of South Sulawesi (Celebes) in the Seventeenth Century,* The Hague, 1981.

—— *The World of Maluku. Eastern Indonesia in the Early Modern Period,* Honolulu, 1993.

Anderson, J., *Mission to the East Coast of Sumatra in 1823* (1826), intro. N. Tarling, Kuala Lumpur, 1971.

—— *Political and commercial considerations relative to the Malay Peninsula and British settlements in the Straits of Malacca,* Prince of Wales Island, 1824 (repr. Kuala Lumpur, 1989).

Andhra Pradesh State Archives, *District Records, Masulipatam. Consultations,* vol. 2837, 1786–vol. 2973, 1799.

Anon., 'Calico printing (in Gujarat)', *Journal of Indian Arts,* vol. 1, no. 16, London, 1886: 128–30.

Anon., 'Kalamkari temple cloth painting and cotton printing at Masulipatam', *Census of India,* 1961, vol. II-VII A-I.

Appadurai, A., *Economic Conditions in Southern India (1000–1500 A.D.),* 2 vols, Madras, 1936.

Appadurai, Arjun (ed.), *The social life of things. Commodities in cultural perspective,* Cambridge, 1986.

Arasaratnam, S., 'Dutch East India Company and the Kingdom of Madura 1650–1700', *Tamil Culture,* vol. IX, no. 1, 1963: 48–74.

—— 'A note on Periathamy Marikkar – a 17th century Commercial Magnate', *Tamil Culture,* vol. X, no. 1, 1965: 1–7.

—— 'Indian Merchants and their Trading Methods, circa 1700', *ISEHR,* vol. 3, no.1, 1966: 85–95.

—— 'The Dutch East India Company and its Coromandel trade, 1700–1740', *BKITLV,* no. 123, 1967: 325–46.

—— 'Some notes on the Dutch in Malacca and the Indo-Malayan trade 1641–1670', *Journal of Southeast Asian History,* vol. X, no. 3, 1969: 480–90.

—— 'The Indian commercial groups and European traders 1600–1800: changing relationships in southeastern India', *South Asia,* (n.s.), vol. 1, no. 2, 1978: 42–53.

—— 'Weavers merchants and Company: the handloom industry in South-eastern India 1750–1790', *IESHR,* vol. XVII, no. 3, 1980: 257–81.

—— *Merchants, Companies and Commerce on the Coromandel Coast, 1650–1740,* New Delhi, 1986.

—— *Maritime Commerce and English Power: Southeast India, 1750–1800,* New Delhi, 1996.

—— 'Blockprinted fabrics of Gujarat for export to Siam: an encounter with Mr Maneklal T. Gajjar', *JSS,* vol. 77, pt 2, 1989: 71–73.

Babu, S., 'Commodity Composition of the English Trade on the Coromandel Coast (1611–1652)', in Mathew, 1995: 261–72.

Baker G. P., *Calico Painting and Printing in the East Indies in the 17th and 18th Centuries,* London, 1921.

Baldaeus, Philippus, *Naauwkeurige Beschryvinge van Malabar en Choromandel,* Amsterdam, 1672.

Baldry, J., *Textile in Yemen. Historical references to trade and commerce in textiles in Yemen from antiquity to modern times,* British Museum Occasional Paper no. 27, London, 1982.

[Bangkok] Taikoku Kokoritsu Hakubutsukan (National Museum of Thailand), *Taikoku Kodai Senshoku* (Old Textiles of Thailand), Tokyo, 1965.

Barbosa, Duarte, *The Book of Duarte Barbosa. An account of the Countries Bordering on the Indian Ocean and Their Inhabitants , 1518,* 2 vols, trans. M. Langworth Dames, London, 1918–21 (repr. New Delhi, 1989).

Barnes, R., *The Ikat Textiles of Lamalema: A Study of an Eastern Indonesian Weaving Tradition,* Leiden, 1989.

—— *Indian Block-printed Cotton Fragments in the Kelsey Museum, The University of Michigan,* Ann Arbor, 1993.

—— 'Indian Trade Textiles', *Hali,* no. 87, July 1996: 80–85.

—— 'From India to Egypt: The Newberry Collection and the Indian Ocean Trade', *Islamische Textilkunst des Mittelalters: Aktuelle Probleme,* Abegg-Stiftung Riggisberg, 1997a: 79–92.

—— *Indian Block-printed Textiles in Egypt. The Newberry Collection in the Ashmolean Museum, Oxford,* 2 vols, Oxford, 1997b.

Barrett Jones, A. M., *Early Tenth Century Java from the Inscriptions,* Dordrecht, 1984.

Bassett, D. K., 'English trade in the Celebes, 1613–1667', *JMBRAS,* vol. 31, pt I, 1958: 1–39.

—— 'English relations with Siam in the seventeenth century', *JMBRAS,* vol 34, pt II, 1961: 90–105.

—— 'British "Country" trade and local trade networks in the Thai and Malay states, c.1680–1770', *Modern Asian Studies,* vol. 23, no. 4, 1989: 625–43.

—— *The British in South-east Asia during the seventeenth and eighteenth centuries,* Hull, 1990.

Bastin, J. S., *The British in West Sumatra 1685–1825: a selection of documents,* Kuala Lumpur, 1965.

Bayly, C. A., 'The origins of Swadeshi (home industry): cloth and Indian society, 1700–1930', in Apparadurai, 1986: 285–321.

Beer, A. B., *Trade Goods. A Study of Indian Chintz,* Washington, D.C., 1970.

Berinstain, V., et al., *Indiennes et palampores à l'Ille Bourdon au XCIIIe siècle,* Maison Française du Meuble Créole, Saint-Louis, La Réunion, 1994.

Bernet Kempers, A. J., *Ancient Indonesian Art,* Cambridge, Mass., 1959.

Bernier, François, *Travels in the Mogul Empire, A.D. 1656–1668,* trans. I. Brock, London, 1891 (repr. Delhi, 1968).

Best, T., *The Voyage of Thomas Best to the East Indies, 1612–1614,* ed. W. Foster, London, 1934 (repr. 1980).

Bhattacharya, B., 'The Dutch East India Company and the Trade of the *Chulias* in the Bay of Bengal in the Late Eighteenth Century', in Mathew, 1996: 347–62.

Bilgrami, N., *Sindh jo ajrak,* Karachi, 1990.

Birdwood, G. and Foster, W. (eds), *The First Letter Book of the East India Company 1600–1619,* London, 1892.

Blair, E. H. and Robertson, J. A. (eds), *The Philippine Islands, 1493–1898,* 55 vols, Cleveland, 1903–9.

Blussé, L., 'Chinese trade in Batavia during the days of the V.O.C.', *Archipel,* no. 18, 1979: 195–214.

—— *Strange Company, Chinese Settlers, mestizo women and the Dutch in VOC Batavia,* Utrecht, 1986.

—— and Gaastra, F. (eds), *Companies and Trade. Essays on Overseas Trading Companies during the Ancien Régime,* Leiden, 1981.

Boussac, M.-F. and Salles, J.-F. (eds), *Athens, Aden, Arikamedu: Essays on the Interrelations between India, Arabia and the Eastern Mediterranean,* Delhi, 1995.

Bowery, T., *A Geographical Account of Countries Round the Bay of Bengal, 1669 to 1679,* ed. R.C. Temple, Cambridge, 1905.

Bowring, Sir J., *The kingdom and people of Siam with a narrative of the mission to that country in 1855,* London, 1857 (repr. Kuala Lumpur, 1969).

Boxer, C. R., *A True Description of the Mighty Kingdoms of Japan and Siam by François Caron and Joost Schouten* (1671), London, 1935 (repr. of the 1883 edn with intro. and notes by Boxer).

—— *South China in the 16th Century, being the Narratives of Galeste Pereira, Fr. Gaspar da Cruz, Fr. Martin de Rada, 1550–1575,* London, 1953.

—— *The Dutch Seaborne Empire 1600–1800,* London, 1965.

—— *The Portuguese Seaborne Empire 1415–1825,* London, 1969.

Breck, J., 'Four 17th century Pintadoes', *Metropolitan Museum Studies,* New York,1929.

Brennig, J. J., *The Textile Trade of Seventeenth-Century Northern Coromandel: A Study of a Pre-Modern Asian Export Industry,* PhD, U. of Wisconsin-Madison, 1975; University Microfilms, Ann Arbor, 1992.

—— 'Chief merchants and European enclaves of 17th century Coromandel', *Modern Asian Studies,* vol. 11, pt 3, 1977: 321–46.

—— 'Joint-stock Companies of Coromandel', in B. B. King and M. N. Pearson (eds), *The Age of Partnership,* Honolulu, 1979: 71–94.

Brett, K. B., 'The flowering tree in Indian chintz', *JITH,* no. III, 1957: 45–49.

—— 'The Japanese style in Indian chintz design', *JITH,* no. V, 1960: 42–50.

Brommer, B., *Bontjes voor de tropen. De export van imitatienweefsels naar de tropen,* Zwolle, 1991.

Bruijn, J. R., Gaastra, F. S., Schoffer, I., et al., *Dutch–Asiatic shipping in the 17th and 18th centuries. Vol. 1,* The Hague, 1987.

—— and Gaastra, F. S. (eds), *Ships, Sailors and Spices. East India Companies and their Shipping in the sixteenth, seventeenth and eighteenth centuries,* Amsterdam, 1993.

Brummelhuis, H. ten, *Merchant, Courtier and Diplomat: A History of the Contacts between the Netherlands and Thailand,* Lochem, 1987.

Buchanan, F. H., *A Journey from Madras through the countries of Mysore, Canara and Malabar,* 3 vols, London, 1807.

Buhler, A., 'Patola Influences in Southeast Asia', *JITH,* vol. 4, 1959: 4–46.

—— *Ikat, Batik, Plangi,* 3 vols, Basel, 1972.

—— Ramseyer, U., and Oygi, N. R., *Patola und Gringsing,* Museum für Volkerkunde, Basel, 1975.

—— and Fischer E., *Clamp Resist Dyeing of Fabrics,* Calico Museum of Textiles, Ahmedabad, 1977.

—— *The Patola of Gujarat,* 2 vols, Basel, 1979.

Calico Museum of Textiles, Ahmedabad, *Treasures of Indian Textiles,* Bombay, 1980.

—— *The Chintz Collection. The Calico Museum of Textiles, India,* 2 vols, Ahmedabad, 1983.

Camoens, L. Vaz de, *The Lusiads,* Harmondsworth, 1952.

Carletti, F., *My Voyage Around the World* (1594–1606), trans. H. Weinstock, London, 1965.

Caron, F., *A True Description of the Mighty Kingdoms of Japan and Siam* (1671), intro. J. Villiers, Bangkok, 1986. See also Boxer 1935.

Carswell, J., 'The port of Mantai, Sri Lanka', in V. Begley and R. D. De Puma (eds), *Rome and India. The Ancient Sea Trade,* Madison and Delhi, 1992: 197–203.

Chandra, M., *Jain Miniature Paintings from Western India,* Ahmedabad, 1948.

—— *Costumes, Textiles, Cosmetics and Coiffure in Ancient and Medieval India,* Delhi, 1973.

Chandra, S. (ed.), *The Indian Ocean. Explorations in history, commerce and politics,* New Delhi, 1987.

Charnvit, K., *The Rise of Ayudhya. A History of Siam in the fourteenth and fifteenth centuries,* Kuala Lumpur, 1976.

Chaudhuri, K. N., *The English East India Company. The Study of an Early Joint-Stock Company 1600–1640,* London, 1965.

—— 'The Structure of the Indian Textile Industry in the Seventeenth and Eighteenth Centuries', *IESHR,* vol. XI, nos. 2–3, 1974: 127–82.

—— *The Trading World of Asia and the English East India Company 1660–1760,* Cambridge, 1978.

—— *Trade and Civilization in the Indian Ocean: an economic history from the rise of Islam to 1750,* Cambridge, 1985.

—— *Asia before Europe: economy and civilization of the*

Indian Ocean from the rise of Islam to 1750, Cambridge, 1990.

Chaudhury, S., 'The Rise and Decline of Hugli, a port in Medieval Bengal', *Bengal Past and Present*, vol. 86, 1967: 33–67.

Chaumont, A. de, *Relation de l'ambassade de Mr. le Chevalier de Chaumont à la cour du Roy de Siam*, Paris, 1686.

Chen Da Zhen and Lu Guisun, *Nan zhi* ('Gazetteer of the South Seas'), Dade period (1297–1307). Ms. photocopy.

Chijs, J. A. van der, *Nederlandsch-Indisch Plakaatboek, 1602–1811*, 17 vols, The Hague, 1885–1900.

Choisy, A., *Journal du voyage de Siam fait en 1685 et 1686* (1687), ed. M. Gascon, Paris,1930.

Chongkol, C. 'Textiles and Costume in Thailand', *Arts of Asia*, vol. 12, no. 6, 1982: 124–31.

Chou Ta-kuan [Zhou Daguan], *Notes on the Customs of Cambodia* (1296–97), Bangkok, 1967.

Churchill, *Collection of Voyages and Travels*, 6 vols, London, 1732.

Cockayne, G., 'Letter from Makassar, 16 July 1615', in *Letters Received by the East India Company from its servants in the East*, ed. F .C. Danvers and W. Foster, London, 1896–1901, vol. III: 136–47.

Cocks, R., *Diary kept by the head of the English Factory in Japan: Diary of Richards Cocks, 1615–1622*, 3 vols, Tokyo, 1978–80.

Coolhaas, W. P., *A Critical Survey of Studies on Dutch Colonial History*, 2nd edn, rev. G. J. Schutte, The Hague, 1980.

—— (ed.), *Generale Missiven van Gouverneurs-General en Raden aan Heren XVII der Verenigde Oostind-ische Compagnie*, 8 vols, The Hague, 1960–85.

Coomaraswamy, A. K., 'A Hamsa-laksana sari', *Bull. of the Museum of Fine Arts, Boston*, vol. 25, 1927: 36–37.

Cousin, F., 'Some data on block-printing in Sind', in H. Khuhro (ed.), *Sind through the centuries*, Karachi, 1981.

Crawford, J., *History of the Indian Archipelago containing an Account of the Manners, Arts, Languages, Religious Institutions and Commerce of its inhabitants*, 3 vols, Edinburgh, 1820 (repr. London, 1967).

—— *A Descriptive Dictionary of the Indian Islands and Adjacent Countries*, London, 1856.

Cruz, Fr G. da: see Boxer, 1953.

Crystal, E., 'Mountain Ikats and Coastal Silks: Traditional Textiles in South Sulawesi', in J. Fischer (ed.), *Threads of Tradition. Textiles of Indonesia and Sarawak*, Berkeley, 1979: 53–62.

Culin, S., 'The Story of the Painted Curtain', *Good Furniture Magazine*, vol. XI, Sept. 1918: 133–48.

Dagh-Register gehouden in't Casteel Batavia, 1642–1682, 31 vols, Batavia and The Hague, 1887–1931.

Dampier, W. *Voyages and discoveries*, ed. C. Wilkinson, London, 1931.

Daniell, T. and W., *A Picturesque Voyage to India by the way of China*, London, 1810

Danvers, F. C., and Foster, W. (eds), *Letters received by the East India Company from its Servants in the East, 1602–1617*, 6 vols, London, 1896–1902.

Das, S., *Fabric Art of India*, Delhi, 1992.

Das Gupta, A., 'Indian Merchants and the Trade in the Indian Ocean', in T. Raychaudhuri and I. Habib (eds), *The Cambridge Economic History of India: c. 1200–c. 1750*, vol. I, Cambridge, 1982: 407–33.

—— *Indian Merchants and the Decline of Surat, 1700–1750*, Wiesbaden, 1979.

—— 'Asian Shipping: A Note', *Indian Ocean Newsletter*, vol. VII, no. 1, 1986: 12–13.

—— and Pearson, M. N. (eds), *India and the Indian Ocean 1500–1800*, Calcutta, 1987.

De Bone, M.G., 'Patolu and its techniques', *Textile Museum Journal*, vol. 4, no. 3, 1976: 49–62.

Depierre, M. J., 'Notice sur un tissu imprimé de l'Inde', *Bull. de la Société Industrielle de Mulhouse*, vol. LXXIX, 1909: 464–66.

Digby, S., 'The Broach coin-hoard as evidence of the import of valuta across the Arabian Sea during the 13th and 14th centuries', *JRAS*, 1980, no. 2.

—— 'The Maritime Trade of India', in T. Raychaudhuri and I. Habib (eds), *The Cambridge Economic History of India, Vol. 1: c. 1200–c.1750*, Cambridge, 1982: 125–59.

Dijk, T. van, and de Jonge, N., 'Basta in Barbar. Imported Asian Textiles in a South-east Moluccan

Culture', in Völger and Welck, 1991: 18–33.

Dodwell, H., 'The Madras Weavers under the Company', *Proc. of the Indian Historical Records

Dohring, K., *Art and Industry in Siam*, 2 vols, Bangkok, n.d.

Downton, N., *The Voyage of Nicholas Downton to the East Indies, 1614–15, as recorded in contemporary narratives and letters*, ed. W. Foster, London, 1938.

Drakard, J., *A Malay Frontier: Unity and Duality in a Sumatran Kingdom*, Ithaca, N.Y., 1990.

East India Company, *Letters Received by the East India Company from its Servants in the East 1602–1617*, 6 vols London, 1896.

Egan, J., *Leaden Cloth Seals in the British Museum's Collections*, British Museum, Dept of Medieval and Later Antiquities, Occasional Paper, London, 1993.

Emery, I., *The Primary Structure of Fabrics*, Textile Museum, Washington, D.C., 1966.

Eredia, M. G. de., 'Eredia's description of Malacca, Meridional India, and Cathay', trans. J. V. Mills, *JMBRAS*, vol. 8, pt 1, 1930: 1–288.

Estrade, C., *Toiles imprimées de la Perse et de l'Inde d'après les documents recueillis par Oberkampf*, Paris, 1925.

Farrington, A., *The English Factory in Japan, 1613–1623*, 2 vols London, 1991.

—— 'English East India Company documents relating to Pho Hien and Tonkin', *Vietnamese Studies*, no. 40 (110), 1993: 125–39.

Fawcett, C. (ed.), *English Factories in India (New Series) 1670–1684*, 4 vols, Oxford, 1936–55.

Ferrier, R. W., 'The trade between India and the Persian Gulf and the East India Company in the 17th century', *Bengal Past and Present*, no. 89, 1970: 189–98.

—— 'The Armenians and the East India Company in Persia in the seventeenth and eighteenth centuries', *Economic History Review*, 2nd ser., no. 26, 1973: 38–62.

Fischel, W., 'The Spice Trade in Mamluk Egypt', *JESHO*, vol. 1, 1958: 157–74.

Floor, W., 'Economy and Society: Fibres, Fabrics, Factories', in C. Bier (ed.), *Woven from the Soul, Spun from the Heart*, Textile Museum, Washington, D.C., 1987: 20–32.

Floris, P., *Peter Floris. His Voyage to the East Indies in the Globe 1611–1615*, ed. W. H. Moreland, London, 1934.

Forge, A., 'Batik Patterns of the Early Nineteenth Century', in Gittinger, 1989: 91–106.

Forth, G. L., *Rindi: An Ethnographic Study of a Traditional Domain in Eastern Sumba*, The Hague, 1981.

Foster, W. (ed.), *The Voyages of Sir James Lancaster to Brazil and East Indies, 1591–1603*, London, 1904.

—— *The English Factories in India…A Calendar of Documents in the India Office, British Museum and Public Records Office*, 9 vols, Oxford, 1906–27.

—— *Supplementary catalogue of the documents in the India Office relating to India or Home Affairs of the East India Company 1600–1640*, London, 1928.

Fox, J. J., 'Roti, Ndao and Savu', in M. Kahlenberg (ed.), *Textile Traditions of Indonesia*, Los Angeles County Museum of Art, 1977: 97–104.

Furber, H., *Rival Empires of Trade in the Orient 1600–1800*, Minneapolis, 1976.

Gaastra, F. S., *De geschiedenis van de VOC*, Leiden, 1991.

Gallop, A. Teh, *Golden Letters. Writing Traditions of Indonesia*, London, 1991.

—— *The Legacy of the Malay Letter*, London and Kuala Lumpur, 1994.

Galvão, A.: see Jacobs.

Geary, P., 'Sacred commodities: the circulation of medieval relics', in Appadurai, 1986: 169–91.

Gervaise, N., *An Historical Description of the Kingdom of Macassar in the East Indies*, London, 1701 (repr. Farnborough 1971).

Gervaise, N., *The Natural and Political History of the Kingdom of Siam*, trans. J. Villiers, Bangkok, 1989 (trans. of *Histoire naturelle et politique du royaume de Siam*, Paris, 1688).

Giles, F. H., 'A Critical Analysis of Van Vliet's Historical Account in the 17th century', *JSS*, vol. XXX, pts 2, 3, 1938; repr. in *JSS Selected Articles*, vol. VII, 1959.

[Gion], *Exhibition of objects from the Gion Festival*, Kyoto Municipal Museum, 1994.

Gittinger, M., *Master Dyers to the World. Technique

and Trade in Early Indian Dyed Cotton Textiles*, Textile Museum, Washington, D.C., 1982.

—— (ed.), *Indonesian Textiles. Irene Emery Roundtable on Museum Textiles*, Textile Museum, Washington, D.C., 1980.

—— (ed.) *To Speak with Cloth. Studies in Indonesian Textiles*, Fowler Museum of Cultural History, U. of California, Los Angeles, 1989.

—— and Lefferts, L., *Tai textiles*, Textile Museum, Washington, D.C., 1992.

Glamann, K., *Dutch–Asiatic Trade 1620–1740*, Copenhagen, 1958.

Glover, I., *Early Trade Between India and South-East Asia: A Link in the Development of a World Trading System*, Hull, 1989.

Goitein, S. D., 'Letters and Documents on the India Trade in Medieval Times', *Islamic Culture*, vol. 37, no. 3, 1963: 188–205.

—— *A Mediterranean Society. The Jewish Communities of the Arab World as Portrayed in the Documents of the Cairo Geniza*, 5 vols, Berkeley, 1967–88.

—— 'A mansion in Fostat: a twelfth-century description of a domestic compound in the ancient capital of Egypt', in H. A. Miskimin et al. (eds), *The Medieval City*, New Haven and London, 1977.

Golombek, L., 'The Draped Universe of Islam', in P. P. Soucek (ed.), *Content and Context of Visual Arts in the Islamic World*, New York, 1988: 25–50.

Graham, P. J., 'Vouchsafing Fecundity in Eastern Flores: Textiles and Exchange in the Rites of Life', in Hamilton, 1994: 194–209.

Grey, E. (ed.), *The travels of Pietro Della Valle in India. From the Old English translation of 1664 by G. Havers*, 2 vols, London, 1892 (repr. New Delhi, 1991).

Groslier, G., *Recherches sur les Cambodgiens*, Paris, 1921.

Guide to the Records of the Masulipatam District from 1682 to 1835, 3 vols, Madras, 1935.

Guy, J., 'Trade Ceramics in Southeast Asia and the Acculturation Process', *Trade Ceramic Studies*, no. 4, 1984: 117–26.

—— *Oriental trade ceramics in South-east Asia. Ninth to sixteenth centuries*, Singapore,1986.

—— 'Commerce, Power and Mythology: Indian Textiles in Indonesia', *Indonesia Circle*, no. 42, 1987: 57–74.

—— '*Sarasa* and *Patola*: Indian Textiles in Indonesia', *Orientations*, vol. 20, no.1, 1989: 48–60.

—— 'Indian Textiles for the Thai Market – A Royal Prerogative', *The Textile Museum Journal*, vol. 39, 1992: 82–96.

—— 'The lost temples of Nagapattinam and Quanzhou', *Silk Road Art and Archaeology*, no. 3 (1993–1994), 1994: 291–310.

—— 'Jain Manuscript Painting', in P. Pal (ed.), *The Peaceful Liberators. Jain Art from India*, Los Angeles County Museum of Art, 1995: 88–99.

—— 'Cloth for the Gods: the *Patola* Trade to Kerala', *Asian Art and Culture*, vol. IX, no. 2, 1996: 27–37.

—— 'Rama, Rajas and Courtesans: Indian Figurative Textiles in Indonesia', in H. P. Ray and J.-F. Salles (eds), *Seafaring Communities in the Indian Ocean*, Delhi, 1998.

—— and Richards, R. J., 'Architectural ceramics of Sukhothai Province', *Transactions of the Oriental Ceramics Society*, vol. 56, 1993: 75–100.

Gwatkin, N. , *Scenes for a Raja: study of an Indian kalamkari found in Indonesia*, Fowler Museum of Cultural History, U. of California, Los Angeles, 1986.

Hadaway, W. S., *Cotton painting and printing in the Madras Presidency*, Madras, 1917.

Haellquist, K. R. (ed.), *Asian Trade Routes*, Copenhagen and London, 1991.

Hall, D. G. E., *Early English Intercourse with Burma 1587–1743*, London, 1938 (repr. 1968).

—— 'The Daghregister of Batavia and Dutch Trade with Burma in the Seventeenth Century', *Journal of the Burma Research Soc.*, vol. XXIX, pt II, 1939: 139–56.

Hall, K. R., *Trade and Statecraft in the Age of the Colas*, New Delhi, 1980.

—— *Maritime Trade and State Development in Early Southeast Asia*, Honolulu, 1985.

Hamilton, A., *A New Account of the East Indies* (1727), ed. W. Foster, 2 vols, London, 1930 (repr. Amsterdam, 1970).

Hamilton, R. (ed.), *Gift of the Cotton Maiden. Textiles

of Flores and the Solor Islands, Fowler Museum of Cultural History, U. of California, Los Angeles, 1994.

Hartkamp-Jonxis, E. (ed.), *Sits. Oost–West Relaties in Textiel*, Zwolle, 1987.

—— *Indian Chintzes*, Rijksmuseum, Amsterdam, 1994.

Havart, D., *Op- en ondergang van de Coromandel*, Amsterdam, 1689.

Havell, E. B., *Arts and Industries of the Madras Presidency, 1885–1888*, Selections from the Records of the Madras Government, New Revenue Ser., no. vi, Madras, 1909.

Hayashiya, T., '*Meibutsu-gire*' or '*Famed Fabrics*' from China, India, and Southeast Asia. Formerly in the collection of the Maeda family, 2 vols, Kyoto National Museum, 1979.

Hedges, W., *The diary of William Hedges 1681–1687*, ed. R. Barlow and H. Yule, 3 vols, London, 1887–89.

Hilgers-Hesse, I., 'Textiles in Early Malay-Indonesian Literature', in Völger and Welck ,1991: 194–96.

Himpunan Wastraprema, *Cindai. Pengembaraan Kain Patola India*, Jakarta, 1988.

Hirth, F., and Rockhill, W. W., *Chau Ju-kua* [Zhou Rukou]: *His Work on the Chinese and Arab Trade in the Twelfth and Thirteenth centuries, entitled Chu-fan-chi*, St Petersburg, 1911 (repr. Taipei, 1967).

Holder, E., *Monograph on dyes and dyeing in the Madras Presidency*, Madras, 1896.

Holmgren, R. G., and Spertus, A. E., *Early Indonesian Textiles for Three Island Cultures: Sumba, Toraja, and Lampung*, Metropolitan Museum of Art, New York, 1989.

Holmgren, R. J., and Spertus, A. E., 'Is Geringsing Really Balinese?', in Völger and Welck, 1991: 59–80.

—— 'Newly Discovered Patolu Motif Types – Extension to Alfred Buhler and Eberhard Fischer (1979), The Patola of Gujarat', in Völger and Welck, 1991: 81–86.

Hooykass, C., 'Patola and Gringsing: An Additional Note', *BTLV*, vol. 134, 1978: 356–59.

Hossain, H., *The Company Weavers of Bengal: The East India Company and the Organization of Textile Production in Bengal 1750–1813*, Delhi, 1988.

Huntington, G. W. B. (trans. and ed.), *The Periplus of the Erythraean Sea*, London, 1980.

Ibn Battuta, *Travels in Asia and Africa 1325–1354*, trans. H. A. R. Gibb, London, 1929 (repr. 1983).

Ibrahim, Ibn Muhammad, *The Ship of Sulaiman*, trans. J. O'Kane, London, 1972.

India Office Records, *Records of the Relations between Siam and Foreign Countries in the 17th Century copied from papers preserved at the India Office*, vols 1–5, 1607–1700, Bangkok, 1915–21.

Irwin, J. C., 'Indian textile trade in the 17th century, Part I, Western India', *JITH*, no. 1, 1955: 5–33.

—— 'Indian textile trade in the 17th century, Part 2, Coromandel Coast', *JITH*, no. 2, 1956: 24–40.

—— 'Indian textile trade in the 17th century, Part 3, Bengal', *JITH*, no. 3, 1957: 59–74.

—— 'Insignia of the English East India Company', *JITH*, no. 4, 1959: 78–79.

—— 'The etymology of chintz and pintado', *JITH*, no. 4, 1959: 77.

—— 'Indian textile trade in the 17th century, Part 4, foreign influences', *JITH*, no. 4, 1959: 1–10.

—— 'Golconda cotton paintings of the early 17th century', *Lalit Kala*, no. 5, 1959: 11–48.

—— and Brett, K. B., *Origins of Chintz*, London, 1970.

—— and Hall, M., *Indian Painted and Printed Fabrics; Vol. 1, Historic Textiles of India at the Calico Museum*, Ahmedabad, 1971.

Irwin, J., and Schwartz, P. R., *Studies in Indo-European textile history*, Ahmedabad,1966.

Isetan, *Ii-ke meiho ten (Exhibition of masterpieces in the Ii family collection)*, Isetan Museum of Art, Tokyo, 1986.

Ishii, Y., 'Seventeenth Century Japanese Documents about Siam', *JSS*, vol. 59, pt 11, 1971: 161–74.

—— 'Religious patterns and economic change in Siam in the sixteenth and seventeenth centuries', in Reid (ed.), 1993: 180–96.

Iwao, J., 'Re-opening of the Diplomatic and Commercial Relations between Japan and Siam during Tokugawa Days', *Acta Asiatica*, no. 4., 1963: 1–31.

—— 'Japanese Foreign Trade in the 16th and 17th Centuries', *Acta Asiatica*, no. 30, 1976: 1–18.

Jacobs, H. (trans. and ed.), *A treatise on the Moluccas (c. 1544), probably the preliminary version of António Galvão's lost Historia das Molucas*, Rome, 1971.

Jacq-Hergoualc'h, M., 'A propos de dessins de Charles le Brun liés à la venue d'Ambassadeurs Siamois à Paris en 1686', *JSS*, vol. 78, pt 2, 1990: 30–36.

Jain, J., 'Saudagiri prints. Textiles from far off Siam', *The India Magazine*, vol. V, no. 11, 1985: 54–63.

Jasper, J. E., and Pirngadie, M., *De inlandsche Kunstnijverheid in Nederlandsch Indie, vol. 2, De Weefkunst*, The Hague, 1912.

Jayakar, P., 'A neglected group of Indian *ikat* fabrics', *JITH*, no. 1, 1955: 55–65.

—— 'Cotton printing of Gujarat and Kathiawar', *Marg*, vol. IV, no. 4, 1950–51: 40–43.

—— 'Gaiety in Colour and Form: Painted and printed Cloths ', *Marg*, vol. 31, no. 4, 1979: 23–34.

Jones, J. W., and Temple, Sir R. (eds), *The Itinerary of Ludovico di Varthema of Bologna from 1502 to 1508*, London, 1928.

Jonxis, E., 'Some Coromandel Chintzes', *Bull. of the Needle and Bobbin Club*, vol. 53, nos. 1, 2, 1970: 37–57.

Jourdain, J., *The Journal of a Voyage to the East Indies 1608–1617*, ed. W. Foster, Cambridge, 1905.

Kaempfer, E., *A description of the kingdom of Siam (1690)*, Bangkok, 1987.

Kajitani, N., and Kojiro, Y. *Gion Matsuri 'Yama' 'Hoko' Kensohin Chosa Hokukusho: Torai Senshokukin no Bu* [Survey Report on Textiles…used to decorate floats in the Gion Festival], Kyoto, 1992.

Kajiyama, N., *Nihon dento isho. Vol. 2. Maeda-ke denrai isho*, Tokyo, 1968.

Karashima, N., 'Trade relations between South India and China during the 13th and 14th centuries', *Journal of East-West Maritime Relations*, vol. 1, 1989: 59–81.

—— 'Indian commercial activity in ancient and medieval Southeast Asia', paper presented to the *Eighth International Conference on Tamil Studies*, Thanjavur, 1995.

Kathirithamby-Wells, J., 'Banten: a west Indonesian port and polity during the sixteenth and seventeenth centuries', in J. Kathirithamby-Wells and J. Villiers (eds), *The Southeast Asian Port and Polity: Rise and Demise*, Singapore, 1990: 106–25.

Katiresu, S., 'Dyeing with chaya root as practised in the Northern Province', *The Ceylon National Review*, July 1906: 214–18.

Kato, E., 'The Japan–Dutch Trade in the Formative Period of the Seclusion Policy – particularly on the Raw Silk Trade by the Dutch Factory at Hirado, 1620–1640', *Acta Asiatica*, no. 30, 1976: 34–84.

Kerlogue, F., *Scattered Flowers. Textiles from Jambi, Sumatra*, Hull, 1996.

Kirihata, K. (ed.), *Meibutsu-gire or 'Famed Fabrics' from China, India and Southeast Asia, formerly in the collection of the Maeda Family*, 2 vols, Kyoto National Museum, 1978–79.

Kobata, A., and Matsuda, M. (trans.), *Ryukyuan Relations with Korea and South Sea Countries. An Annotated Translation of Documents in the Rekidai Hoan*, Kyoto, 1969.

Kobe City Museum, *Sarasa No Sekai Ten*, 1984.

Kondo, O., 'Japan and the Indian Ocean at the time of the Mughal empire, with special reference to Gujarat', in S. Chandra, 1987: 174–90.

Kotilainen, E.-M., *'When the bones are left.' Study of the Material Culture of Central Sulawesi*, Helsinki, 1992.

Kuhn, D., *Textile Technology*, in *Science and Civilization in China*, ed. J. Needham, vol. 5, *Chemistry and Chemical Technology*, pt IX, Cambridge, 1988.

Kuwabara, J., 'P'u shou-ken...A general sketch of the trade of the Arabs in China during the T'ang and Sung eras', *Memoirs of the Research Department of the Toyo Bunko*, vol. 7, 1935: 1–104.

La Loubère, S. de, *A New Historical Relation of the Kingdom of Siam (1691)*, Bangkok, 1986 (trans of *Du royaume de Siam*, Paris, 1691).

Laarhoven, R., *The textile trade of the VOC in Asia, 1600–1780*, paper presented at the World History Assn Second International Conference, Honolulu, June 1993.

—— *The Power of Cloth: The Textile Trade of the Dutch East India Company (VOC) 1600–1780*, PhD, Australian National U., Canberra, 1994

(unpublished).

Lach, D. F., *Asia in the Making of Europe*, vol. 1, *The Century of Discovery*, 2 vols; vol. 3, *A Century of Advance, Bk 3: Southeast Asia*, Chicago, 1965, 1993.

Lancaster, Sir J., *Voyage to the East Indies* (1600–1603), ed. C. R. Markham, London, 1940.

Latham, R. (trans.), *The Travels of Marco Polo*, Harmondsworth, 1958.

Le Bonheur, A., *Phra Narai, Roi de Siam, et Louis XIV*, Paris, 1986.

Lee, Chor Lin, 'Textiles in Sino-South East Asian Trade: Song, Yuan and Ming Dynasties', in Scott and Guy, 1995: 171–86.

Legge, J., *A Record of Buddhist Kingdoms*, Oxford, 1886 (repr. New York, 1965).

Leksukhum, S., *The Stucco Motifs of the Late Ayutthaya Period (1629–1767 A.D.)*, Bangkok, 1989.

Leur, J. V. van, *Indonesian Trade and Society: Essays in Asian Social and Economic History*, The Hague, 1955.

Linschoten, J. H. van, *The Voyage of John Huyghen van Linschoten to the East Indies from the Old English Translation of 1598*, ed. A. C. Burnell and P. A. Tiele, 2 vols, London, 1885 (repr. New Delhi, 1988).

Lo Hsiang Lin, 'Islam in Canton in the Sung period. Some Fragmentary Records', in F. S. Drake (ed.), *Symposium on Historical, Archaeological and Linguistic Studies on Southern China, South-East Asia and the Hong Kong Region*, Hong Kong, 1967: 176–79.

Lodewycksz, W., *De eerste Schipvaart der Nederlanders naar Oost-Indie onder Cornelis de Houtman 1595–1597*, I. Linschoten-Vereeniging, vol. VII, The Hague, 1915.

Lohuizen, J. van, *The Dutch East India Company and Mysore*, The Hague, 1961.

Lohuizen-De Leeuw, J. E. van, 'An early 16th century link between Gujarat and Java', in Ba Shin et al. (eds), *Essays Offered to G. H. Luce*, vol. II, Ascona, 1966: 89–93.

Lombard, D., *Le carrefour javanais: Essai d'histoire globale*, 3 vols, Paris, 1990.

Ludden, D., *Peasant History in South India*, Delhi, 1989.

Mackie, L., 'Textiles', in W. Kubiak and G. Scanlon (eds), *Fustat Expedition, Final Report*, vol. 2, *Fustat C*, American Research Center in Egypt, Winona Lake, 1989.

Ma Huan, *Ma Huan's Ying-yai Sheng-Ian (The Overall Survey of the Ocean's Shores, 1433)*, trans. J. V. G. Mills, Cambridge, 1970.

Majlis, B. K., *Indonesiche Textilen. Wege zu Gottern und Ahnen*, Deutsches Textilmuseum, Krefeld, 1984.

Manrique, F. S., *Travels of Fray Sebastien Manrique 1629–1643* (1649), ed. C. E. Luard, 2 vols, Oxford, 1927.

Manucci, N., *Mogul India or Storia do Mogor*, trans. W. Irvine, 4 vols (repr. New Delhi, 1989).

Marchal, S., *Costumes et parures Khmèrs d'après les devata d'Angkor-vat*, Paris, 1927.

Marsden, W., *The History of Sumatra* (1811), intro. J. Bastin, Kuala Lumpur, 1966.

Mathew, K. S. (ed.), *Mariners, Merchants and Oceans. Studies in Maritime History*, Delhi, 1995.

Maxwell, R., *Textiles of Southeast Asia: Tradition, Trade and Transformation*, Melbourne, 1990.

—— 'The Tree of Life in Indonesian Textiles: ancient iconography or imported chinoiserie?', in Völger and Welck, 1991: 104–22.

Meilink-Roelofsz, M. A. P., *Asian Trade and European Influence in the Indonesian Archipelago between 1500 and 1630*, The Hague, 1962.

—— 'The structure of trade in Asia in the 16th and 17th centuries', *Mare Luso-Indicum*, IV, 1980: 1–43.

—— (ed.), *De VOC in Azie*, Fibula-van Dishoeck, 1976.

—— (Inventaris), Raben, R., and Spijkerman, H. (eds), *De archieven van de Verenigde Oostindische Compagnie. The Archives of the Dutch East India Company (1602–1795)*, The Hague, 1992.

[——] *All of one company. The VOC in biographical perspective. Essays in honour of Prof. M. A. P. Meilink-Roelofsz under the auspices of the Centre for the History of European Expansion, Rijksuniversiteit, Leiden*, Utrecht, 1986.

Mellott, R., *Tai No Senshoku – Senshoku To Kinran*, Kyoto, 1983.

Mendonça, M.J. de, *Embroidered quilts from the Museu*

Nacional de Arte Antiga, Lisbon, 1978.

Metha, R. N., 'Bandhas of Orissa', *JITH*, vol. VI, 1961: 62–73.

Methwold, W., *Relations of the kingdome of Golconda and other neighbouring nations*, in Moreland, 1931.

Middleton, H., *The Voyage of Sir Henry Middleton to the Moluccas, 1604–1606*, ed. W. Foster, London, 1943.

Miller, J. I., *The spice trade of the Roman empire, 29 BC to AD 641*, Oxford, 1969.

Mills, J. V. G., 'Manuel Godinho de Eredia, "Description of Malacca and meridional India and Cathay"', *JMBRAS*, vol. VIII, pt 1, 1930: 1–227.

Moffat, A. L., *Mongkut, the King of Siam*, Ithaca, N.Y., 1961

Mohan Das, T., 'Andhra textile industry in the eighteenth century', *Journal of the Andhra Pradesh State Archives*, vol. XIV, no. 1, 1988: 131–35.

Mollat, M. (ed.), *Sociétés et compagnies de commerce en Orient et dans l'Océan Indien*, Paris, 1970.

Moreland, W. H., 'Indian Exports of Cotton Goods in the Seventeenth Century', *Indian Journal of Economics* (Allahabad), vol. V, pt III, 1925: .... [pc]

—— *From Akbar to Aurangzeb. A study in Indian Economic History*, London, 1923 (repr. New Delhi, 1990).

—— (ed.), *Relations of Golconda in the early seventeenth century*, London, 1931.

—— see Floris, P.

Mortel, R. T., 'The mercantile community of Mecca during the late Mamluk period' *JRAS*, vol. 4, pt 1, 1994: 15–35.

Mouhot, H., *Travels in the Central Parts of Indo-China (Siam), Cambodia and Laos*, 2 vols, London, 1864 (repr. Singapore, 1989).

Mundy, J., *Travels of John Mundy*, ed. R. C. Temple, London, 1914–19.

Murphy, V., 'The Bengal Export Market', in V. Murphy and R. Crill, *Tie-dyed Textiles of India*, London, Victoria and Albert Museum/Ahmedabad 1991.

Nabholz-Kartaschoff, M.-L., *Golden Sprays and Scarlet Flowers. Traditional Indian Textiles from the Museum of Ethnography, Basel*, Kyoto, 1986.

—— 'A Sacred Cloth of Rangda. Kamben Cepuk of Bali and Nusa Penida', in Gittinger, 1989: 181–98.

—— et al. (eds) *Weaving Patterns of Life. Indonesian Textile Symposium 1991*, Museum of Ethnology, Basel, 1993.

Nagtegaal, L., *Riding the Dutch Tiger. The Dutch East Indies Company and the northeast coast of Java, 1680–1743*, Leiden, 1996.

Nakamura, K., 'Yamada-Nagamasa. Japanese Warrior in Old Siam', *Cultural Nippon*, vol. 7, no. 4, 1939: 79–94.

Navarrete, D., *The Travels and Controversies of Friar Domingo Navarrete, 1618–1686*, trans. J. S. Cummins, Cambridge, 1962.

Nicholl, R., *European sources for the history of the Sultanate of Brunei in the sixteenth century*, Brunei Museum, 1975.

Niessen, S. A., *Batak Cloth and Clothing. A Dynamic Indonesian Tradition*, Kuala Lumpur, 1991.

Nieuhof, J., *Voyages and Travels to the East Indies, 1653–1670* (1682), Singapore, 1988 (repr. of the second part of the 1732 edn).

Nishida, H. (ed.), *Namban and Shimamono*, Tokyo, 1993.

No Na Pak Nam, *Evolution of Thai Ornament*, Bangkok, 1981.

—— *Khoi Manuscript Paintings of the Ayutthaya Period*, Bangkok, 1985

Nooy-Palm, C. H. M., *The Sa'dan Toraja: A Study of their Social Life and Religion*, 1, *Organization, Symbols and Beliefs*, The Hague, 1979.

—— 'The Role of the Sacred Cloths in the Mythology and Ritual of the Sa'dan- Toraja of Sulawesi, Indonesia', in Gittinger, 1980: 81–95.

—— 'The sacred cloths of the Toraja. Unanswered questions', in Gittinger, 1989: 163–80.

Ogasawara, S., *Hikone sarasa*, Hikone Castle Museum, 1989.

—— 'Re-consideration of "Hikone sarasa"', *Museum* (Tokyo National Museum), no. 510, Sept. 1993: 12–31.

Osumi, T., *Printed Cottons of Asia*, Tokyo, 1963.

Ovington, J., *A voyage to Surat in the year 1689*, ed. H. G. Rawlinson, London, 1929.

Pankhurst, R., 'Imported textiles in Ethiopian Sixteenth and Seventeenth Century Manuscript Bindings in Britain', *Azana*, vol. XV, 1980: 434–56.

Parpola, M., 'Textiles from Celebes and Sangir at the National Museum of Finland', in J. Siikala (ed.), *Oceanic Studies. Essays in honour of Aarne A. Koskinen*, Helsinki, 1982: 253–64.

Pearson, M. N., *Merchants and rulers in Gujarat. The response to the Portuguese in the sixteenth century*, New Delhi, 1976.

—— *Coastal Western India. Studies from the Portuguese Records*, New Delhi, 1980.

Pelrus, C., *The Bugis*, Oxford, 1995.

Pereira, G.: see Boxer, 1953.

The Periplus of the Erythraean Sea: see Huntington, 1980, and Schoff, 1912.

Pfister, R., 'Tissus imprimés de l'Inde médiévale', *Revue des Arts asiatiques*, vol. X, no.3, 1937: 161–64.

—— *Les Toiles imprimées de Fostat et l'Hindoustan*, Paris, 1938.

—— 'The Indian art of calico-printing in the Middle Ages', *Indian Art and Letters*, no. XIII, 1939: 22–23.

Phan Huy Le, 'Pho Hian. The Centre of International Commerce in the XVII–XVIII centuries', *Vietnamese Studies*, n.s., no. 40 (110), no. 4, 1993.

Pigafetta, A., 'Account of Magellan's Voyage', in Lord Stanley of Alderley (ed.), *The Voyage Around the World by Magellan*, New York, 1874: 35–163 (repr. Hakluyt Soc., 1963).

Pinto, F. M., *The Voyages and Adventures of Ferdinand Mendes Pinto* (1614), trans. H. Cagon, London, 1891.

Pires, Tomé, *The Suma Oriental of Tomé Pires* (1512–15), trans. A. Contesão, 2 vols, London, 1944.

Pliny, *Natural History*, trans. H. Rackham, London, 1950.

Pol, A., *Schepen met geld. De handelsmunten van de Verenigde Oostindeische Compagnie 1602–1799*, The Hague, 1989.

Polo, M.: see Latham.

Pombejra, D. na, *Court, Company, and Campong. Essays on the VOC presence in Ayutthya*, Ayutthaya Historical Study Centre, Occasional Paper no. 1, 1992.

—— 'Ayutthaya at the end of the seventeenth century: was there a shift to isolation?' in Reid (ed.), 1993: 250–72.

Porter, V., 'The Rasulids in Dhofar in the VIth–VIIIth/XII–XIVth Centuries (Pt II): Three Rasulid Tombstones from Zafar', *JRAS*, 1988, 1: 32–43.

Prakash, O., 'Bengal Textiles in 17th Century International Trade', in W. M. Gunderson (ed.), *Studies on Bengal*, East Lansing, Mich., 1976.

—— *The Dutch Factories in India, 1617–1623*, New Delhi, 1984.

—— *The Dutch East India Company and the Economy of Bengal, 1630–1720*, Princeton, 1985.

Ptak, R., 'China and Calicut in the early Ming period: envoys and tribute embassies', *JRAS*, 1989, no. 1: 81–111.

—— and Rothermund, D. (eds), *Emporia, Commodities and Entrepreneurs in Asian Maritime Trade, c. 1400–1750*, Stuttgart, 1991.

Quiason, S. D., *English 'Country Trade' with the Philippines 1644–1765*, Querzon City, 1966.

Quaritch Wales, H. G., *Siamese State Ceremonies*, London, 1934.

Rada, Fr M. de: see Boxer, 1953.

Raffles, T. S., *The History of Java*, 2 vols, London, 1830; plates vol. 1844 (repr. of 1817 edn Kuala Lumpur, 1965, 1978).

Ramaswamy, V., *Textiles and Weavers in Medieval South India*, Delhi, 1985.

Ray, H., *Trade and diplomacy in India–China relations. A study of Bengal during the fifteenth century*, New Delhi, 1993.

—— 'The South East Asian Connection in Sino-Indian Trade', in Scott and Guy, 1995: 41–54.

Ray, H. P., *Monastery and guild: commerce under the Satavahanas*, Delhi, 1986.

—— *Winds of Change: Buddhism and the early maritime links of South Asia*, Delhi, 1994.

Raychaudhuri, T., *Jan Company in Coromandel 1605–1690: A Study in the Interrelations of European Commerce and Traditional Economies*, The Hague, 1962.

Rea, A., 'Monumental Remains of the Dutch East India Company in the Presidency of Madras', *Archaeological Survey of India. New Imperial Series, Vol. XXV, Southern India, Vol. IX*, Madras, 1897.

Reddy, W. M., 'The structure of a cultural crisis: thinking about cloth in France before and after the Revolution', in Appadurai, 1986: 261–84.

Reid, A., 'A great seventeenth century Indonesian family: Matoaya and Pattingalloany of Makassar', *Masyarakat Indonesia*, vol. 8, no.1, 1981: 1–28.

—— *Southeast Asia in the Age of Commerce 1450–1680. Volume One: The Lands Below the Winds*, New Haven and London, 1988.

—— *Southeast Asia in the Age of Commerce 1450–1680. Volume Two: Expansion and Crisis*, New Haven and London, 1993.

—— (ed.) *Southeast Asia in the Early Modern Era. Trade, Power, and Belief*, Ithaca, N.Y., 1993

Richards, D. S. (ed.), *Islam and the Trade of Asia: A Colloquium*, Oxford, 1970.

Richards, J. F., 'European city-states on the Coromandel coast', in P. M. Joshi (ed.), *Studies in the foreign relationships of India. Prof. H.K. Sherwani Felicitation Volume*, Hyderabad State Archives, 1975: 508–21.

Robson, S. O., 'Notes on the cultural background of the Kidung literature', in N. Philips and K. Anivar (eds), *Papers on Indonesian Languages and Literature*, Paris, 1981: 105–20.

Rockhill, W. W., 'Notes on the relations and trade of China with the eastern archipelago and the coast of the Indian Ocean during the fourteenth century', *Tu'ong Pao*, vol. 15, 1914: 419–47; vol. 16, 1915: 61–159, 236–71, 374–92.

Roe, T., *The embassy of Sir Thomas Roe to India 1615–1619*, ed. W. Foster, London, 1926.

Roessingh, M. P. H., *Sources of the history of Asia and Oceania in the Netherlands. Part 1: Sources up to 1796*, Netherlands State Archives Service, Royal Institute of Linguistics and Anthropology; Munich, 1982.

Rothermund, D., *Asian trade and European expansion in the Age of Mercantilism*, Delhi, 1981.

Rouffaer, G. P., and Juynboll, H. H., *De Batik-kunst in Nederlandsch-Indië en haar Geschiedenis*, 2 vols, Utrecht, 1914.

Roxburgh, W., *Plants of the Coast of Coromandel*, 3 vols, London, 1795–1819.

Sainsbury, E. B. (ed.), *A Calendar of the Court Minutes of the East India Company 1635–1679*, 11 vols, Oxford, 1907–38.

Sandbukt, O., 'Resource management and relations of appropriation among tropical forest foragers: the case of the Sumatran Kubu', *Research in Economic Anthropology*, vol. 10, 1988: 117–56.

Sangar, S. P., 'Export of Indian textiles to the Middle East and Africa in the seventeenth century', *Journal of Historical Research*, vol. XVII, no. 1, 1974: 1–5.

—— 'Cloth fabrics of the Coromandel Coast in the seventeenth century', *Panjab University Research Bulletin (Arts)*, vol. V, no. 1, 1974: 37–50.

Santoso, S., *Ramayana Kakawin*, 3 vols, New Delhi, 1980.

Sarasin, V., *Tribute and Profit: Sino-Siamese Trade, 1652–1853*, Cambridge, Mass., 1977.

Saris, J., *The Voyage of Captain John Saris to Japan, 1613*, ed. E. M. Satow, London, 1900.

Sarkar, H. B., *Trade and commercial activities of southern India in the Malayo-Indonesian world*, Calcutta, 1986.

Sastri, K. A. N., 'A Tamil Merchant-Guild in Sumatra', *Tijdschrift voor Indische Taal-, Land- en Volkenkunde*, vol. 63, no. 2, 1932.

—— *Foreign Notices of South India. From Megasthenes to Ma Yuan*, Madras, 1939.

Sauvaget, J., *Ahbar As-sin Wa l-Hind. Relation de la Chine et de l'Inde, rédigee en 851*, Paris, 1948.

Scheurleer, P., and Klooke, M. (eds) *Divine Bronzes*, Leiden, 1988.

Schlingloff, D., 'Cotton-Manufacture in ancient India', *JESHO*, vol. XVII, pt 1, 1974: 81–90.

Schoff,.W. H. (trans.), *The Periplus of the Erythraean Sea*, New York, 1912 (repr. New Delhi, 1974).

Scholten, C., *The Coins of the Dutch Overseas Territories 1601–1948*, Amsterdam, 1953.

Schorer, A., *Brief Relation of Trade of the Coromandel Coast*, in Moreland, 1931.

Schouten, J., 'A report by Commissary Justus Schouten of his visit to Malacca, 7 September 1641', in P. A. Leupe (ed.), 'The Siege and Capture of

Malacca from the Portuguese in 1640–1641', *JMBRAS*, vol. 14, pt 1, 1936: 69–144.
—— *A True Description of the Mighty Kingdoms of Japan and Siam* (1671), intro. J. Villiers, Bangkok, 1986. See also Boxer, 1935.
Schwartz, P. R., 'French Documents on Indian Cotton Painting: I, The Beaulieu ms.', c. 1734', *JITH*, no. II, 1956: 5–23.
—— 'French Documents on Indian Cotton Painting: II, New Light on Old Material', *JITH*, no. III, 1957: 15–44.
—— *Printing on cotton at Ahmedabad, India in 1678*, Calico Museum of Textiles, Ahmedabad, 1969.
—— 'The Roxburgh account of India cotton painting: 1795', *JITH*, no. IV, 1959: 47–56.
Scott, R., and Guy, J. (eds) *South East Asia and China: Art, Interaction and Commerce*, Percival David Foundation of Chinese Art Colloquies on Art and Archaeology in Asia, no. 17, London, 1995.
Sen, S. P., 'The Role of Indian Textiles in Southeast Asian Trade in the Seventeenth Century', *Journal of Southeast Asian History*, vol. 3, no. 2, 1962: 92–110.
Serrao, V., 'Quadros de Vida de S. Francisco Xavier', *Oceanos*, no. 12, 1992: 56–58.
Shahriyar, Buzurg Ibn, *The Book of the Wonders of India*, ed. G. S. P. Freeman-Grenville, London, 1981.
Shunzo, S., 'Ryukyu and Southeast Asia', *Journal of Asian Studies*, vol. XXIII, no. 3, 1964: 383–89.
Siam Society, *Selected Articles from the Siam Society Journal. Volume VIII. Relationship with France, England and Denmark*, Bangkok, 1959.
Simmonds, E. H. S., 'The Thalang Letters, 1773–94: Political Aspects and the Trade in Arms', *Bull. of the School of Oriental and African Studies*, vol. 26, no. 3, 1963: 592–619.
—— 'Francis Light and the ladies of Thalang', *JMBRAS*, vol. XXXVIII, pt 2, 1965: 213–28.
Singh, O. P., *Surat and its trade in the second half of the seventeenth century*, New Delhi, 1977.
Smart, E. S., 'A preliminary report on a group of important Mughal textiles', *Textile Museum Journal 1986*, vol. 25, 1987: 5–23.
Smith, G. V., *The Dutch in Seventeenth Century Thailand*, DeKalb, Ill., 1977.
Smithies, M. (ed. and trans.), *The Discourse at Versailles of the First Siamese Ambassadors to France 1686–7*, Bangkok, 1986.
—— 'The travels in France of the Siamese Ambassadors 1686–7', *JSS*, vol. 77, pt 2, 1989: 59–70.
—— *The Siamese Embassy to the Sun King. The Personal Memorials of Kosa Pan*, Bangkok, 1990.
Solwyn, G., and Solwyn, B., 'Cosmic Symbolism in Semen and Atasalasan Patterns in Javanese Textiles', in Gittinger, 1980: 248–74.
Specker, K., 'Madras handlooms in the nineteenth century', *IESHR*, vol. 26, no. 2, 1989.
Srinuan, J., *Mural Paintings of Thailand Series: Wat Yai Suwannaram*, Bangkok, 1984.
Steensgaard, N., *The Asian trade revolution of the seventeenth century*, Chicago, 1973.
Stein, B., 'Coromandel Trade in Medieval India', in J. Parker (ed.), *Merchants and Scholars*, Minneapolis, 1965: 47–62.
Steinmann, A., *Batik. A Survey of Batik Design*, Leigh-on-Sea, 1958.
Stern, S. M., 'Ramisht of Siraf, a merchant millionaire of the twelfth century', *JRAS*, 1967: 10–14.
Stillman, N. A., 'The eleventh century merchant house of Ibn 'Awkal: a Geniza study', *JESHO*, vol. 16, 1973: 15–88.
Stuart-Fox, D., 'Textiles in Ancient Bali', in Nabholz–Kartaschoff et al. (eds): 1993: 85–98.
Subrahmanyam, S., *Improving empire. Portuguese trade and settlement in the Bay of Bengal 1500–1700*, Delhi, 1990(a).
—— *Merchants, markets and the state in early modern India*, Delhi, 1990(b).
—— *The Political Economy of Commerce: Southern India, 1500–1650*, Cambridge, 1990(c).
Sudhir, P., and Swarnalatha, P., 'Textile traders and territorial imperatives: Masulipatnam, 1750–1850' *IESHR*, vol. 29, no.2, 1992: 145–69.
Sumaryoto, W. A., 'Textiles in Javanese Texts', in Nabholz-Kartaschoff et al. (eds): 1993: 31–50.
Sutherland, H., and Bree, D. S., *Quantitative and qualitative approaches to the study of Indonesian trade: the case of Makassar*, Rotterdam School of

Management, Management Report Series, no. 17, 1987.
Tachard, P. G., *A Relation of the Voyage to Siam* (1688), Bangkok, 1981 (trans. of *Voyage de Siam des Peres Jesuites Envoyez par le Roy aux Indes & à la Chine*, Paris, 1686).
Tatsumara, K., *Nampo senshoku zuroku* (Dyed and printed textiles from India and Indonesia), Kyoto, 1964.
Tavernier, J.-B., *Travels in India* (1640–67), 2 vols, ed. W. Crooke, London, 1925 (repr. New Delhi, 1977).
Taylor, K. W., 'Nguyen Hoang and the Beginning of Vietnam's Southward Expansion', in Reid (ed.), 1993: 42–65.
Taylor, L. M. 'Articles of Peculiar Excellence. The Siam Exhibit at the U.S. Centennial Exposition (Philadelphia, 1876)' *JSS*, vol. 79, pt 2, 1991: 13–23
Temple, R. C. (ed.), 'The Scattergoods and the East India Company', *Indian Antiquary*, 1921, suppl.
Terpatra, H., *De vestiging van de Nederlanders aan Kust von Korromandel*, Groningen, 1911.
Thomaz, L. F. F. R., 'The Malay Sultanate of Melaka', in Reid (ed.)., 1993: 69–90.
Thurston, E., 'The Cotton fabric industry of the Madras Presidency', *JIAI*, vol. 7, no. 59, 1897 (repr. *Art and Industry Through the Ages*, III, New Delhi, 1982).
Tibbetts, G. R., *A study of the Arabic texts containing material on South-East Asia*, London, 1979.
—— *Arab Navigation in the Indian Ocean before the Coming of the Portuguese*, London, 1981.
Tolat, P., 'Depth & Brilliance. Indigo in resist printing', in C. Kagal (ed.), *Shilpakar*, Bombay, 1982: 94–99.
Urano, R., *Edo sarasa komo watari*, Tokyo, 1977.
Valentijn, F., *Oud en Nieuw Oost-Indien* (1724–26), ed. S. Keizer, 3 vols, Dordrecht and Amsterdam, 1858.
Varadarajan, L., 'Figurative Kalamkari and its locale', in A. Krishna (ed.) *Chhavi–2, Rai Krishnadasa Felicitation Volume*, Varanasi, 1981: 67–70.
—— *South Indian traditions of Kalamkari*, Ahmedabad, 1982.
—— 'Indian textile technology in the pre-industrial period', *Indica*, vol. 21, no. 2, 1984: 61–69.
—— 'Commodity structure and Indian participation in the trade of the Southern Sea, circa ninth to thirteenth centuries', in S. Chandra, 1987: 90–108.
Varthema, L. di: see Jones.
Vassallo e Silva, N., *No Caminho do Japão*, Lisbon, Museu de S. Roque, Santa Casa da Misericordia, 1993.
Veldhuisen-Djajasoebrata, A., 'On the origin and nature of Larangan: forbidden batik patterns from the Central Javanese principalities', in Gittinger, 1980: 201–21.
—— *Bloemen van het heelal. De kleurrijke wereld van de textiel op Java*, Amsterdam/Rotterdam, Museum voor Land- en Volkenkunde, 1984.
—— *Weavings of Power and Might. The Glory of Java*, Museum voor Land-en Volkenkunde, Rotterdam, 1988.
—— 'Snakeskin Motifs on some Javanese Textiles. Awe, Love and Fear for Progenitrix Naga', in Nabholz-Kartaschoff et al. (eds), 1993: 51–70.
Vermeulen, A. C. J., and van der Velde, P. (eds), *The Deshima Daghregisters*, 3 vols, Leiden, 1986–90.
Vlam, G. A. H., 'Sixteenth century European tapestries in Tokugawa, Japan', *Art Bulletin*, vol. LXIII, no. 3, 1981: 476–95.
Vliet, J. van, 'Description of the Kingdom of Siam' (1636), trans. L. F. von Ravensway, *JSS*, vol. VII, pt 1, 1910.
—— see Giles, 1938 and 1959.
Vogelsang-Eastwood, G. M., *Resist-dyed textiles from Quseir al-Qadim, Egypt*, Paris, 1990.
Völger, G., and Welck, K. v. (eds), *Indonesian Textile Symposium 1985*, Cologne, 1991.
Walker, D., *Flowers Underfoot. Indian Carpets of the Mughal Era*, Metropolitan Museum of Art, New York, 1997.
Wardle, T., 'The Indian Silk Culture Court (at the Colonial and Indian Exhibition' (1886), *JIA*, vol. 1, no. 15, 1886: 115–23.
Wassing, R., *Weefsels en Adatkostuums vit Indonesie*, Museum Nusantara, Delft, n.d.
Watson Andaya, B., 'The Indian "Saudagar Raja" in traditional Malay courts', *JMBRAS*, vol. LI, pt 1, 1978: 13–35.

—— 'The cloth trade in Jambi and Palembang society during the seventeenth and eighteenth century', *Indonesia*, 48, 1989: 26–46.
—— 'Cash Cropping and Upstream–Downstream Tensions: The Case of Jambi in the Seventeenth and Eighteenth Centuries', in Reid (ed.), 1993: 23–41.
—— *To live as brothers: southeast Sumatra in the seventeenth and eighteenth centuries*, Honolulu, 1993.
Watson, J. F., *Collection of Specimens and Illustrations of the Textile Manufactures of India*, 15 vols, India Museum [Victoria and Albert Museum], London, 1872–1877.
Weiner, A. B., and Schneider, J., *Cloth and human experience*, Washington, 1989.
Wheatley, P., 'Geographical notes on some commodities involved in Sung maritime trade', *JMBRAS*, vol. XXXII, pt 2, no. 186, 1959: 1–140.
—— *Nagara and commandery. Origins of the southern Asian urban traditions*, U. of Chicago Dept. of Geography, Research Paper nos. 207–8, Chicago, 1983.
Whitcomb, D. S., and Johnson, J. H., *Quseir Al-Qadim 1980 Report*, American Research Center in Egypt Inc., Malibu and Cairo, 1982.
White, G., 'Report on the trade of Siam' (1678), in J. Anderson, *English intercourse with Siam in the seventeenth century*, London, 1890: 421–28 (repr. Bangkok, 1981).
White, S., *John Thomson. A Window to the Orient*, London, 1986.
Wijetunga, W. M. K., 'South Indian corporate commercial organizations in South and South-east Asia', in *Proc. of the First International Conference Seminar of Tamil Studies, Kuala Lumpur, April 1966*, vol. 1, International Assn of Tamil Research, Kuala Lumpur, 1968: 494–508.
Winius, G. D., and Vink, M. P. M., *The Merchant Warrior Pacified. The VOC and its Changing Political Economy in India*, Delhi, 1991.
Wink, A., *Al-Hind. The making of the Indo-Islamic world*, vol. I, *Early medieval India and the expansion of Islam 7th–11th centuries*, Leiden, 1990.
Wisseman Christie, J., 'Texts and Textiles in "Medieval" Java', *BEFEO*, vol. 80, no. 1, 1993: 181–211.
Wolters, O. W., *Early Indonesian commerce. A study of the origins of Srivijaya*, Ithaca, N.Y., 1967.
—— *The fall of Srivijaya in Malay history*, Ithaca, N.Y., 1970.
Wong, G., 'A Comment on the Tributary Trade between China and Southeast Asia', *Southeast Asian Ceramic Soc. Transactions*, no. 7, 1979.
Woodward, H. W., 'A Chinese silk depicted at Candi Sewa', in K. L. Hutterer (ed.), *Economic exchange and social interaction in Southeast Asia*, Ann Arbor, 1977: 233–43.
—— 'Indonesian textile patterns from a historical point of view', in Gittinger, 1980: 15–35.
Wyatt, D. K., 'Persian Missions to Siam in the Reign of King Narai', *JSS*, vol. 62, 1, 1974: 151–57.
—— 'Family politics in seventeenth and eighteenth century Siam', in R. J. Bickner et al. (eds), *Papers from a conference on Thai Studies in honor of William J. Gedney*, Ann Arbor, 1986: 257–61.
Yoshimoto, S., *Sarasatic Design Collection*, Kyoto, 1975.
—— *Kain Perada. Gold-printed textiles of Indonesia: the Hirayama Collection*, Tokyo, 1991.
—— *Batik and Sarasa* [Japanese text], Tokyo, 1993.
—— *Sarasa. The Okada, Nishimura and Nomura Collections* [Japanese text], Osaka, 1996.
Yoshioka, T., *Sarasa no Seikai-ten* ('The World of Sarasa'), Kobe, 1984.
—— *Sarasa, printed and painted textiles*, Kyoto, 1993.
—— and Yoshimoto, S., *Sarasa of the World. Indian chintz, European print, Batik, Japanese stencil*, Kyoto, 1980.
Yule, H., and Burnell, A. C., *Hobson-Jobson. A glossary of colloquial Anglo-Indian works and phrases*, London, 1886 (repr. New Delhi, 1984, and London, 1996).
Zhongwai jiaotong shiji congkan ('Selected materials on the history of China's overseas trade'), Beijing, 1981.
Zhou Daguan: see Chou Ta-kuan.
Zhou Rukuo: see Hirth.

The following data is the result of accelerated radiocarbon analysis of Indian cotton textile samples – all originating in Gujarat – undertaken by the Research Laboratory for Archaeology and the History of Art, Oxford, between 1994 and 1996, and the Institute of Geological and Nuclear Sciences, New Zealand, in 1997.

The analysis at Oxford was organized by Dr Ruth Barnes, of the Ashmolean Museum, and samples were supplied by that museum, the Victoria and Albert Museum, London, and Dr J. Luth of Hanover. The testing of the Ashmolean Museum samples was funded by the Advisory Panel of the Oxford Radiocarbon Accelerator Unit; that of the Victoria and Albert Museum samples was generously supported by Dr Luth.

Results of the 1994 and 1995 analyses, pertaining to the Egyptian-provenanced samples, are published in Barnes, 1996, 1997a, 1997b; for Indonesian-provenanced examples, see Guy, 1998.

• Radiocarbon dates are expressed in AD
• ± = statistical error range, expressed in years
• OxA = Oxford analysis report
• NZA = New Zealand analysis report
• V&A = Victoria and Albert Museum

Egyptian provenance

895 ± 75   [46]
Elephant, rider and vine
Block-printed resist-dyed blue
Ashmolean Mus., Newberry Coll. 1990.250
OxA-6530, 1996
Barnes, 1997b, cat. 241

1010 ± 55
Interlocking lotus-vine medallions
Block-printed resist-dyed blue
Ashmolean Mus., Newberry Coll. 1990.247
OxA-4953, 1994
Barnes, 1997b, cat. 238

1255 ± 55   [cf. 73]
Interlocking spirals
Block-printed resist-dyed blue, mordant-dyed red and brown
Ashmolean Mus., Newberry Coll. 1990.305
OxA-4960, 1994
Barnes, 1997b, cat. 296

1265 ± 40   [47]
Stylized flowering trees and vines
Block-printed mordant-dyed brown, resist- and mordant-dyed blue and brown
Ashmolean Mus., Newberry Coll. 1990.823
OxA-6523, 1996
Barnes, 1997b, cat. 821

1325 ± 40   [58]
Repeat design of *hamsa* encircling a medallion
Block-printed resist-dyed and mordant-dyed light and dark red and brown
Ashmolean Mus., Newberry Coll. 1990.807
OxA-6576, 1996
Barnes, 1997b, cat. 805

1340 ± 40   [45]
Continuous landscape of trees with pearl borders
Resist-dyed and mordant-dyed red
Ashmolean Mus., Newberry Coll. 1990.1129
OxA-6479, 1996
Barnes, 1997b, cat. 1122

1390 ±75
Interlace design based on Arabic script
Block-printed resist-dyed light and dark blue
Ashmolean Mus., Newberry Coll. 1990.215
OxA-6521, 1996
Barnes, 1997b, cat. 207

1460 ±70
Leaves and quatrefoils
Block-printed resist-dyed and mordant-dyed red and brown
Ashmolean Mus., Newberry Coll. 1990.804
OxA-4956, 1994
Barnes, 1997b, 797

1555 ±55   [cf. 36]
Rosette design and tab border
Block-printed mordant-dyed red and brown, resist-dyed blue
Ashmolean Mus., Newberry Coll. 1990.1085
OxA-4958, 1994
Barnes, 1997b, 1078

1595 ±50
Flower-in-circle repeat pattern
Block-printed and painted mordant-dyed red and brown
Ashmolean Mus., Newberry Coll. 1990.712
OxA-6522, 1996
Barnes, 1997b, 705

1690 ± 90   [52]
Interlocking stepped squares
Mordant-dyed red and brown and block-printed resist-dyed
Ashmolean Mus., Newberry Coll. 1990.473
OxA-4954, 1994
Barnes, 1997b: cat. 473

Indonesian provenance

1340 ± 40   [44, 137]
Forested landscape
Block-printed mordant-dyed red and block-printed and painted resist-dyed blue
V&A IS 96-1993
OxA-6482, 1996

1370 ± 40   [26, 146]
Double-register repeat design of a woman with attendants
Block-printed mordant-dyed black and red, painted resist-dyed blue
V&A IS 95-1993
OxA-6481, 1996
Guy, 1998

1400 ± 40   [cf. 59]
Hamsa and flower medallion design
Block-printed mordant-dyed
Ashmolean Mus., 1995.61
OxA-5769, 1995
Barnes, 1997b, pl. 13

1411 ± 64   [cf. 146]
Repeat design of a woman with attendants
Block-printed mordant-dyed red and painted resist-dyed blue
Private coll., London
NZA-8090, 1997

1510 ± 40   [59]
Hamsa and flower medallion design
Block-printed mordant-dyed red and brown
V&A IS 94-1993
OxA-6480, 1996
Guy, 1998

1595 ± 40   [cf. 148]
Repeat design of a female musician
Block-printed mordant-dyed black and red and painted resist-dyed blue
Coll. J. Luth, 273-80
OxA-6484, 1996
Barnes, 1997b, pl. 41

1605 ± 40   [cf. 59]
Hamsa and flower medallion design
Block-printed mordant-dyed red and brown
Coll. J. Luth, 1789-90
OxA-6485, 1996

1645 ± 45
Repeat design of peacocks
Block-printed mordant-dyed red and painted resist-dyed blue
Coll. J. Luth, 2513-95
OxA-6588, 1996

1655 ± 55   [cf. 148]
Repeat design of a female musician
Block-printed mordant-dyed red and painted resist-dyed blue
Coll. J. Luth, 2512-95
OxA-6587, 1996

1720 ± 40   [128]
Repeat floral design
Block-printed mordant-dyed red and painted
V&A IS 100-1993
OxA-6483, 1996

1750 ± 45   [150]
Theatrical scene within a floral border
Block-printed and painted mordant-dyed red and painted resist-dyed blue
Coll. J. Luth, 2318-94
OxA-6586, 1996

GLOSSARY

(A)	*Arabic*	(Pe)	*Persian*
(D)	*Dutch*	(Po)	*Portuguese*
(E)	*English*	(Sk)	*Sanskrit*
(G)	*Gujarati*	(Ta)	*Tamil*
(H)	*Hindi*	(Te)	*Telugu*
(Ja)	*Javanese*	(Th)	*Thai*
(M)	*Malay*		

allegaes (G) Striped or checked cotton cloth, sometimes mixed with silk, typically red or blue and white, supplied as uncut lengths up to 16 yds (14.6 m). Made in Gujarat and also on the Coromandel Coast (cotton only).

aloes wood (Sk) Corruption of *agaru*, an aromatic wood. From Southeast Asia, especially Champa (Vietnam).

bafta / baffeta (Pe) Literally, 'woven'. Plain cotton cloth, either white or dyed – most commonly red, blue or black for the Southeast Asian market; typically 13 x 1 yds (11.9 x 0.9 m). Manufactured in Gujarat (especially Broach) and later in Bengal and on the Coromandel Coast.

batik (Ja) From *tik*, 'dot'. Cotton cloth decorated by a complex process of repeated wax-resisting and dyeing. The wax may be put on with a spouted applicator (*canting*), which produces *tulis* ('hand-drawn' batik), or with a copper stamp (*cap*), a method chiefly associated with Java.

bethile / betille / bettella (Po) From *beatilha*, 'veiling'. Muslin, sometimes embroidered, associated with the Coromandel Coast around Golconda and nearly Warangal. Typically 15–25 x 1.5 yds (13.7–22.8 x 1.4 m).

calico From the name of the port of Calicut. Cotton cloth from the Malabar Coast.

Cambay cloth Checked fabric traded from Cambay, Gujarat, widely worn in Southeast Asia; on the Indian east coast known as *gingham* (q.v.).

camphor (A) From *kafur*. An aromatic resin harvested in the forests of Sumatra and Borneo for its pharmaceutical benefits.

chappa / cap / chop (H, D) A copper stamp or seal, applied as a mark of authorization by trading companies to ensure control of specified commodities, especially textiles. Used by both the English and Dutch East India Companies.

chay (Ta) From *chaya-ver*. A red dye extracted from the root of *Oldenlandia umbellata*, found in the delta areas of Coromandel Coast, used with madder (q.v.).

chela / chillae (H) Poor-quality checked or striped cotton cloth, patterned on the loom, produced in the Madras area and exported to Southeast Asia.

chetti (Ta) / **chetty** (E) South Indian merchant caste, usually Tamil-speaking Hindus, widely involved in the Southeast Asian market textile trade.

chinde (M) / **cindai** (Ja) Terms for *patola* (q.v.). In Dutch records they are used in counterdistinction to *patola*, possibly denoting a cheaper version available in both silk (single ikat) and cotton.

chintz Etymology uncertain; most probably derived from Sanskrit *chitra*, 'variegated', via Hindi *chint* and Gujarati *chit*, 'spotted cloth'. In Portuguese *chita*, Dutch *sits*, French *cite*, *chitte*, Malay *chita*. The term came to be applied equally to painted and printed cloths; these are, however, distinguished in the trade records, commanding different prices. Widely produced, but the finest quality is associated predominantly with the Coromandel Coast, principally Masulipatam and Pulicat.

chulias Term current throughout Southeast Asia for Muslim Tamil merchants.

corge (H) From *kori*, a score. A bundle of cloths packaged for shipment, consisting of twenty lengths.

Daghregister (D) Daybook recording the commercial transactions of the VOC (q.v.).

dhoti (H) A full-length skirt-cloth, sometimes drawn up between the legs and secured at the waist; worn principally by Hindu males.

dragam / dragon (Ja) Poor-quality cotton, dyed red and black.

dupatty / dopatta (H) From *dupatta*, 'a cloth in two widths'. A textile designed in two loom widths. Usually exported as a painted cotton to Indonesia.

gingham Etymology uncertain; probably anglicized from an Indian term, possibly from the Tamil *kindam*. A striped or checked cotton cloth, woven from pre-dyed yarn with double-threaded warps and wefts. Average roll 20–22 x 1.5 yds (18.3–20 x 1.4 m). See also cambay cloth.

godown (M) From *gadong*. A warehouse or storeroom, usually for securing goods prior to sale.

guinees / guinea cloth Plain, checked or striped cotton produced in large quantities on the Coromandel Coast and Gujarat for both the Indonesian and African markets.

ikat (M) Literally, 'to bind'. Cloth in which the pattern is pre-dyed by resist-binding bundles of yarns in the warp or weft threads. When done in both, as in *patola* (q.v.), the process is known as double ikat.

indigo From Sanskrit *nila* and Arabic *al-nil*, via the Portuguese *anil*; widely referred to in trade records as *nil*. A dye extracted from the leaf of *Indigofera tinctoria*, producing a great variety of hues of blue.

kain (M) 'Cloth'. *Kain panjang*, literally 'long cloth', is worn as a skirt-cloth in the Malay world. Historically a painted cotton import, it was gradually displaced by batik substitutes. *Kain gulong* or *caingoulons*, from *kain* plus *gulong*, 'rolled', is a cloth patterned on the loom and often incorporating gold thread in the *kapala*, intended for use as Malay sarongs (q.v.), produced on the Coromandel Coast around Thanjavur and Pulicat. See also *sembagi*.

kalamkari (Pe) From *qalam*, 'pen', and *kari*, 'workmanship'. In trade records, used to identify hand-painted resist- and mordant-dyed cotton textiles, produced to high standards (painted on both sides). Produced on the Coromandel Coast and around Surat.

Kling (M) South Indian merchants who traded from the Coromandel Coast to Southeast Asia.

long cloth (E) Cotton cloth from the Coromandel Coast renowned for its length, typically 37 x 1.25 yds (33.8 x 1.1 m).

lungi / lungee (Pe, H) From the Persian/Urdu *lunggi* or Hindi *lungi*. Length of unstitched fabric worn as a skirt-cloth in South India.

madder The root of *Rubia tinctorum*, which yields alizarin. This produces a red dye when combined with the mordant (q.v.) alum, a black dye when mordanted with iron, and hues of violet when alum and iron are mixed.

mordant Ingredient used for fixing dyes in cloth, usually a metal oxide. It is applied to the cloth and combines with the dye in the bath, making the colour adhere to the treated areas.

muri Fine-quality plain weave cotton suitable for chintz painting, associated with the Coromandel Coast centres of Masulipatam, Pulicat and Nagapattinam. Possibly employed by the Javanese for batiking.

painted cottons Cloths decorated through a variety of combinations of mordant- and resist-dyeing to produce colourfast designs, typically floral, geometric or figurative. 'Painted' cloths may be produced by the use of the *qalam* (q.v.) or by block-printing.

palampore (Pe, H) Anglicized from *palang-posh*, 'bedcover', which describes the principal use of these cloths. Painted or printed cottons, usually decorated with a flowering tree or large-scale floral design, in demand in Europe and in Asia, where they circulated in Indonesia in the eighteenth century and later.

patola (G) Singular *patolu*. Silk cloth decorated by the double-ikat technique (see ikat). An expensive product, unique to Gujarat, where it is specially associated with the weaving centre at Patan, but was also made at Ahmedabad and probably Cambay. Specific designs were supplied to the Indonesian market.

pattas Inexpensive cloths of silk and cotton blend, widely traded in eastern Indonesia in the seventeenth century, and modified to local taste, e.g. *patta macasser* for the Makassar (Ujang Pandang) market.

percalla High-quality plain cotton cloth, suited for chintz (q.v.). Typically 8 x 1 yds (7.3 x 0.9 m). The best quality came from Madras and Golconda.

pha kiao / phaa kiao (Th) Literally, 'pillar cloth'. Cloth with deep end-panels and side-borders, for use as a pillar, wall or floor covering.

pha lai yang (Th) 'Garment designed with patterns'. Typically, Indian cloth with Thai designs.

pha nung / phaa naa nang (Th) Skirt length of cloth, wrapped in front with both ends folded in pleats, and secured with a belt. When worn gathered up between the legs and tucked into the waist at the back, in a style reminiscent of the Indian *dhoti* (q.v.), known as *pha nung chong* (or *chung*) *kraben*.

phra khlang (Th) The Thai king's representative in his dealings with foreigners, especially in matters of diplomacy and trade.

piece goods Cloths intended for attire, supplied to order in measured lengths.

pintado (Po) Literally, 'painted'. Term used in trade records to denote painted cottons.

prada (M) Cloth with glued gold leaf decoration, popular in Sumatra, Java and Bali.

rumal (Pe) Literally, 'handkerchief'. A fine cloth, made in a single loom length in multiples of a ¾-yard (68 cm) square.

sabai (Th) Cloth worn loosely around the upper body by Thai women.

salempore / sallampore Plain and dyed cotton cloth in a range of qualities made on the Coromandel and Malabar coasts and also in Sri Lanka; typically 16 x 1 yds (14.6 x 0.9 m). Referred to in the fourteenth-century Javanese text, the *Nagara-kertagama*, as being worn as a shawl by women.

sappanwood / sapan wood (M) A red dye source (also known as brazilwood), from the wood of *Caesalpina sappan*.

sarasa / sarassa (M, J) Probably derived from Hindi *sarasa*, 'superior'. Term used in trading records from the sixteenth century onwards, and still current in Japan. Strictly, denotes cottons finely hand-painted on both sides; used as skirt-cloths and as curtaining, and often produced in pairs. Major production centre around Thanjavur.

sari (H) An untailored length of cloth, typically 5–6 metres, worn by women as a wrapped garment, sometimes extended over the head.

sarong (M) Skirt-cloth worn by Malays and Indonesians; identical in function to the *lungi* (q.v.).

saudagar raja (M) A Malay ruler's merchant.

saudagiri (G) Literally, 'trade goods', from *saudagar*, 'merchant'. Painted cottons, typically heavily glazed, produced in Gujarat in the nineteenth century for the Thai market.

selendang (M) A multi-purpose shoulder-cloth worn by Indonesian women.

sembagi (M) Term used in western Indonesia for painted and printed cotton cloth of Indian origin, often in the form *kain sembagi*.

shahbandar (Pe) / **syahbandar** (M) Port official/harbourmaster, with responsibility for the conduct of foreign merchants, collecting duties, and liaison with the local ruler.

tapi / tape (Ja) From *tapih*, 'skirt'. Relatively inexpensive painted cottons produced for the Indonesian, Malay and Thai markets; coloured piece-goods (q.v.) widely used in Southeast Asia as skirt-cloths. Specifications varied according to the intended market. Varieties are distinguished in records by the use of place-names, e.g. *tapi jambi*, *tapi ternate*. *Tapi cindai* is a cotton decorated with a *patola* pattern (cf. *chinde*), usually of coarse painted cotton, popular for use as sarong (q.v.) skirt-cloths in Southeast Asia.

tumpal (M) Literally, 'teeth'. A row of elongated triangular elements, typically in an end-panel, characteristic of cloths worn in Southeast Asia.

VOC (D) Vereenigde Oost-Indische Compagnie. The Dutch United East India Company, founded in 1602 as a consortium of existing Dutch trading companies under a charter granted by the States-General, and dissolved in 1800.

vrijburger (D) Literally, 'free merchant'. Typically, a former VOC employee trading on his own account in Asia.

◆◇◆◇◆◇◆◇◆◇◆◇◆◇◆◇◆◇◆◇

ILLUSTRATIONS:
CREDITS AND NOTES

◆◇◆◇◆◇◆◇◆◇◆◇◆◇◆◇◆◇◆◇

• Unless otherwise stated, photographs were supplied by the holding collections. The author and publishers are grateful to them and to the photographers cited.
• Accession numbers are given only for textiles.
• Additional measurements are given here, where known, for cloths of which only details have been reproduced. An asterisk (*) indicates that the cloth is incomplete in that dimension.

A.E.D.T.A.   Association pour l'Etude et la Documentation des Textiles d'Asie, Paris
KIT   Koninklijk Instituut voor de Tropen, Amsterdam
KITLV   Koninklijk Instituut voor Taal-, Land- en Volkenkunde, Leiden
V&A   Victoria and Albert Museum, London

p. 1   Kobe City Museum
title page   See below, 29
pp. 4–5   V&A, IS 74-1993 [480 x 100 cm]
1   KITLV
2, 3   Museu de São Roque, Santa Casa de Misericordia, Lisbon.
4   KIT
5   Stephen White
6   Private coll., London
7   V&A, IS 149-1984 [244 x 80 cm]
8   National Gallery of Victoria, Melbourne, Abbott gift, 1985 [565 x 90 cm]
9   V&A, IS 13-1960 [197 x 76 cm]
10   Diane Daniel, Los Angeles
12   V&A, IS 53-1991 [114* x 88 cm]
13   V&A, IS 9-1997 [40* x 79 cm]
14, 15   V&A
16, 17   Photo John Guy
18   From Irwin and Hall, 1971
19–21   Photo John Guy
22   V&A, IS 189-1960 [432 x 157 cm]
23   Photo John Guy
24   Photo Ecole Française d'Extrême-Orient, Pondicherry
26   V&A, IS 95-1993 [487 x 99 cm]
27   V&A, IS 32-1994 [258* x 41* cm]
28   Idemitsu Museum of Art, Tokyo
29   V&A, 434-1897(IS) [73* x 52*]
30   V&A, D 76-1907
31   From Baldaeus, 1672
32   British Library, London
33   Photo John Guy
34, 35   Saraswati Mahal Library, The Palace, Thanjavur. Photo John Guy
36   V&A, IS 94-1990 [244 x 132 cm]
37   See 34, 35
38–41   V&A, T1a, d, f, g
42   Cora Ginsberg LLC, New York. Photo Spink & Son [272 x 221 cm]
43   Bibliothèque Nationale, Paris
44   V&A, IS 96-1993
45   Ashmolean Museum, Oxford, Newberry Coll. 1990.1129 [39.5* x 23* cm]
46   Ashmolean Museum, Oxford, Newberry Coll. 1990.250
47   Ashmolean Museum, Oxford, Newberry Coll. 1990.823
48   V&A, IS 89-1936 [137 x 110.5 cm]
49   V&A
50   Photo John Guy
51   V&A
52   Ashmolean Museum, Oxford, Newberry Coll. 1990.480 [22* x 16* cm]
53   V&A, IS 72-1972
54   Museum der Kulturen, Basel III.14040 [75* x 59* cm]
55   National Gallery of Australia, Canberra, Abbott gift, 1988 [492 x 91 cm]. Photo V&A
56   V&A, IS 68-1950
57   Prince of Wales Museum, Bombay
58   Ashmolean Museum, Oxford, Newberry Coll. 1990.805 [25.5* x 13* cm]
59   V&A, IS 94-1993 [416 x 91.5 cm]
60   From T. Ono, *Pagan. Mural Paintings of the Buddhist Temples in Burma*, Tokyo, 1978
61   From Lodewycksz, 1598

62   From Ba Shin, *The Lokahteikpan*, Rangoon, 1962
63   Rossi and Rossi, London. Photo Raymond Forth Studios
64   See above, 60
65   V&A, IS 90-1990 [271 x 106 cm]
66, 67   Photo John Guy
68   V&A, IS 57-1991 [104* x 78* cm]
69   Asian Art Museum of San Francisco
70   Private coll., London [137* x 220 cm]
71   From N. J. Krom, *De Tempels van Angkor*, Amsterdam, n.d.
72   Museum Nasional, Jakarta. Photo National Gallery of Art, Washington, D.C.
73   Ashmolean Museum, Oxford, Newberry Coll. 1990.1099 [35* x 23.5* cm]
74   From N. J. Krom, *Inleiding tot de Hindoe-Javaansche Kunst*, The Hague, 1923
75   J. Luth, Hanover. Photo V&A
76   Asian Civilisations Museum, Singapore
77   Algemeen Rijksarchief, The Hague
78, 79   KITLV
80   V&A, IS 100-1990
81   V&A, IS 101-1993
83   KIT
84   V&A, IS 102-1993 [288 x 106 cm]
85   Thomas Murray, California [373 x 130 cm]
86, 87   V&A, 5344 (IS) [184* x 127 cm]
88   V&A, IS 53-1997
89   KIT
90, 91   V&A, IS 41-1988 [316 x 238 cm]
92   From Linschoten, 1598/1885
93   Yu-chee Chong Fine Art, London. Photo V&A
94   From J. P. Cortemünde, *Dagbog fra en Ostindiefart 1672–5*, Kronborg, 1953
95, 96   British Museum, London
97, 98   Yu-chee Chong Fine Art, London. Photo V&A
99   From Nieuhof, 1662
100   National Gallery of Australia, Canberra, Abbott gift, 1988. Photo John Guy
101   G. Nishimura, Kyoto. Photo John Guy
102   National Gallery of Australia, Canberra, Abbott gift. Photo V&A
103   British Museum, London
104   Christie's, Amsterdam
105   KIT
106   Mangkaunagaran Palace, Surakarta
107   A.E.D.T.A., 2798 [400 x 114 cm]
108   V&A, IS 5-1989 [392 x 100 cm]
109   Louvre, Paris
110   Anita Spertus and Robert J. Holmgren, New York [347 x 85 cm]
111   Irwan Holmes, Jakarta
112   KITLV
113   V&A, IS 34-1994 [223* x 40* cm]
114   V&A, IS 33-1994 [220* x 38* cm]
115   KITLV
116   V&A, IS 31-1994 [436 x 119 cm]
117   KIT
118, 119   KITLV
120   Photo Penelope Graham
121–126   I. Hirayama, Kamakura. Photo Ancient Art Yamazaki, Tokyo
127   V&A
128   V&A, IS 100-1993
129   Drawn by Graham Parlett
130   National Gallery of Victoria, Melbourne, Abbott gift, 1985 [634* x 75 cm]
131   Drawn by Graham Parlett
132   V&A, IS 92-1990 [285 x 89.5 cm]
133   Jeevak and Banoo Parpia, Ithaca, N.Y.
134   V&A, IS 95-1990 [295 x 102 cm]
135   National Gallery of Australia, Canberra. Photo National Gallery of Victoria, Melbourne
136   KITLV
137   See above, 44
138   Courtesy Spink & Son, London
139   V&A, IS 98-1993 [305 x 193 cm]
140   From Rea, 1897
141   V&A, IS 81-1988 [241 x 202 cm]
142   V&A, IS 99-1993 [324 x 210 cm]
143   Thomas Murray, California
144   Mary Kahlenberg, Santa Fe, N.M.
145   V&A, IS 2-1972
146   See above, 26
147   National Gallery of Australia, Canberra, Abbott gift, 1989. Photo V&A
148   A.E.D.T.A., 2610 [496 x 107 cm]
149   Kobe City Museum [495 x 95 cm]
150   J. Luth, Hanover. Photo V&A [472* x 77.5 cm]
151   V&A, IS 23-1996
152   National Gallery of Australia, Canberra, Abbott

gift, 1988 [580* x 91 cm]. Photo V&A
153   V&A, IS 97-1990 [435 x 95.5 cm]
154   Museum of International Folk Art, Neutrogena Coll., Santa Fe, N.M. [264* x 81 cm]. Photo courtesy Mary Kahlenberg
155   Yu-chee Chong Fine Art, London. Photo V&A
156   Vlisco BV, Helmond. Photo John Guy
157   From Rouffaer and Juynboll, 1914
158   V&A, T 53-1909 [215 x 114 cm]
159   V&A, D 557-1901
160   Siam Society, Bangkok
161   See above, 70
162   Museum für Indische Kunst, Staatliche Museen Preussischer Kulturbesitz, Berlin
163   See above, 70
164   National Library, Bangkok
165   A.E.D.T.A., 2837
166   V&A, IS 51-1991 [33.5* x 70* cm]
167   V&A, IS 52-1991 [143* x 84 cm]
168   V&A, IS 37-1991 [343 x 113 cm]
169   See above, 68
170   V&A, IS 58-1991 [211* x 132 cm]
171   V&A, IS 54-1991 [181* x 73* cm]
172   From Dohring, n.d.
173   V&A, IS 40-1991 [131* x 102 cm]
174   See above, 68
175   See above, 171
176   See above, 173
177   V&A, IS 60-1991 [55* x 111 cm]
178, 179   Drawn by Graham Parlett
180   See above, 12
181   Royal Museum of Scotland, Edinburgh. Photo courtesy Jonathan Hope
182   Photo courtesy Muang Boran Publishing House, Bangkok
183   V&A, IS 346-1992 [282 x 108 cm]. Photo courtesy Spink & Son, London
184   Chester Beatty Library, Dublin
185, 186   From La Loubère, 1691
187   V&A IS 43-1991 [96.5* x 51* cm]
188   Royal Ontario Museum, Toronto.
189   From Dohring, n.d.
190   National Library, Bangkok
191   Bibliothèque Nationale, Paris
192   National Museum, Bangkok. Photo Tettoni, Cassio and Associates/Photobank
193   National Library, Bangkok
194   V&A, IS 50-1991 [206 x 107 cm]
195   Photo John Guy
196   Chester Beatty Library, Dublin
197   V&A, IS 55-1991
198   Photo courtesy Muang Boran Publishing House, Bangkok
199   V&A
200   V&A, IS 35-1987 [270 x 81 cm]
201   V&A, IS 81-1991 [396 x 94 cm]
202   V&A, 6631 (IS)
203   V&A, 1707 (IS)
204   V&A, IS 48-1991 [107* x 98 cm]
205   V&A, IS 62-1991 [84* x 85* cm]
206   V&A, IS 46-1991 [75* x 53* cm]
207, 208   National Crafts Museum, New Delhi. Photo John Guy
209   From Baldaeus, 1672
210   From Baron, 1685
211   V&A, IS 46-1991 [each page 75* x 53* cm]
212   Kanebo Museum of Textiles, Osaka
213   Kobe City Museum
214   British Museum, London
215   Algemeen Rijksarchief, The Hague
216   Maeda Ikutokukai Foundation, Tokyo
217   V&A, IS 97-1993 [434 x 71 cm]
218   Tokugawa Art Museum, Nagoya
219   Tokyo National Museum, Ii Coll.
220   Tokyo National Museum
221   Prefectural Museum of Art, Yamaguchi City
222   Toyama-Kinenkan Museum, Saitama-Ken, T. Yamanobe Coll.
223   Kobe City Museum
224   Photo John Guy
225   Private coll., Kyoto. Photo John Guy
226, 227   Tokyo National Museum, Ii Coll.
228   Kyoto National Museum, Maeda Coll. [107 x 42 cm]
229, 230   Tokyo National Museum, Ii Coll.
231   Photo G. Vlam
232   Minami-kannonyama Festival Preservation Society, Kyoto
233   V&A, T 63-1948
234, 235   Tokyo National Museum, Ii Coll.
236–238   See above, 211

190

ACKNOWLEDGMENTS

This study has been in the making over the past fifteen years, stimulated by the appearance in Southeast Asia of Indian textiles of unfamiliar designs and of uncertain antiquity. It gradually became clear that these cloths were the legacy of Asia's great spice trade, and that many of them dated from that trade's heyday, when they were employed as a commodity in the markets of Southeast Asia.

In the course of my research, I was assisted by many colleagues and friends. Above all, I wish to acknowledge my debt to the work of the late John Irwin, former Keeper of the Indian Department at the Victoria and Albert Museum, who pioneered the integrated study of historical trade records and Indian textiles. I must also record my appreciation of the support of Mme Krishna Riboud, who has promoted the preservation and study of Asian textiles through her private foundation in Paris, the Association pour l'Etude et la Documentation des Textiles d'Asie (A.E.D.T.A.). I must make an acknowledgment of the contribution of Dr Mattiebelle Gittinger of the Textile Museum in Washington, D.C., who broadened the scope of this field of study with her innovative exhibition, *Master Dyers to the World*, in 1982.

I have pursued fieldwork on this subject in India, Indonesia, Thailand, Cambodia, Vietnam, China and Japan, as well as in the archives and historical collections of Europe. Concurrently, I have worked towards assembling a comprehensive collection of Indian trade textiles for the Victoria and Albert Museum. The results of these efforts are published here for the first time.

The Victoria and Albert Museum has generously supported this project, for both fieldwork and archival research. I am particularly grateful to Dr Deborah Swallow who supported my requests for time, as did colleagues in the Museum's Research Department, to which I was attached for a period. Other colleagues who assisted in various ways include Rosemary Crill, who fielded my many questions on textile technology, Dr Graham Parlett, who produced the line drawings, Divia Patel, who managed the Museum's photography, Dr Rupert Faulkner, and Verity Wilson. Mike Kitcatt is responsible for the excellent photographs of the Museum's textiles.

My thanks must go to the following colleagues outside the Museum: Dr Ruth Barnes, Dr Valerie Berinstain, Professor K. N. Chaudhuri, Dr Craig Clunas, Francesca Gallaway, Annabel Gallop Teh, Dr Henry Ginsburg, Patricia Herbert, Jonathan Hope, Dr J. Luth, Yu Chee Chong, Dr Venetia Porter, Dr Remco Raven, and Dr Nuno Vassallo e Silva. I owe a particular debt to Ebeltje Hartkamp-Jonxis of the Rijksmuseum, Amsterdam, who gave me encouragement and invaluable guidance to Dutch collections. Assistance was provided by staff of the State Archives in The Hague, the University of Leiden, and Vlisco BV, Helmond.

To the following individuals who assisted in various ways I wish to record my appreciation: in India, Dr Françoise L'Hernault, Dr R. Nagaswamy, Gira Sarabhai, Martand Singh, Dr Jyotindra Jain and Dr Lotika Varadarajan; in Thailand, Natthapatra Bhujjong-Chandavij, Dr Pisit Charoenwongsa, Professor Dhiravat na Pombejra and Paothong Thongchua; in Japan, Noriko Katsumori, Yoshio Kikuya, Shojiro Nishimora, Sae Ogasawara, Shigeko Tanaka, Tomoyuki Yamanobe, Sachio Yoshioka and Dr Shinobu Yoshimoto; in the U.S.A., Louise Cort, Diane Daniel, Mary Kahlenberg, Dr Ruurdje Laarhoven, Dr John Listopad, Richard Mellott and Thomas Murray; in Australia, Michael and Mary Abbott, the late Professor Anthony Forge, Dr Penelope Graham, Robyn Maxwell and Dick Richards. I wish also to thank the staff at Thames and Hudson for their faith in this book and support in its realization.

Finally, my greatest debt is to Judy and Stella, who had to put up with my long absences, in the field and at my desk, and who supported this work in so many ways.

John Guy *London, 1998*